# THE SECRETS OF D-DAY

*Below is a statement by Hitler's Chief of Staff, Field Marshall Wilhelm Keitel, after he had been condemned to death by the Nuremberg Tribunal . . .*

'Our Intelligence was completely at fault (with regard to the Normandy Invasion), although a few untrustworthy reports had indicated that the Allies' preparations were complete. An invasion of northern France had been expected since the spring of 1944, as soon as the weather was favourable. The Normandy landings were reported, but the troops were only put on the usual alert – as they had been so often before . . .

German Military Intelligence knew nothing of the real state of the Allies' preparation. The full alert was not ordered even when the Allied invasion fleet was approaching the Normandy coast.'

## A CORGI D-DAY SPECIAL

# Gilles Perrault

# The
# Secrets of D-Day

Translated from the French
by
Len Ortzen

**CORGI BOOKS**
A DIVISION OF TRANSWORLD PUBLISHERS LTD

# THE SECRETS OF D-DAY
## A CORGI BOOK 0 552 09540 0

Originally published in Great Britain
by Arthur Barker Ltd.

PRINTING HISTORY
Arthur Barker edition published 1963
Corgi edition published 1966
Corgi edition reissued 1974

This book is set in Linotype Times

Corgi Books are published by Transworld Publishers Ltd,
Cavendish House, 57–59 Uxbridge Road,
Ealing, London, W.5.
Made and printed in Great Britain by
Hunt Barnard Printing Ltd., Aylesbury, Bucks.

# Contents

# THE SECRET OF D-DAY

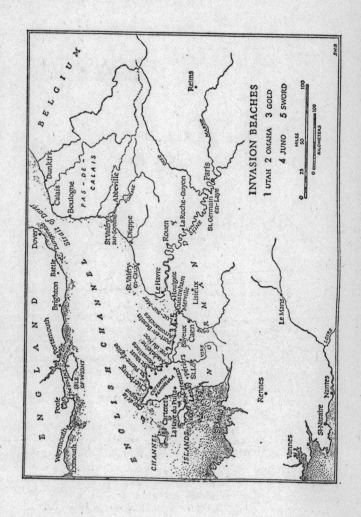

INVASION BEACHES

1 UTAH  2 OMAHA  3 GOLD
          4 JUNO  5 SWORD

# MARCH

## 1. The Supreme Gamble

On March 20, 1944, the commanders of the German Army, Navy and Air Force in the west—Field Marshal von Rundstedt, Admiral Krancke and Field Marshal Sperrle—were summoned to Hitler's headquarters. The Führer ended the meeting with these words:

"The forty-five divisions now stationed in Europe are badly needed in Russia. They must be transferred there as soon as victory has been won in the west, so that the situation can be completely reversed. The outcome of this war and the fate of the Reich depend on every soldier on the western front, the number-one theater of operations. Each officer and man must therefore be made to feel that everything depends on his individual effort."

This time it was not the usual blustering, the trite exhortation to be killed rather than give ground, "for wherever a German soldier plants his foot, he keeps it there"—a disastrous principle which had resulted in several hundred thousand of those German soldiers dragging their lives out in the Siberian tundras. This time it was a deliberate strategic gamble. The Führer had stopped ranting and recovered the tone he had used when explaining his great politico-military decision to his generals. In 1939 he had seized Poland, betting—against the advice of his general staff—that the 110 divisions of the British and French armies would not attack the 23 German divisions left to guard the Rhine. He had won. In 1941, finding British opposition too determined, he had gambled on defeating Russia in five months, which would have assured him of final victory ("If we crush Russia, the last chance of success for the British will have disappeared, and Germany will become master of Europe."). He had lost. And now he was chancing everything on a last throw of the dice: an Allied defeat in the west.

On that very day, March 20, Zhukov crossed the Dniester and prepared to thrust into Rumania, and Koniev drew near Czechoslovakia. The Germans had to pull back so hurriedly that the Russians captured 500 tanks and 12,000 trucks intact. All along the Russian front the Germans were outnumbered three to one, and the enemy's strength in tanks, guns and planes was five times their own. Yet in spite of the great danger from the coming summer offensive of the Russians, which the German commanders already knew would soon extend along the whole eastern front, Hitler was giving absolute priority to the west. He was not just waiting for an Allied invasion: he was hoping it would come.

The Allies were completing their preparations with resolution, but also with fear and trembling for the result. Roosevelt, who was to run for a fourth term five months after D-Day, had told Churchill that he would not survive politically if the invasion failed. Churchill himself had his doubts and fears. He had been reluctant to agree to OVERLORD. He would have preferred to let German power crumble away, limit frontal attacks on "Fortress Europe" to scattered commando raids, gain a foothold in Yugoslavia and advance into the Balkans. There were no doubt political reasons in his mind, but he also believed that a cross-Channel attack against the Atlantic Wall would be foolish. It would mean risking all the hard-won gains since Dunkirk, and although Churchill had been bold when defeat was near, he became cautious when victory was in sight. Eisenhower later wrote that Churchill often warned him they must make sure the beaches would not be covered with the bodies of Allied soldiers.

The American generals were confident, but they had also been full of optimism in 1942, when they had wanted to cross the Channel and attack the all-powerful Wehrmacht. The British had firmly vetoed any such attempt then, and Eisenhower had declared that the day of their refusal "could well go down as the blackest day in history." He later acknowledged that such a premature attack would have been sheer folly. The Americans had again wanted to invade across the Channel in 1943, and had gotten Churchill to agree in 1944 only by threatening to turn all their might against Japan and leave Europe a secondary theater of operations. "They make war as though they were playing rugby," commented a British diplomat. But Bedell Smith, Eisenhower's chief of staff, gave OVERLORD only a fifty per cent chance of success. The British were inclined to be pessimistic too, except for Montgomery, who was confident because Montgomery had a hand in it.

The troops were afraid. British Army Intelligence reported that "the average young officer is expecting to die in the assault, and among the rank there is that same heavy weight of apprehension and dismal foreboding." The uneasiness went so deep that Montgomery abandoned his maps, took up his pilgrim's staff and preached a new crusade with the theme: "We're the best team, and with God's help we shall win." He addressed the men of the invasion forces, often making six or seven speeches a day to a division at a time.

The morale of the American 1st Division was collapsing. The men were asking to be sent back to the States. This was the toughest, proudest and most seasoned of the American divisions in Europe. It had known two "D-Days" already: in North Africa and in Sicily. When counterattacked by the crack armored division the *Hermann Goering*, soon after landing in Sicily, the men of the First had dug in and let the enemy tanks go through. Then they attacked the German infantry following up, and put them to flight. But now the "Big Red One" refused to take part in a third D-Day. It wanted to go home. The morale of the 29th, the other division due to go into the assault on Omaha Beach, was just as low. It had never been under fire, and casualties of ninety per cent were predicted. Eisenhower sent General Bradley, who was no orator, to talk to the men. "This stuff about tremendous losses is tommyrot," he told them. "Some of you won't come back—but it'll be very few." The staff reporters of *Stars and Stripes* and other army publications were told to write enthusiastic articles on the great strides that had been made in military medicine. They wrote optimistically about the chances of survival of the wounded.

On both sides of the Channel, propaganda was concentrated on the invasion, on the Second Front. Goebbels proclaimed: "We have fortified the coast of Europe from the North Cape to the Mediterranean and installed the deadliest weapons that the twentieth century can produce. That is why any enemy attack, even the most powerful and furious possible to imagine, is bound to fail." Goebbels made his forecast: "At Dieppe they held on for nine hours, and there was no Wall. If they hold on for nine hours next time, they'll do well." Goebbels kept broadcasting the slogan which helped the German people to forget the Russian menace and the terror of air attacks: "The final victory will be won on the western front."

The Allies kept repeating this too. The war was dragging on, and the Allied forces were creeping up Italy at a snail's pace, but there was this great sledgehammer blow about to fall on the Germans. America was waiting for it. Russia, exhausted, was waiting for it. So was Britain, which had become so packed with troops and material that people were saying the tight little island would sink without the thousands of barrage balloons to hold it up. Occupied Europe, where the Resistance groups were being hounded by the Gestapo, was waiting for it. In France, in 1944, an active Resistance member was reckoned to have only another six months of freedom before arrest and inevitable death. Battles were going on in Russia, Italy and the Pacific. There was fighting on the seas and in the air. But the enemy peoples, drugged by propaganda, held their breath as they waited for news of the decisive clash which was to take place on a few miles of beach. Both sides saw this battle as the "moment of truth" of the whole war, and so that was what it would be.

If the Germans threw the Allies back into the sea, Hitler would gain a long respite and all his plans would again become possible. Another Dunkirk would not shatter Anglo-American strength, but would paralyze it for a long time. The psychological consequences in particular would be incalculable. People's hopes had been raised so high by propaganda that morale was likely to fall correspondingly. Much time would be needed to reorganize the Allied forces, to make new plans for another combined operation (OVERLORD took nearly two years to prepare in all its minute detail), and for the troops to recover their spirits. For even if the losses in men and materiel were comparatively slight, the Allied war machine would be like a powerful motor with a battery that needed recharging.

For Hitler, this respite would make all the difference between possible victory and certain defeat. His U-boat packs had been driven out of the Atlantic by the British, but he was building electrically powered submarines whose speed and underwater endurance would enable them to escape pursuit. The Luftwaffe had been overwhelmed by the Allied air forces, but Messerschmitt was making the Me–163 jet, which would sweep the enemy from the skies. These were not secret weapons which might turn out to be illusory, but materiel that would soon be ready for use in the war, and in sufficient quantity to wrest from the Allies the air and sea mastery indispensable for a fresh invasion attempt. There were the V–1's and V–2's, which would rain down on proud London and reduce her to submission. Finally, there was the possibility of driving a wedge between the Allies by negotiating with a Russia disappointed by the Anglo-American failure and reeling under the pressure of German divisions transferred from the west.

All this was at stake for the Führer in the coming clash, and it was in order to explain the situation to his western commanders that he had brought them to his Rastenburg lair on that twentieth of March, 1944. He thought they had understood. He was possibly disappointed when Rommel told him that his infantry divisions had no mobility and could have no role in modern warfare. Hitler coldly replied, "Their role is to be killed behind their fortifications, so they don't need to be mobile." For the Wall had to be held, come what might. The Wall was where victory had to be won.

The Wall was a myth. As von Rundstedt was to write: "Nothing in front of it, nothing behind—a mere showpiece. The best that could be hoped for was that it might hold up an attack for twenty-four hours, but any resolute assault was bound to make a breakthrough, anywhere along it, within a day at most. And once this had been done, the rest of it could be taken from the rear, for it all faced out to sea and so became quite useless."

The guns had been mounted in concrete casemates instead of moving turrets because of the shortage of steel. This limited their field of fire. They had come from ten defeated countries and were of twenty-eight different calibers. Spare parts were almost unobtainable; there were very few fire-control instruments, which were necessary for firing at moving ships. The average age of the gunners was forty-five. In some sectors there were auxiliary units of *Marinehelfer* and *Marinehelferinnen,* composed of students of both sexes who continued their studies by correspondence.

The German Seventh Army, which was to take the whole weight of the Allied assault, was equipped with 92 different models of weapons using 252 kinds of ammunition, of which 47 were no longer being made—and so could not be wasted on practice firing. The battalion commander had no cars: they were supposed to go into battle on horseback. The 6th Parachute Regiment, a crack unit with an average age of seventeen and a half, had 70 trucks of 50 different makes. When its commander, Colonel von der Heydte, asked for much-needed weapons he received the reply: "Come now, Heydte, all that paratroopers need are daggers!"

A more serious weakness than the assorted and outdated arms and equipment was the poor quality of the troops. The best men and units were being thrown into the Russian cauldron. The west received only the elderly and the very young, the disabled and the sick, soldiers who had suffered third-degree frostbite on the Russian front. The 70th Division, called the "White Bread Division," was made up entirely of dyspeptics on a strict diet. Since there were not enough German soldiers, contingents of foreigners had been enrolled to fight under the swastika banner. In 1944 the Wehrmacht, sword of a nation proud of its racial purity, included Negroes and Indians in its ranks, Cossacks, Armenians and Tartars, as well as Frenchmen, Belgians and Mongolians, and others. In the future invasion area there were twenty-three battalions of Russians, former prisoners of war who had been given a choice between starvation and the German uniform. They had preferred the uniform, but, as General von Schlieben, the commander at Cherbourg, said: "It seems doubtful that Russians can be made to fight in France, for Germany, against Americans and Englishmen."

And since this was still not enough, German children had been rounded up. In November, 1943, the Comtesse de Maupertuis saw a new contingent of soldiers arrive at her requisitioned château near Bayeux. They were fourteen years old. They practiced hand-to-hand combat in the park, then danced and played tag during their rest periods.

But there were also the armored divisions, the paratroopers and the S.S.

The German tanks were superior to all but the Stalin tank. The Sherman's shells could not penetrate the seven-inch thickness of steel that protected the Tiger, and they glanced off the angled armor of a Panther. The only way of knocking out these German monsters was by a flank attack, but a shell from one of their 88's or 75's could stop any Allied tank. Von Rundstedt had ten armored divisions under his command on D-Day, strategically disposed behind the Wall. They had all been forged on the Russian anvil; the Panzer Lehr was the strongest in the German army, and the 12th S.S. Hitler Jugend was commanded by the fanatical Kurt Meyer—in August his infantrymen would fight the Canadians with shovels when their ammunition gave out.

Only these tanks and these men could throw the Allies back into the sea.

If von Rundstedt was to set his trap in the right place, if his armored divisions were to avoid having to make long journeys on roads and rails bombed by Allied planes and harassed by the Resistance, and if their steel jaws were to close on the invasion forces in time, German intelligence would have to answer this double question: "Where and when?"

## 2. At the Foot of the Wall

THE periscope emerged off the French coast. Thirty feet below, a British lieutenant commander had his eye glued to the eyepiece. At first he saw only water streaming across the lens, then the dark outline of the shore against the sky. He turned the periscope from left to right. Steep cliffs came into view, then rolling hills, then more cliffs. He lowered the periscope and gave his crew the order to proceed at reduced speed.

The crew normally consisted of two men, but that night a commando officer and sergeant were also in the midget submarine, so there were five men packed into a space five feet wide and eight feet long. The height was only five feet, which kept the men bent when standing. The commando sergeant suffered the least discomfort, being short. The underwater crossing from England had made the air almost unbreathable. The thought of mines was visible on each face.

The motor was purring gently, driving the submarine towards the hostile coast. The lieutenant commander had another look through the periscope, then gave the order to surface. The hull broke through the dark water some three hundred yards from the beach. Having unbolted the hatch, the lieutenant commander went up into the conning tower, drawing in lungfuls of fresh air. Everything was calm. He bent over the hatchway and motioned to the two commandos, who joined him on the narrow deck. They were wearing frogmen's rubber suits. Their equipment consisted of a flashlight, a compass, an auger, some little bags, a reel of fishing line and a few brass pegs. They also carried a dagger and a .45 automatic in their belts. Experiments had shown that the .45 Colt automatic withstood salt water and sand better than any other pistol in the world.

Without a word, the two commandos slid into the icy water, careful to avoid the slightest splash. The lieutenant commander watched them swimming towards the beach until they were swallowed up by the night.

Major Logan Scott-Bowden and Sergeant Bruce Ogden Smith were excellent swimmers, but the icy temperature of the water and their sluggish circulation from the hours spent huddled in the midget submarine could easily cause cramp. They also knew that the sound of a hand slapping the water could bring a burst of fire in their direction from German sentries. The difficulty lay in swimming swiftly yet noiselessly.

After a few minutes they reached the edge of the forest of obstacles which, on Rommel's orders, had been growing since January all along the shore. They worked their way between the stakes until they touched bottom. They continued on their hands and knees and crawled the last few yards on their bellies. When they reached dry sand they lay still and scanned the beach for German sentries.

One of Sergeant Ogden Smith's peculiarities was that he was a sergeant. At the beginning of the war it had been a fad among certain stylish young Englishmen to refuse to accept a commission, from a kind of inverted snobbery. They were called "the long-haired brigade." Most of them, in time, had given in to the advantages and attractions of officer rank. But Ogden Smith had remained a sergeant. It pleased him not to be an officer, as it pleased him to wage his own little war within the big one. He shed no blood, and he had some exciting moments. No one knew exactly what he did, not even his wife, who had a responsible job at a factory in Wales. She may have believed he was having a cushy, safe war in some army office, and probably she thought at times, after an exhausting day, that he was better off than she was.

The beach appeared to be deserted. The only sound was the lapping of the waves. No sentry could be seen. The two men began moving up the gentle slope of the beach. This was surely the most nerve-racking moment of their mission. Slipping overboard from the submarine was at least an escape from confined quarters. And the water was a kind of protection. But now steel nerves were needed to move away from the water's edge and advance towards the enemy-held positions. Ahead of them were land mines, batteries, machine-gun nests and automatic flamethrowers—the whole arsenal of weapons ready to throw back entire armies.

The strangest part of it was that the major and the sergeant might have been there for nothing. Soldiers often die for nothing, but it is relatively rare for their leaders to accept this possibility, and even rarer for them to create it deliberately. Yet these two men's superiors, now lying peacefully in their beds, might well have sent them on a mission which they knew to be useless. Scott-Bowden and Ogden Smith had already reconnoitered a score of beaches. There was of course no question of making D-Day landings on twenty beaches, and the five to be used had long since been decided upon. But there was always the chance that the two men might be captured, handed over to the Gestapo and tortured. If they talked, the enemy would be able to concentrate forces on the areas where they had reconnoitered the beaches. So they were deliberately sent to beaches a hundred miles and more away from the area chosen for the invasion. They could not therefore reveal the great secret if captured and tortured, for they did not know which of the many beaches they had visited were the selected ones.

On this particular night they were on a beach about two miles long, set between steep cliffs with a line of low hills ahead. The sands they were crawling over would be soaking up the blood of American soldiers before three months had passed. They were on "Bloody Omaha."

They attached one end of the fishing line to a peg which they stuck in the sand. The line had come from the shop of Ogden Smith's parents, who sold fishing supplies near St. James's Palace. A lead bead had been attached to it every fifty yards. The two men were crawling along one behind the other. The first was digging at the sand with his dagger, feeling for mines. The second was unwinding the line; each time he came to a bead he fixed the line in the sand with one of his brass pegs, so that he marked exactly the path being taken. They would thus have no mines to fear on the return journey. At each bead he also dug into the ground with his auger, brought up a sample of sand and put it into one of his little bags.

Suddenly the two commandos dropped flat, their hearts thumping and their foreheads moist. Behind them, they had heard a crunching sound. Slowly turning their heads, they saw a German sentry. On several previous occasions they had sighted sentries, but always up the beach in front of block-houses or casemates. This one was between them and the sea. He was walking too casually to have had his suspicions aroused. But he was headed straight toward the line they had strung out behind them. They drew their pistols.

It had all begun a few weeks earlier, when an officer on General Montgomery's staff began thinking about vacations he had spent at seaside resorts in Normandy before the war. These musings were, however, in line of duty; he was help-ing to plan an invasion which must begin on the beaches where he had passed many happy days. Thoughts of good old times at the seaside had reminded him of seeing large patches of clay on those Normandy beaches. No sooner had he men-tioned this to his superiors than the question at once arose: would the assault tanks get bogged down in this clay? An answer could not be given until its exact consistency was known.

The solution was brought nearer by a clerk at the British Museum. He discovered in the 1938 *Bulletin de la Société Préhistorique Française* a detailed description of a patch of clay on the beach at Luc-sur-Mer, which was one of the beaches where the British were to land. Geologists were consulted, and reported that there were similar patches on the beach at Brancaster, in Norfolk. Tanks were driven over the clayey patches at Brancaster, and got stuck. This was a disaster. There was only one thing left to do: call in Hobart.

Percy Hobart was a professional soldier and had been one of the pioneers of tank warfare. He had always maintained that tanks would play a major part in the next war, so his annoyed superiors put him on the retired list as soon as the next war broke out. In 1940 he joined the Home Guard; he was given the rank of corporal and placed in command of a few farmers armed chiefly with pitchforks. Winston Churchill had plucked him away from these activities, and with the rank of major general he had given all his time to inventing and perfecting a number of special tanks for the Normandy invasion.

There was the "Crab," a tank equipped with a revolving drum in front and heavy chains which beat on the ground ahead, exploding mines before they could do any harm. There was the "Crocodile," which had a flamethrower; and a tank which carried logs to fill in antitank ditches. Hobart also thought up a tank to place thirty-foot gangways across bomb craters or streams, and another, the "Ramp," with a sloping body designed for surmounting seawalls and earthworks. He was the inventor of the amphibious tanks used in the assault, and of grenade-tanks, bang-alore-tanks, and other special kinds. In fact, it seemed that Major General Sir Percy Hobart was able to make anything out of a tank, except a tank.

His answer to the patches of clay was the "Bobbin" tank, which unrolled long strips of steel matting ahead of it, thus making a firm path for itself and for the ordinary tanks following later.

Then began the task of checking the position of the clay patches on the five chosen landing beaches, so that Hobart's "Bobbin" tanks could be given priority there.

The sentry stepped on the fishing line and it sank into the

sand. He noticed nothing amiss and went peacefully on his way, completely unaware of having provided the enemy with an important piece of information: the beach was not mined. Scott-Bowden and Ogden Smith lay flat on the ground for a minute or two longer. It had been a close call, but they had walked under the muzzles of German guns so often that they had acquired a feeling of invulnerability. Three months previously, they had been exploring the beach of La Rivière, near Bayeux. Scott-Bowden had slipped along to the seawall and listened to a couple of Germans talking. A few seconds before midnight, Ogden Smith had remembered it was December 31. He had crawled over to Scott-Bowden, put his mouth to his ear and wished him "Happy New Year," ten feet away from the enemy soldiers.

The German sentry had now disappeared, but he might return. The two commandos cautiously withdrew down the beach, taking the line with them. Then, making their way between the obstacles, they slipped into the water. After swimming for a few minutes they signaled with their flashlights. The midget submarine emerged from the darkness and took them safely on board. Thus ended their second visit to Omaha Beach. On the first occasion they had drawn a clinometer behind them, measuring the slope of the beach. They were to make a third visit, which would be by far the most spectacular and dramatic. Instead of arriving like thieves in the night, they went in at dawn, leading an army brought by five thousand ships. For at the last minute General Omar N. Bradley requested that the two commandos be assigned to guide the American assault troops to the beach they knew so well.

It was likewise at General Bradley's request that they made this second visit. During a staff conference some hours earlier the general had noticed a suspicious mark in aerial photographs of Omaha Beach. British Intelligence were asked if they had any information as to the consistency of the beach at that spot. The request reached Nigel Willmott, the officer commanding the special reconnaissance unit, and he immediately ordered Scott-Bowden and Ogden Smith to prepare to leave. Thanks to them, Willmott was able to give General Bradley, the very next day, a glass tube containing a sample of the sand from the suspicious-looking spot. He handed it over with studied indifference, as though it were the most natural thing in the world, delighting in surprising these Americans who were surprised at nothing. When Bradley wrote his memoirs years later, he still remembered the slim, taciturn British officer who had casually given him the sample gathered the previous night from under the boots of German sentries.

During those winter and spring nights Allied commandos frequently prowled along the foot of the Wall. A few were captured and shot, in accordance with the Führer's Most Secret Order No. 00/3830/42. Two were saved by Rommel, who plucked them out of the Gestapo's clutches. But most of them, protected by some special providence, returned safe and sound from their nocturnal expeditions. The information they brought back was equaled only by the risks they ran—and they alone were able to obtain it.

The French Resistance was everywhere except on the beaches. To reach them, men would have had to crawl through minefields several hundred yards wide, cut a gap in the barbed wire, slip between the blockhouses, jump trenches and clamber over the antitank wall—in short, they would have had to get through the whole thickness of the Wall without being seen by the sentries. It was impossible. The beaches were accessible only from the sea. Or from the air.

Every yard of beach had been photographed. Reconnaissance planes flying high or skimming the waves had taken millions of pictures. The number of stakes that Rommel had planted was known, as was the thickness of the antitank wall, the position and shape of offshore reefs, the location of sandbanks and their variations at times of very high tides. The coast had been photographed in all weathers and at every hour of the day. It was known that a given wind caused waves of such-and-such a height in a certain area. Scrutinized, assembled and classified by experts, the aerial photos had supplied a large crop of information. But they could not reveal whether the clayey sand of Omaha Beach would bog down the Allied war machine, or what metal had been used to make the obstacles called "Belgian barn doors," the strongest and largest of the obstacles that Rommel had installed along the shore. They could not solve the mystery of April 23. On that day a bomber attacking the batteries at Houlgate dropped one of its bombs into the sea, close to the beach. To their astonishment, the crew saw the water thrown up by a series of terrifying explosions. The Allied Command, fearing some new German invention which might mean postponing the Normandy invasion, sent a professor and a senior officer with special photographic equipment, protected by commandos, to the coast. They found that the explosions had been caused by mines and grenades attached to the tops of the underwater obstacles.

Oddly enough, although these beaches were to be the scene of the first assault, all this information was essential not so much for H-Hour as for the hours that would follow. Rommel's obstacles would hinder the assault troops but could not stop them. The obstacles might, however, hold up the flow of reinforcements and materiel, thus blocking the vital arteries to the beachhead. In the American sector alone, the equivalent of two hundred trainloads of troops had to be gotten ashore in the first eighteen hours. To enable the landing craft to reach the beaches, and the tanks and trucks to reach the roads, special engineer units had been training for months, working by the stopwatch, in order to clear the beaches in the first few hours. They were to suffer fifty per cent casualties, but each minute saved justified the loss of a man's life.

It was to facilitate their task that five French commandos, led by Vourch and Klopfenstein, landed on the beach at Biville on the night of December 26, 1943. Their faces and hands had been blackened by burnt cork. There was a white band on the back of each man's jacket, to enable them to distinguish each other at a few yards' distance. While one group gathered samples of the sand, the others, with Francis Vourch, groped their way between the obstacles. They were looking for one of the "Belgian barn doors," those huge obstacles strong enough to stop a landing craft going at full speed. They found one. Cautiously making certain that no grenade was attached to it, they cut off a piece of it with a hacksaw. One man collected some seaweed to hide the cut, then they all withdrew to their rubber dinghy, rowed quietly out to sea, and were picked up a mile off shore by the motor launch which had brought them across.

A staff officer of Combined Operations was waiting for them on the dock at Newhaven. He took the piece of steel to London that same night, and it was submitted to a laboratory analysis. The exact dimensions of the obstacle were known from aerial photographs: three meters square, with a horizontal base four meters long and three meters wide. A model of it could therefore be built to exact size and, because of the analysis of the metal, to exact weight. This model was taken to the camp where the Beach Clearance Units of the Royal Engineers were training, and in the next few days specialists determined the size of the explosive charges needed to blow up one of these three-ton steel monsters, and where they had to be placed.

A strange problem arose in connection with the antitank obstacles known as "Czech hedgehogs." These were made of three steel bars cut from rails. The bars, 1.2 meters long, were joined at the middle, perpendicular to one another. Similar "hedgehogs" were set up in an army camp in England, due account being taken of the weight of French rails: 75 pounds. These obstacles were crushed by the engineers' bulldozers. But then an officer discovered that in 1918 the United States had sent some 100-pound rails to France. Models were made with this American material. The bulldozers were powerless against them. There was only a very slight chance that Rommel's "hedgehogs" had been made from the American rails, but that chance remained, and it had to be checked.

Everything had to be checked: the strength of the offshore currents, the depth of the water, the slope of the beaches, the thickness and consistency of the land, the shape and weight of the obstacles. Before the armies, whose ultimate objective was the heart of Germany, could be launched, Sherlock Holmeses with blackened faces and hands had to go and examine the beaches of France in the dark, for the success of the invasion might depend on any one of the clues they brought back.

But to make sure that this elaborately and minutely planned invasion would fail, the Germans had only to know a date and the name of a French province.

## 3. The Man from Stockholm and the Man from Oslo

ON a bitterly cold night in that same month of March, 1944, a few men were huddled together in a truck taking them to the edge of the Stockholm airport. The wind was sweeping across the runways, swirling the snow. The truck came to a stop a few yards from an enclosure protected by barbed wire, marked off by portable barriers and glaringly illuminated by six floodlights. In the middle stood the British airplane which made the weekly flight between Scotland and Sweden. There were Swedish sentries with rifles on their shoulders pacing back and forth along the barriers. This warlike display, a surprising sight in a neutral country, often made the British airmen smile; and the Swedish soldiers assigned to guard duty in the arctic temperatures were probably dismayed by it. Neither the airmen nor the sentries, nor even the Swedish authorities, had any idea that on another cold night two German saboteurs had crawled close to the barriers with the intention of blowing up the plane. The order had come from Hitler, who could not stand the idea of this plane making its regular run and insolently flying over occupied Norway. But the sight of the Swedish sentries had made the two saboteurs retreat and the plan had been abandoned.

The passengers in the truck got out and ran toward the gangway, bending double against the gusts of air from the whirling propellers, and climbed into the plane. The crew was already aboard. The sentries moved the barriers and the plane taxied to the end of the runway. Two minutes later it had taken off and was turning westward.

The lights were on inside the plane but there were thick curtains screening the windows. The half-dozen passengers wrapped themselves in blankets and sought a comfortable position for sleeping. One of the six was a regular, the courier with the diplomatic pouch from the British embassy in Stockholm; four were R.A.F. men who had been shot down over Norway and had succeeded in crossing into neutral Sweden. The sixth passenger was a small, elderly man with a sad, lined face, who made a painful contrast to the youthful buoyancy of the airmen. When the man beside him struck up a conversation with him, he said his name was Joseph Jan Vanhove and that he was a Belgian. Then he pulled a little bundle of newspaper clippings from his pocket and passed them to the airman one at a time, translating each one into English. They proved to the airman that one should never judge by appearances. The clippings came from the German-controlled Belgian newspapers and described his puny companion as one of the chief Resistance leaders, responsible for the finances of the underground groups. He had barely escaped arrest, there was a price on his head, and the Germans threatened to execute anyone caught helping him. As an aid to a possible Judas, the papers had published a photograph of the Resistance leader being sought.

The astonished airman plied him with questions. How had Vanhove managed to escape the Gestapo? How had he gotten to Sweden? The little Belgian refused to answer. He explained that at the British embassy in Stockholm he had been told to be discreet and save the story of his adventures for the intelligence officers who would question him in London.

While the passengers gradually dropped off to sleep, Joseph Vanhove was probably thinking that the idea of the newspaper clippings had been a stroke of genius. The airman had reacted in the same way as his compatriots at the embassy. The members of the French Resistance whom Vanhove had contacted a few months earlier had also shown fraternal enthusiasm when he had shown them the clippings. Their credulity had still been unshaken when they faced a German firing squad. That success had decided the German Secret Service to send Vanhove after its supreme objective and obsession: the date and place of the Allied invasion.

Everything had gone well so far. Unless, by some bitter misfortune, a German night fighter shot down the plane on its way to Scotland, Vanhove would be in London within a few hours. He expected to be questioned there by experts whose eyes would not fill with tears when they read his clippings. But he had no great fear of this final screening, for the Germans had never before used the Stockholm route to introduce their agents into Britain. So far they had sent them, usually disguised as Resistance fighters, by way of Spain or Portugal.

Oswald John Job had gone that way. In October, 1943, he had arrived at the British embassy in Madrid, ragged, hungry and penniless. It had not even been necessary to give him a cover story. Job was of British nationality. The story he told on arriving in England, on November 1, 1943, was that he had escaped from the camp at St.-Denis, just outside Paris, where British civilians captured during the swift German advance in 1940 were interned. This story was accepted. However, the Spanish escape route was so suspect that everyone who came that way was kept under discreet watch for many months by the counterespionage services. And the latter became very curious about the great number of communications sent by Job, through the Red Cross, to his recent fellow internees. His letters were intercepted and examined, and were discovered to carry secret messages written in invisible ink. The internees to whom Job had written never received his letters: they had all gone straight to the German Secret Service.

Oswald John Job, aged fifty-nine, was hanged at Pentonville Prison on March 16, 1944.

The original plan had been to put Vanhove on one of the Spanish freighters that took oranges to England and have him slip ashore while the cargo was being unloaded. But since German agents had started placing booby traps in the crates of oranges, these ships were given a thorough search on arrival in a British port. Then some clever person had remembered that Spanish ships also took oranges to Stockholm. Why not make use of the Swedish route? The British carefully screened everyone coming from Spain, but would probably be less on their guard against someone arriving by way of Sweden.

Vanhove had become a spy not from inclination but from necessity. He had been a waiter at the Hôtel Métropole in Brussels when it was requisitioned by the Germans, and he had subsequently become associated with a certain Captain von Eilenberg who was running a flourishing black-market business. The German police discovered it, and von Eilenberg was sent to the Russian front. As for Vanhove, he was offered the choice between death by firing squad or work as a spy. Heroism was not his strong point.

Would Vanhove have recognized Hans Schmidt again if he had met him at some street corner in England? He had waited on Schmidt at the Métropole, but that had been in August, 1940, and since then thousands of customers had eaten in the restaurant. Hans Schmidt, with his hard features, fair hair and gray eyes, was apparently no different from the other victorious warriors having a good time in Brussels. Yet he was not German but Danish; and while the other officers were speculating about their chances of landing on English soil, he was sure of being in London before the end of the month. For he had been brought to Brussels to be parachuted over England, after being instructed in his new profession of spy.

Hans Schmidt, twenty-six, mechanic by trade, jumped from a Heinkel one moonless night at the end of August, 1940, and landed safely in England. He was still there in March, 1944. He was working on a farm in the southwest, and had become perfectly integrated into English life. In 1942 the Germans had even received a radio message from him, one of the most unusual ever received by any Secret Service: "Will be out of touch for two weeks. Just got married. Going on honeymoon." Another message was sent in 1943, just as unusual though quite logical: "Am father of a seven-pound boy." Hans Schmidt was obviously out of danger. After such a long time, why should British counterespionage take any interest in him. Yet Hans Schmidt, who had been sent to England in 1940 to help prepare for the German invasion, was to send the Germans information about the plans for the Allied invasion nearly four years later.

The parachutist, lying face down on the floor of the plane, heard the pilot shout into the intercom: "England!" The three members of the crew all started yelling "Booo! Booo! Booo!" The radio operator, seated just above the parachutist, explained to him that they were imitating the sound of a Stuka making a dive-bombing attack, and that it was the war cry of the Luftwaffe. Aircrews shouted it when they arrived over England.

The Junker-11 was actually flying over Scotland, but to the parachutist there was very little difference. Spies got hanged whether caught in England or Scotland. He rubbed his legs together to get some warmth into them. It was about the only movement he could make; the Junker-11, a reconnaissance plane, was not intended to carry a passenger, and even less one making a parachute jump. He was wedged between a machine gun and various instruments. One of the three machine guns had been removed to enable the jump to be made, and a trapdoor was fitted in its place. When the parachutist received the signal he would pull a lever to open the trap and plunge down head first. Of all the ways of leaving an aircraft in flight this was undoubtedly the least agreeable, especially as the opening was narrow and the parachutist would have to wiggle and twist frantically in order to get through it.

An hour before takeoff he had stripped naked in a hut on the airfield and Secret Service men had given his civilian clothes a thorough inspection. His knees had been bandaged to limit the risk of an accident on landing, and he had dressed again knowing there was nothing in his clothes to betray him as a German agent. He had put on a flying suit over his civilian clothes, then buckled on his parachute, which he had previously folded and packed himself, as required by Luftwaffe regulations.

The radio operator now tapped him on the shoulder; he unfastened his oxygen mask, exchanged his airman's helmet for a parachutist's, then hooked up the ripcord of his parachute. At the second tap he pulled the lever and managed to extricate himself from the plane. A few seconds later he was swinging below his open parachute in the empty, peaceful sky.

He was an ordinary man, a Norwegian miner who had enthusiastically joined Quisling's Nazi Party; he had been easily persuaded to go on a spying mission to Britain. It was the mission that was extraordinary. His task was to spy on two of his compatriots, Jack Berg and Olaf Klausen, who were already in Britain working for the Germans.

These two, young, daring and handsome, had long been the great pride of their masters, and even the German High Command was full of admiration for their exploits. They had been taken by seaplane to within a mile or two of the Scottish coast, and had gone ashore by rubber dinghy without difficulty; they had cycled to London, and a few weeks later several reports of sabotage in southern England had appeared in the newspapers. That had been in the spring of 1941. Since then, unbelievable luck seemed to have been with them. On February 20 and again on June 18, 1943, money and explosives were dropped to them by parachute, enabling them to carry out two more series of sabotage. At the same time they were regularly sending back by radio important information about troop movements in Britain.

But there were skeptics in Berlin who were beginning to think this was all too good to be true. Considering the rate at which German agents sent to Britain were caught and hanged, it was amazing that Berg and Klausen should have evaded capture for three years. They must have been caught and persuaded to become double agents. Yet was not Hans Schmidt a living proof that it was possible to carry on for four years without falling into the enemy's net? To this the skeptics replied that the two cases were not comparable. The two Norwegians were supposed to be wandering about the country, with no fixed address, no job, and liable to be caught in a security check, whereas the Dane had a home and even a family, which warded off suspicion and ensured his safety.

The Norwegians' supporters retorted that the Luftwaffe had bombed two towns in Scotland as a diversion when money and explosives were being dropped on February 20, 1943. The civilian casualties had been heavy. And the Norwegians had been previously informed of the raid to be made on the towns near the drop zone. Would the British have deliberately sacrificed the lives of dozens of women and children in order to make the enemy believe that the two agents were still operating freely?

As the controversy continued, the heads of the German Secret Service asked a special committee, including psychiatrists and other specialists, to give an opinion on the problem. The members studied every message received from the two Norwegians since 1941 but discovered no indication that they were being forced to send false information. Then catch-questions were sent to them. Their replies were quite candid. The committee concluded that they were sincere, but that was not considered sufficient by high authority. However, in March, 1944, the need for information about the enemy's intentions was so great that the slightest opportunity could not be neglected. And Berg and Klausen, having been so long in enemy territory, were capable of discovering the replies to the two questions on which Germany's fate depended. But it was still necessary to know with absolute certainty that they could be trusted.

Such was the mission of the Norwegian Nazi. The task of this spy was to spy on other spies.

## 4. Lily in Lisbon

IN Lisbon, March evenings already have a springlike mildness. Lily Sergueiev, young and blor.de, was finishing a very good dinner in the restaurant of the Avenida Palace. She sat for a few more minutes listening to the South American tunes of the orchestra, then went up to her room and tidied some of her things. She became less tense as the time for her rendezvous approached. She took off her black dress, slipped into a tweed skirt and a brown sweater, and combed her hair. At half-past eight she put on a coat and left the hotel, joining the crowd strolling down to the Plaza Rossio. But when she got there she jumped on a streetcar which took her back to her starting point. She got off and, hands thrust into her coat pockets, walked slowly up the wide avenue. A warm breeze was rustling the two lines of palm trees. The tamarisk was in bloom and the air was fragrant with jasmine. It was hard to realize that in England it was still winter.

She came to the Plaza Pombal, which was unlit. She walked around it, stopped behind the statue of the Marquês de Pombal and looked at the luminous dial of her watch. Her "contact" in Lisbon had set their rendezvous for nine o'clock.

One minute after nine a car came speeding out of a dark street. Its headlights were dimmed. It swung round the square with a grinding of tires and jerked to a stop beside her. At the same time the headlights were turned off.

The rear door opened and Lily Sergueiev was yanked into

the car by her arm. As she fell on to the back seat the car shot forward, completed its turn around the square and headed down the street it had appeared from.

The dim light from the streetlamps was not enough for her to distinguish either the driver's face or that of the man next to her. But when the driver spoke she knew he was not Kliemann. He asked her how she had got out of England. She refused to answer: she would talk only to Kliemann. The driver said she was being taken to him, and stopped questioning her. Then the man next to her asked if her name was Nina and if she had been born in Kiev.

"No," she replied.

"It's strange, I once met a girl who had the same name as you. She was very gay. I brought her from Danzig to Rouen."

"Take your hat off."

The man raised the soft hat that was hiding his eyes. "Why do you want me to do that?" he said in surprise.

"To see if you've changed at all, Captain Büking. What have you done with the *Adel Traber?*"

He uttered an exclamation of surprise, seized her hands and squeezed them. The next few minutes were very friendly and animated, as the two recalled the good old times before the war and that voyage on the *Adel Traber,* of which Büking had been captain. Lily, an adventurous young French girl, had gone off to Estonia to visit an uncle, then found herself without any money to return to France. It was a situation that many girls would have found embarrassing, but not Lily Sergueiev. She had always traveled on foot from Paris to Warsaw, and then cycled around Europe; and the outbreak of war had caught her at Beirut while on her way, still by bicycle, from Paris to Saigon.

In Estonia she had gone to the Worms Company and asked for free passage on one of their freighters. Captain Büking now reminded her that she had been seasick all the way to the mouth of the Seine. On recovering she had organized a terrific pillow-fight among the crew; feathers had been found even down in the bunkers. Büking and Lily agreed that it was indeed a small world and that times had certainly changed. Still, it was strange to meet again in Lisbon, both working for the German Secret Service.

A little later Lily Sergueiev climbed the stairs of a rooming house that smelled of rancid oil, at 23 Traversa Sao, and found Major Kliemann, her superior on this mission, waiting for her. He was still as fat as ever, still red-faced and well dressed. He was lying on the divan with his mustache drooping, looking sorry for himself. The two stared at each other in silence for a long time.

"I've been very ill," he said at length. "And how about you? You wrote and said you were in bad shape. Are you better?"

"It seems I've had it. The doctors in England gave me another six months to live. I must hurry up and live them."

"Do you want to go back to France?"

"Why? Haven't I been successful?"

"Beyond all our hopes. You got into England, you've come out, and now you're going back again. Do you realize you're the first to have succeeded in such an exploit? I'm very proud of you, Lily!"

He had met her through a mutual friend, a Berlin journalist. She had at once agreed to work as a German agent. She was a good recruit, intelligent and amazingly resourceful, as her travels proved. For two long years she had been taught ciphering, the use of invisible ink, the economic and strategic geography of Great Britain, the organization of her armed forces, with their uniforms, ranks and insignia, and the silhouettes of British tanks, aircraft and warships. By the spring of 1943 she had been fully prepared and briefed. She had first been taken to the unoccupied zone of France, from where she had crossed into Spain with the discreet help of the German authorities. The plan was for her to go to Madrid and apply for a British visa. She had an English cousin, a member of an upper-class family, whose name she could give as a reference. Everything had gone well. Thanks to her cousin's influence she had even obtained a job at the Ministry of Information, in the office of a man named Bernstein.

"Sydney Bernstein is head of the Films Division," she explained to Kliemann. "He's sent me to Lisbon to contact script writers and novelists who've escaped from France. The British intend to make propaganda films to be shown in European countries as soon as they're liberated, right after the invasion. Bernstein wants to outdo the Americans, who've already made a series of such films. I've seen some of them—they're awful, enough to make the French and Belgians die laughing . . . That's why Bernstein wants to

employ script writers who've lived under the German occupation."

"Excellent," said Kliemann. "If this comes off. I can send you as many script writers as you want. And how about the radio? How are you going to get it into England?"

The transmitter was concealed in a cheap old-fashioned radio. Technicians had hidden the crystals in one of the tubes.* The whole set would have to be taken to pieces to discover the sockets for the transmitting key. Kliemann's reason for coming to Lisbon from Paris had been to bring the transmitter to Lily Sergueiev. Previously she had used invisible ink to send her information in letters. The letters were sent to Lisbon, and from there were forwarded via Madrid to Paris. It took much too long. Lily was working in a British Ministry. Through her cousin, she met British and American officers socially. In the past few months she had given the Germans much information on troop concentrations in Britain. She was capable of discovering the secrets of the invasion, but that would be no use unless she could send them on with the shortest possible delay. The transmitter would enable her to do so. But Kliemann was skeptical about her chances of getting it to England.

"I've thought of another plan," she told him. "Tomorrow morning I'm going to see a young man I know at the British embassy here. His name is Stewart. I'll ask him to get me a secondhand radio; they're impossible to get in London. Two or three days later I'll tell him I've found one, but that I'd like to avoid paying duty on it. He'll send it on for me in the diplomatic pouch. I'm sure he won't refuse to do that for me."

"You're wonderful! But what if he does refuse?"

"We'll think of something else."

"All right. Now, when are you going to transmit?"

It was decided that Lily would transmit her messages on Mondays, Wednesdays and Thursdays, at twelve-thirty in the afternoon and eleven in the evening. If she was discovered by British counterespionage and forced to send false information, she was to signal this with a dash after her call sign. Kliemann ended his instructions by urging her to be very careful. Berlin was highly satisfied with her work. She

---

* Each transmitter had its own crystal which could be plugged into the set and gave out the particular wave-length that the set worked on [TRANS. NOTE].

must run no risk, especially not to obtain information of a secondary nature. She must concentrate all her activities on the coming invasion and pay particular attention to the region between Bristol and Salisbury, where her cousin lived. If the Allies had decided to invade across the Straits of Dover they would be concentrating troops and materials in southeastern England. But if she should notice heavy troop concentration in the Bristol-Salisbury area, it would indicate Normandy as the invasion target.

Lily flew to London on March 23, taking a huge basket of bananas and pineapples with her. As for the transmitter, it would be sent to her in the diplomatic pouch. It was bitterly cold in the plane, and Lily sat shivering in spite of her four blankets. She was leaving Lisbon and its warm sunshine, exchanging the advancing spring for the last of a London winter. Perhaps she had felt the caress of real sunshine on her body for the last time. Six months to live before the final attack of uremia, she had told Kliemann. But she had learned that from Dr. Robertson on January 3, so there were little more than three months left to her. Yet the American doctor had told her: "Robertson wasn't very generous. You may easily live for a year." Three months or a year, the alternative did not disturb her; it was as though a few weeks more or less were of small importance beside the black certainty she possessed. She went to carry out her mission with the lofty and prodigiously effective detachment of those who have nothing to lose.

In that month of March, 1944, when agents from Stockholm, Lisbon and Oslo were converging on Britain to discover the great secret, most German embassies and legations received a cable from von Ribbentrop, the Minister of Foreign Affairs, which was headed "Highly Confidential and Most Secret." It asked them to find out as soon as possible, and at any price, the meaning of the code name OVERLORD.

This cable must have puzzled all members of the diplomatic staffs except Ludwig Moyzisch, the representative of the German Secret Service at the German embassy in Ankara, for he was one of the relays that the word OVERLORD had passed through on its way to von Ribbentrop's office. The departure point had been in the Foreign Office in London; documents relating to Operation OVERLORD were sent from there to the British ambassador in Ankara, Sir Hughe

Knatchbull-Hugessen. Locked by him in the embassy safe, the documents had been taken out and photographed by his valet, Elyesa Bazna. A few hours later, Moyzisch had sent the photographs to Berlin, having paid Bazna the impressive sum of ten thousand pounds for each roll of film. The traffic had been going on for six months. Photographs of several hundred secret documents had been sent to Berlin. Many were of the utmost importance, for Knatchbull-Hugessen was a top-ranking diplomat and the Foreign Office sent him information that went beyond his function in Ankara. He was kept informed of decisions made at the highest level, where Stalin, Churchill and Roosevelt were shaping the postwar world. He was sent copies of the proceedings at the conferences of Moscow, Teheran and Casablanca. In Bazna, who was called "Cicero" because of the eloquence of the documents he made available, the Germans had the most effective agent of all their espionage network.

On receipt of von Ribbentrop's cable, Moyzisch got out his file of all the microfilms received from Cicero. After studying them closely for several hours he reached the conclusion that OVERLORD was the name for a military operation on the largest scale: the opening of the second front by the Allies. He immediately sent a coded message to Berlin; as a professional he fully realized the importance of his discovery. The German agents operating in Britain must be warned without delay that the invasion whose date and location they were seeking bore the code name OVERLORD.

At that time the small German colony in Turkey was still recovering from the incredible event that had happened two months earlier at the consulate in Istanbul. Two members of the German Secret Service had defected and were said to have taken some documents to the English. The incident had shaken German Intelligence from top to bottom. But Moyzisch was of the opinion that, regrettable though it was for psychological reasons, its practical consequences were not very serious—certainly of no comparison with the importance of the message he had just sent to Berlin.

How could Moyzisch have guessed that the treachery of two minor officials had placed the whole German Secret Service in jeopardy?

## 5. The Gorilla and the Fox

PEPE, an austere killer, stabbed the German sentry, and Dominique Ponchardier, who killed with feeling, saw him come back wiping his hands. Aided by Pineau, they had cut a hole in the fence and slipped into the factory grounds. They had seen a sentry outside one of the buildings, but thanks to Pepe that problem was now removed. Pistols in hand, they moved towards the main building. Two men armed with submachine guns had been posted at another entrance; their task was to create a diversion in the event of an attack by the Germans. There were another two in the rear, to cover the retreat. The five motorcycles, three of which had sidecars, had been left about a quarter of a mile away, hidden just off the roadside.

The factory was in a quarry several miles from Saint-Servan. It had been requisitioned by the Germans and served as a command post. If the information which had reached the Resistance group was correct, the strongroom in the main building held documents of the highest importance.

One of the three men gently tried the handle of the door while the other two covered him with their weapons. The door was not even locked. They burst in and exchanged a few shots with two officers who appeared, sleepy-eyed and clutching pistols, and who fell dead, one in his pajamas, the other in his nightshirt. Then they smashed the transmitter that was in the room. The telephone wires had been cut at the very beginning, so the factory was now theoretically out of touch with the outside world. There still remained an officer and two men, whose lack of reaction was reassuring or else disquieting.

The explosives they had brought with them proved unnecessary; there was no strongroom, not even a safe to blow open. Just cupboards, with enough documents on the shelves to fill a couple of trucks. This unexpected abundance was the first setback of the night: the three men had brought only a potato sack. How was any sorting to be done?

They plunged into the mass of paper. Only one of the three could read even a little German, which did not help matters. When the sack was stuffed full they began thrusting papers into their pockets, then between their overcoats and their jackets, then between jacket and vest, then vest and shirt. Looking like fat Buddhas, they continued ripping open files and scattering documents, treading on the growing layer of papers spread around their feet. As the minutes went by the silence of the three Germans became decidedly alarming. If they gave the alarm and the quarry was surrounded, no one would be able to escape from the trap. Yet there was that fascinating mass of documents which had the men almost stupefied, so that they went on tossing papers about like archivists suddenly gone mad.

They had become far more used to dramatic episodes, since 1940, than to such burlesque scenes. Dominique Ponchardier was a hard-headed Auvergnat with the build of a young gorilla and a dark look from under thick eyebrows. Although not yet thirty, he had become one of the big names in the French underground movement; he was the leader, with his brother Pierre, of the Resistance group *Sosies*. It was he who had organized the French end of Operation JERICHO, on February 18, 1944, when Mosquito planes bombed Amiens prison, and dozens of Resistance members under sentence of death escaped from the gaping buildings. Since then, Ponchardier had figured at the head of the list of men sought by the Gestapo. He ought not to have been taking part in this attack on the factory. He knew too much, and a Resistance leader had no right deliberately to risk being captured. But Ponchardier considered it was at times his duty. Not so much for the grand gesture as for the invigorating effect upon his group. So he had led the attack instead of his lieutenant, Pepe, who was just as capable of doing it.

Pepe, a Communist who had fought in Spain with the International Brigade, was a small, wiry, dark-haired man with rather stern features. Like a Stakhanovite of violence, he killed coldly and quickly, as though it were part of some urgent Five-Year Plan, whereas Ponchardier was more like a surly but good-hearted bear in such matters. In another age they would have been successful war-barons, but the needs of their day had obliged them to become part secret agents and part killers, and for three years they had been mixed up in espionage, murder and sabotage. The Ponchardier-Pepe combination was probably the worst possible one for any German soldier to meet.

A burst of firing jerked the plunderers out of their frenzied obsession with papers. They stood still and located the sound. It had come from where the two men had been posted to create a diversion. So retreat was still possible. The three dashed towards the opening they had made in the fence and joined the other two left as a rear guard. To reach their motorcycles they had to go down into a bushy ravine. But they could not find the path again without using their flashlights, and this brought an enemy patrol in their direction. They shot three of the Germans and plunged into the ravine. Just then Ponchardier felt a violent blow on his right leg and knew he had been hit. They could hear the firing of their last two men coming gradually nearer, but accompanied by shots and bursting grenades from German pursuers. They dared not use their flashlights again, and none of them had noticed earlier that the ravine split into two branches. The rearguard men took the right fork, but Ponchardier, Pepe and Pineau, slowed down by the sack and their wads of documents, took the wrong turn and came up against a thick mass of branches.

Pineau, exhausted, handed the sack to Ponchardier. The Germans must have reached the fork by now; it was impossible to turn back. They forced their way through the brambles and, scratched and torn, reached the top of the ravine, where they found the last two men. A hail of bullets greeted this meeting. The pursuers had caught up, but remained under cover. What point was there in taking risks? The alarm had been given and all the roads would soon be blocked by armored vehicles. All they had to do was pin down the Frenchmen and wait for reinforcements.

Ponchardier knew that too. He told the men he had just rejoined to press on towards the motorcycles, to link up with the other two and be ready for them all to make a dash for it. The hardest was still to come: to get away from the area of Saint-Servan which would soon be swarming with German uniforms.

He started off again, firing at the Germans who followed. Pepe went on ahead, acting as a scout. Ponchardier was left alone with Pineau. There was a burst of fire. Ponchardier felt a burning pain in his right buttock and Pineau collapsed. Pepe continued walking, unaware of what had happened. The Germans were advancing through the undergrowth, closing in.

Ponchardier bent over the wounded man, almost hoping he was dead; but he was not quite. He could not be left there, that was impossible. Ponchardier got him over his left shoulder, grasped the sack with his right hand, and staggered forward again, stumbling over loose stones. His trousers were wet with blood and stuck to his thighs, shortening his stride. There was no feeling left in his right leg and buttock; it was as though they had ceased to exist. He kept going. There could be no question of abandoning a wounded man to the enemy. Never. But the sack? If he dropped it, he could go twice as fast and reach the motorcycles. The full sack was as heavy as Pineau. It got stuck between stones and caught on bushes. It was a detestable, odious burden. Ponchardier told himself he would certainly have dropped it if he had not been from Auvergne. Instead, he gripped it more tightly and staggered on.

The sack contained a whole mass of papers just good enough for the toilet. The three men's minds had reeled at the sight of such a wealth of documents, and they had grabbed blindly at them. Ponchardier's sweat was saturating a French newspaper and an old German magazine which he had thrust inside his shirt, without realizing what he was doing. But right at the bottom of the sack was a bundle of special documents relating to the Atlantic Wall. Ponchardier was as yet unaware of all this, of course; he had no idea either that he was finishing in his own way, by sheer strength, a cunning, crafty piece of work begun two years earlier by the old fox Duchez.

Duchez would have been valuable to any school of espionage: he was the perfect example of the kind of man not to be used in intelligence work at any price. A house painter with a wife and children, he was loquacious and careless. A good fellow, and one of the bravest in his home town of Caen, but . . . Every day, the people in the cafés he visited were entertained by his latest account of the fight between

René Duchez and Adolf Hitler. It was usually the latter, in spite of the means at his disposal, who got the worst of it. At apéritif time he always had a crowd of listeners; they smiled and laughed, and clapped him on the back. Good old Duchez! They told each other that if he were really in the Resistance he would have been taken long ago to visit the cellars of the Gestapo headquarters at 25 Rue des Jacobins.

Most of the members of the Resistance group *Centurie,* to which Duchez in fact belonged, firmly believed that such a visit could not long be delayed. The painter was their constant worry. But it was in vain that they implored and warned him. Duchez's reply was to tell them to keep calm. "Keep calm and cool, now and always!" was his favorite saying. He was disastrous. There were probably only two categories of people who did not lose any sleep over Duchez: the leaders of his Resistance group, especially Léonard Gille, a Caen lawyer, because they knew his great cunning; and the local Gestapo officers, because they thought he was too stupid to be dangerous.

During the morning of May 7, 1942, Duchez read an official notice on the board outside the town hall. It said that the Todt Organization—which had begun building the Wall —needed some of its offices redecorated and asked for estimates, which had to be submitted by five o'clock on the evening of May 6. Duchez was therefore too late. But he disliked missing an opportunity of penetrating one of the Todt lairs. That was the kind of exploit which built up his legend. His friends would shudder retrospectively and tell him that the first duty of an intelligence agent was to remain in the shadows, to which he would reply: "Keep calm and cool, now and always!" Moreover, one had to trust in Providence; some unexpected chance of doing harm might present itself.

Duchez drove his old Peugeot truck to the Todt headquarters in Caen. This was on the Rue de la Geôle,* a name that might have stirred dark forebodings in a timorous heart. There was barbed wire in front of the building and a sentry at the door. Duchez was asked for his pass. He put on the smile of a satisfied idiot which usually disarmed people and gave them a false feeling of intellectual superiority. But it had no effect on the sentry. Duchez tried in vain to

---

* "Street of the Jail."

explain; the sentry was forcing him back into the street when a sergeant came out of the guardroom, drawn by the commotion.

"It's about the estimates!" cried Duchez. "The painting you want done!"

The German did not seem to understand, so Duchez stepped across to the sentry-box and made broad, eloquent gestures of painting it. The results were entirely unexpected and unfortunate. The sergeant struck Duchez on the back of the neck with his forearm, knocking him to the ground, and the sentry gave him several kicks on his behind. Then the two dragged him into the guardroom. There an officer sternly asked him if he knew what it cost to make fun of the Führer. Duchez, bruised and baffled, did not know what to say in spite of all his calmness. But when the officer started raising the spector of the firing squad, Duchez remembered that his sworn enemy, Adolf Hitler, had also been a house painter, and realized that his demonstration at the sentry-box had been misunderstood. Explanations followed, with laughs of goodwill on the German side, of relief on the French side; and then Duchez was taken to see the young lieutenant responsible for the upkeep of the building.

When asked his price for papering two offices, Duchez named a sum low enough to be sure of being given the job. The officer, beaming at this, took him along to the office of *Bauleiter* Schnedderer.

Schnedderer, a burly man with a scar on his face, had definite tastes in wallpaper. He wanted either blue horsemen on a light yellow background or silver cannons on a dark blue background. Duchez declared that his choice showed good taste, swore he would do all he could to satisfy him, and offered to return with some samples the next day. This was accepted. Duchez spent the afternoon looking through his stock of wallpaper, and the evening telling friends in the Café des Touristes how he had succeeded in getting among soldiers of that other house painter.

The next morning, just before ten, he entered the office of *Bauleiter* Schnedderer for the second time, with a roll of samples under his arm.

## 6. A Map and a Trump Card

PONCHARDIER thought it was the last straw when Pepe started shooting at him, mistaking him in the darkness for the Germans. He momentarily forgot his pains and dashed into the undergrowth, shouting curses. The shooting stopped. The Germans were still following but keeping their distance. Now and then they fired a burst of shots to harass their quarry.

All of Ponchardier's men had reached the motorcycles, which had been left under the guard of a local Resistance member. He now lay dying on the ground, face down, with his flashlight in his hand. A stray bullet, perhaps—or had he rashly turned on his flashlight when he heard the shooting? They lifted him into one of the sidecars, along with the sack. Pineau was carefully placed in another, and Ponchardier fitted himself into the third, then fainted. The unwounded men jumped onto the motorcycles and were about to roar away when Pepe, with icy calmness, ordered them to push their machines. He sent one man on ahead. The others followed on foot, exhausted by the fight and still doubtful of escape. They had covered about five hundred yards when the scout came rushing back. There was a German roadblock ahead—two armored cars and soldiers with automatic weapons. If it had not been for Pepe's foresight they would have sped blindly and helplessly into the machine guns.

They turned off the road and plunged into the woods. They could hear German armored vehicles taking up positions on all the roads. There were seven of them, and two were badly wounded. Their grenades had all been used during the first skirmish, and they had only a few loaded magazines left for their submachine guns. If they moved on they were almost certain to run into the enemy; if they remained where they were, the net would close in on them. Pepe crept ahead a little, through the trees, towards the roadblock; but he was soon back, without having gotten near it. The forest was alive with German soldiers. They were spread out, combing the area; and in a few minutes they would be upon the fugitives. A brief council of war was held with Ponchardier, who had revived. More of the enemy must certainly be combing the area behind them. The only hope of escape was a lateral flight through the forest, between the advancing lines. The motorcycles would have to be abandoned.

They moved off westward, Pepe supporting Pineau, Ponchardier hobbling along, the others carrying the dying man and the sack. Daybreak was near. They came to a river. An old boat with a deck was tied to the bank. It was half full of water, but they concealed themselves in it. Ponchardier lost consciousness again, then came to. Despite Pepe's protests he gave orders that it was to be every man for himself. The unwounded men would try to reach the forester's lodge that was to serve as their emergency shelter. He would stay in the boat with the dying man. The others would come back for them later, if possible.

Ponchardier, left alone in the icy water with the dying man, was so cold and exhausted that he had no reaction when he heard the voices of the Germans who were searching the river bank. He was beyond fear, beyond hope. His head was throbbing feverishly. Lying there in the muddy water, he was convinced his wounds would become gangrenous. The face of the dying man, who was still conscious, was close beside his own. The man had a bullet in one of his lungs. With each breath he spat blood, which dribbled down his chin and formed a pinkish beard. Ponchardier kept wiping the beard away with the back of his hand. Face to face, they lay watching each other dying. Beside them was the sack.

Duchez later said that it had all happened as if in a dream. His hands had seemed to move of their own accord, and he had merely watched them.

He was standing three paces from the desk where *Bauleiter* Schnedderer was bent over the samples of wallpaper, showing his bald head. It was already due to a series of lucky breaks that Duchez had gotten this far. Only by chance had he read the Todt notice outside the town hall; and, having read it, he ought never to have thought of applying, because it was too late. If it had not been for the scene with the sentry he would never have been taken to the lieutenant. But the most extraordinary thing was for a *Bauleiter* to have interested himself in the minor matter of a choice of wall-paper. Duchez's luck might well have stopped there, but . . .

"Come in!" cried Schnedderer without raising his head.

The officer who had knocked entered the room, saluted with a click of his heels, and put a large bundle of maps on the *Bauleiter's* desk. These were acknowledged with a curt nod of the bald head, and the officer at once withdrew. Schnedderer pushed the samples of wallpaper aside and picked up the top map of the bundle. He sat back in his chair to unfold it, but it was too long for him to do so en-tirely. The map was drawn on thin tracing paper, and Duchez recognized the outline of the Normandy coast. Schnedderer looked at it for only a few seconds, then put it down on his desk and returned to the samples. But there came another knock on the door. A sergeant, standing stiffly at attention, made some sort of report to the *Bauleiter*. Duchez did not understand a word.

Schnedderer got up and opened a door at the back of the room. The sergeant had gone out again. Schnedderer was leaning against the doorway, speaking evenly and distinctly as though dictating to someone in the further room, whom Duchez could not see. Keeping his eyes on the German's broad back, in case he should suddenly turn around, Duchez took a step forward. He put out his hand and drew the map toward him. It was covered with annotations and my-sterious signs. He was able to make out a few words: "Block-house," "Main Defense Line." In thick red letters in one corner was *Streng Geheim*. He knew that meant "Top Secret."

He knew, of course, that he should not try to steal the map. The first duty of a Resistance member was to remain at liberty, for upon that depended the security of his whole group. And Duchez had not one chance in a thousand of succeeding. He did not even know whether all the maps in the bundle were the same. If they were not, and if, when Schnedderer had finished dictating he looked for the map he had been examining, Duchez would be seized in a mat-ter of seconds. Even if the maps were all the same, it would soon be discovered that one copy had disappeared from the *Bauleiter*'s office, and an investigation would inevitably lead to the painter.

Duchez took the map. Because he thought it was worth risking his life? Because he was foolhardy? Because he was a prisoner of his own legend and had to do what no one else would have done? He did not know, and never would know exactly. Sweating profusely, with his heart in his mouth and his stomach tied in knots, he saw his hands reach forward and take the map. He was powerless to prevent this mad act. Schnedderer was still dictating, leaning against the doorway. And now what was he to do with the map? Just behind him was a large mirror hanging from a nail. Duchez stealthily moved back a step, felt about with his right hand, still keeping his eyes on the German and slipped the map between the mirror and the wall. He moved back to the desk, looking as haggard and worn as someone who had been tortured. Schnedderer at last turned around, glanced at him rather absent-mindedly, and noticed nothing wrong. He showed him the wallpaper he had chosen and told him to start the job on Monday.

It had all been like a dream, or a nightmare. The hardest thing for Duchez was to go back at eight o'clock Monday morning. He had no hope that the theft would have gone unnoticed, and knew that suspicion was bound to fall on him. Going back to the Todt offices was almost equivalent to committing suicide. A professional secret agent might have been persuaded to do it at gunpoint. But Duchez was only an amateur who knew nothing of the rules. With his pot of paste in one hand and the rolls of paper under the other arm, he walked briskly past the guardroom and went in to start papering the first of the rooms. For two hours he worked away, singing in his squeaky voice, until a soldier came to tell him that it annoyed the officers. Duchez put on his sorry smile and asked when he could see *Bauleiter* Schnedderer. He felt reassured by now; the theft had not been discovered, and all he had to do was to retrieve the map.

"*Bauleiter* Schnedderer isn't here," replied the soldier. "If you want to see him," he added slyly, "you'll have to take the train to Saint-Malo."

"I'd rather wait," said Duchez with a hearty laugh. "Will he be back tomorrow?"

"Neither tomorrow nor the day after. He's been transferred. His place here has been taken by *Bauleiter* Keller."

It was goodbye to the map; Duchez would never see the inside of the office with the mirror again. He was more likely to see the inside of a Gestapo cell before very long. Schnedderer's sudden transfer must have been a disciplinary measure, following the disappearance of the map. But why had Duchez not already been arrested? There was no point in trying to understand; the whole situation seemed insane. He finished his work by five o'clock and was allowed to leave without hindrance. He had a good dinner and slept like a log. Next morning, he went back with his papering equipment and asked to see the young lieutenant responsible for the work done to the building.

"It's about *Bauleiter* Keller's office," Duchez said to him. "When shall I start work on it?"

"But you're not supposed to do it at all! Your job was the two offices you did yesterday."

"*Bauleiter* Schnedderer personally asked me to do it. He must have said something about it to the officer who replaced him . . ."

The lieutenant, disconcerted, took Duchez to the office with the mirror and reported to the new *Bauleiter*.

"I know nothing about it," thundered Keller. "And anyway, we've spent all our allowance for repairs."

Duchez, with his smile of a misunderstood idiot, explained that there had been no question of money between himself and *Bauleiter* Schnedderer. He had offered to repaper the office for nothing, as a token of his friendship for the German army. Genuine emotion softened the lieutenant's face. Duchez modestly lowered his eyes. Keller gave him a friendly thump on the back and told the lieutenant to have all the furniture taken out of the office so that the obliging decorator could go to work. Duchez protested strongly. He did not want to put German soldiers to all that trouble. Besides, there was no need; he would stack the furniture in the middle of the room and put a cover over it. That was what he usually did when papering a room. The *Bauleiter* appreciated this extra thoughtfulness; the lieutenant was overflowing with goodwill. They were all good fellows together.

It was a poor devil of an electrician who had done some work in the Todt building whom the Germans manhandled, a few days later, to make him confess to the theft. "What map?" he kept repeating. They finally released him. Duchez was never molested.

The map, which was ten feet long and more than two feet wide, arrived in London on June 21, 1942, with other documents brought out of France by the renowned Colonel Rémy; he was the head of the Resistance organization *Confrérie Notre-Dame,* upon which Duchez's group relied for its liaison with England. The map revealed what the Wall would eventually be like between Cherbourg and Honfleur, with its blockhouses, flamethrowers and gun batteries. The technical specifications of the principal fortifications were marked on it, as well as the range and firing angles of each battery, and the position of the ammunition and supply dumps, the telephone communications and the command posts.

Allied intelligence officers studied this wonderful gift with admiration tinged by sadness. For it was certain that the Germans, after the theft of the map, would alter their plans and this section of the Wall when completed would have little resemblance to the original conception of the Todt engineers. Such a conclusion was only logical; yet from beginning to end of this crazy episode there was no place for logic. The heads of the Todt organization were so dismayed that they did not report the loss of the map to the Gestapo, or to army headquarters or even to their immediate superiors. The work was begun in accordance with the original plans. Some weeks later, when the first reports on the fortifications being built reached London, it was the turn of Allied Intelligence officers to think the whole thing was crazy. But the evidence provided by aerial photographs removed all doubt: the Allies were actually in possession of a complete and detailed plan of the section of the Atlantic Wall being built in the future invasion area.

When the detestable sack disgorged its treasures in the dining room of a Paris apartment, nearly two years had passed since René Duchez's sleight-of-hand exploit in Caen; but the Allied Command was still deeply interested in the fortifications of the Wall. Discreet inspectors were being sent, as though by some conscientious architect, to report on the progress of the work. To discover the position and shape of a blockhouse was commendable; but to find out the quality of the concrete used, the weight of its iron reinforcement and the size of the gunslits was even better. René Duchez excelled at obtaining such items of information. He dropped into the little cafés used by the Todt workmen along the coast and chatted with them about building work, making out with a silly smile of vanity that in the past he had helped build defense works which would stand for centuries. His insinuations against their competence would rouse the men to argument; there was always some clever fellow who would seize a piece of paper to make a sketch and prove to Duchez that he was an ignorant fool. Duchez would agree glumly, pay for a round of drinks and leave, stuffing the piece of paper into his pocket.

The Ponchardier brothers' Resistance group *Sosies* was equally interested in the Wall. They were in touch with a French engineer who worked for the Todt organization and had a subgroup of thirty agents. Information kept coming in, adding to and keeping up to date the group's "Guide to the Atlantic Wall." It told a story of slackness, disloyalty, waste and muddle. The forced foreign labor was of little use to the Germans. Minor acts of sabotage were constantly occurring. Some of the concrete fortifications had been made with far too much sand for the cement used, and were likely to crumble at the first shell. All the relevant information sent to London by Resistance groups confirmed that, formidable though the Wall was on Duchez's map, it would prove a great fiasco when put to the test. But London was skeptical; the news was too good to be true. London thought the Resistance groups were believing what they wanted to believe, and asked them to check this information, even though it had already been confirmed a dozen times. This was why Dominique Ponchardier, exasperated, had organized the raid on the command post near Saint-Servan: since the men in London would not believe reports from French sources, he would send them information taken from German sources.

There must have been a cubic yard of papers and documents heaped on the dining-room floor. The survivors of the raid and some members of the group who knew German were sitting about the room. Ponchardier's behind had grown enormous: his right buttock was twice its usual size and felt as though it weighed a ton. The previous day a surgeon had taken some splinters of tibia from his right leg. The man with a perforated lung had died in his arms; it was not until night had fallen again and the Germans had abandoned their search that Pepe had been able to return to the waterlogged boat and rescue Ponchardier.

When the heap of papers had been sorted, the amount retained looked disappointing: just a bundle of handwritten notes. But they had been written by Field Marshal Erwin Rommel himself. They formed the text of an angry report he had composed after an inspection of the Atlantic Wall. Instruction No. 51 from the Führer had sent Rommel on a long journey in December, 1943, and the following January. He had traveled all round the perimeter of the European Fortress, from Denmark to the Mediterranean, to report on the state of the coastal defenses and to make suggestions for their improvement where necessary. Energetic, keen and implacable, Rommel had swept down like some avenging angel upon the somnolent headquarters in the west, where the chief preoccupation was to avoid being transferred to the Russian front. This ever-present menace had caused the many officials responsible for the Wall to make no mention of the inferior work and defects, the sabotage and the delays. Tacit though it was, one order was respected from top to bottom of the hierarchy: "Don't make any trouble."

Rommel soon roused this dormant ant-heap, lashing out right and left. Ponchardier and his men gleefully read through his scathing notes, which contained touches of cruelty at times, stigmatizing some Todt official for having allowed insufficient space for recoil in a gun casemate. His remarks on a fortification at St. Valéry-en-Caux were that it had not been given proper foundations, that it lacked iron reinforcement, and would most likely sink into the ground with the first heavy rains. Elsewhere, the firing angles were inadequate or the guns had been badly mounted. The work had been botched in many places, due either to carelessness or poor materials.

Ponchardier was overjoyed, and opened some bottles of wine. He almost felt like proposing a toast to Rommel, whose evidence was a trump card that would silence criticism from London. But Rommel had not noticed everything; much of the inferior work and the sabotage was then invisible and became apparent only in the course of time. Even so, Rommel had written enough for London to be convinced that the French Resistance had not been exaggerating. The Allied Command, which had been in possession of the plan of the fortifications before work was even begun on them, could now believe that it knew more than the German General Staff did about the real value of the Atlantic Wall.

Rommel owed this compensation to the *Sosies* group, for he had given them a bitter disappointment a few weeks earlier. He was then staying at von Rundstedt's headquarters at Saint-Germain-en-Laye, and frequently went walking alone in the nearby forest. Pepe, hidden among the bushes, had him within range of his Mauser several times. But London had forbidden the assassination, although Ponchardier had repeatedly reported the opportunity. Enclosed in their world of fear, treachery, torture and death, the *Sosies* group could see no difference between the Gestapo, the S.S. and the Wehrmacht. All Germans were enemies, and Ponchardier and his men could not understand why they were prevented from shooting the most famous German military leader. Was it fear of reprisals? There had been occasions when the Allied Command had shown little concern over that. It must have been something like a chivalrous reaction. But the men of *Sosies* were not making war with gloves on, and they had some unkind things to say about the gentlemen in London who would not agree to a senior officer being killed like a rabbit.

# 7. A D-Day Specialist: Admiral Canaris

Such scruples did not exist among the Nazis, and their intelligence services were always certain of having a free hand. Even in peacetime, they were not tied down by considerations of legality and morality, as in the democratic countries. They had no fear of being treated like the American deciphering experts who, in 1929, when Secretary of State Henry Stimson learned with horror that they had broken the Japanese secret code, were dismissed because "a gentleman does not read other people's letters." The head of the Abwehr, the intelligence service of the German Army, was under the orders of a cunning, rascally government which was unscrupulous in its use of lies, blackmail and intimidation.

When Hitler had come to power he had soon broken the opposition of the traditionalist general staff by a false accusation of homosexuality against General Baron von Fritsch and by charging Marshal von Blomberg with having married a prostitute. Hitler had wiped out Roehm and the S.A. on the pretext of an imaginary plot. The Reichstag fire, which was probably started by Goering's henchmen, had enabled Hitler to destroy the German Communist party. In 1937, by undermining Stalin's confidence with forged documents showing that Russian military leaders were preparing a revolt against the regime, Hitler had been able to look on with satisfaction while the Red Army was decapitated and thousands of its officers were liquidated.

After having had the Austrian chancellor, Dollfuss, assassinated, Hitler had broken the resistance of his successor, Kurt von Schuschnigg. The new Austrian leader went to Berchtesgaden for a meeting with Hitler on February 12, 1938, and entered the "eagle's nest" making pleasant remarks about the splendid view and the fine weather. A few hours later, fearing for his life, Schuschnigg signed his country's death warrant—just as the President of Czechoslovakia, Hácha, did a year later. Hácha was subjected to such pressure that at one point he fainted, and had to be revived with injections in order to sign Czechoslovakia's death certificate. Hitler, searching for a pretext to invade that country, had considered having the German ambassador assassinated. To justify his invasion of Poland he had an attack made on the German radio station at Gleiwitz, near the border, by some of his S.S. shock troops dressed in Polish Army uniforms. Eight months later, his advance troops crossed into Holland disguised as Dutch soldiers; and soon the bewildered French were imagining enemy parachute troops dropping all over the country. Hitler was not even deterred by the Vatican, that sanctuary of the West. In 1943 he thought of kidnapping the Pope, and told his General Staff: "I'll enter the Vatican. Do you think I'm daunted by the Vatican? We'll seize it. All the diplomatic corps is there—that rabble! We'll throw that bunch out. Later, we'll express our regrets."

Such methods, which are hardly irreproachable from a moral standpoint, have a certain attraction for the professional secret agent. He is not concerned with defining his country's foreign policy, only with providing the means for its execution. At that level, moral considerations are not his concern. Even if he is the finest man in the world, or working for some noble cause, his functions will darken his soul. He has accepted, once and for all, to dirty his hands and be the instrument of deplorable but necessary deeds. Since there is nothing exalted about his aims, he finds his glory in the cunning ways he achieves them. In every country, the secret agent has his head full of master-strokes which he is prevented from pulling off by the fainthearted-ness or even the rectitude of politicians. But in Nazi Germany there were no such handicaps. If there was one head of a secret service who ought to have felt he had a free hand and could give his imagination and audacity free rein it was Wilhelm Canaris, whom Hitler put at the head of the Abwehr in January, 1935.

Nine years later, the Abwehr of Admiral Canaris had become the world's leading D-Day specialist.

On February 28, 1940, Canaris's chief assistant, Colonel Oster, informed his friend J. G. Sas, the Dutch military attaché in Berlin, of the forthcoming invasion of Denmark and Norway. The date was to be March 9. Sas passed the information to the Danish naval attaché, Captain Kjölsen, who warned Copenhagen. But the Danish authorities considered it implausible. The Norwegian attaché, whom Sas had also informed, had so little belief in it that he did not even bother to notify Oslo.

In October, 1939, a member of the Abwehr, Joseph Müller, was sent to the Vatican to contact British and Belgian diplomats. Müller, a huge man nicknamed "Joe the Ox" by his friends, was one of the most brilliant lawyers in Munich. He warned the Belgian and Dutch representatives that Hitler was about to invade their countries, beginning on November 12. But Müller was not believed. On November 7 Hitler decided to postpone the offensive. He put it off fourteen times during the winter.

On May 1, 1940, Müller told a Belgian diplomat that,

the invasion had been set for May 10. The diplomat sent the information to Brussels by cable, but it was not believed. The Gestapo had intercepted the message and decoded it. Hitler, when informed, ordered the Abwehr to discover the traitor. With remarkable audacity, Canaris officially gave Müller the task of inquiring into the Müller leak. The tracks were covered up.

Colonel Oster gave his friend Sas the same information at the same time. Although Sas's warning about the invasion of Denmark and Norway had proved to be correct, he was not believed either when he told The Hague that Germany would violate Dutch neutrality on May 10.

Oster and Sas were having dinner together on May 9 in the Berlin suburb of Zehlendorf. Oster confirmed that the Germans would attack at dawn. He went to Army G.H.Q. after dinner, to make sure that no postponement had been ordered. The attack was still due to take place at dawn, and Hitler was already on his way to the front. Oster called Sas: "The swine has left for the western front." Sas informed the Belgian military attaché as he had done at the beginning of the month, without effect—and called the War Ministry at The Hague. He said to the duty officer: "The surgeon has decided to operate at dawn." This was a pre-arranged signal to announce an imminent German attack. At midnight a Dutch officer called Sas from The Hague and said. "Do you mean the Germans are about to invade us?" Sas knew that his telephone was permanently tapped by the Gestapo. He tried to make himself understood while at the same time remaining vague enough not to be cut off by the Gestapo. The officer hung up. At dawn, the Dutch government tried to contact Sas again, but the telephone wires had been cut. A few days later the leak was being widely discussed in diplomatic circles in Berlin. Colonel Oster was rumored to be its source. Canaris immediately told the Gestapo that he had started the rumor himself, so that it would reach the ears of the enemy agents who had warned the Dutch; thus reassured, they would neglect to take precautions.

In June, 1940, Joseph Müller was back in the Vatican, and he gave a British diplomat the German Admiralty's plan for the invasion of England. He was unable to give the date of this operation, for it had not been set, and never was. But, thanks to Müller, Churchill was later able to write in his memoirs that he knew about SEA LION—the code name for the German invasion—before the German General Staff did. At the time it was in fact known only to Admiral Raeder and a dozen other officers. A few months later Müller informed the British of the date of Operation BARBAROSSA: the invasion of Russia.

Toward the end of March, 1941, Canaris warned the Yugoslavs that Operation PUNISHMENT was about to fall on Belgrade. Hitler was annoyed by a pro-British government coming to power and had decided to send his bombers to devastate the Yugloslav capital, as a prelude to invading the country. On April 3 the government declared Belgrade an open city, but this did not prevent German bombers from carrying out a mass raid on April 6 and wiping out large areas of the capital, which had no anti-aircraft defenses. Seventeen thousand dead were among the ruins.

In October, 1942, Canaris informed the Swiss that Hitler was preparing to invade their country. The Swiss army immediately took such effective defense measures that the German plan was abandoned. The Abwehr, after so many vain efforts to prevent war or limit its ravages, had at last obtained a positive result. But it was also the last time it gave warning of a German attack. The Wehrmacht, pummeled in North Africa and bled at Stalingrad, was on the defensive. The task of the Abwehr, which had been giving away the secrets of all German D-Days with remarkable persistence, was now to discover the date and location of the Allied assaults. At the beginning of 1944 the fate of Germany, insofar as it depended on the success or failure of the invasion, appeared to rest with the mysterious and disconcerting Admiral Canaris.

During World War I, Wilhelm Canaris had been the lover of Mata Hari, whom he persuaded to act as a spy in France. When her activities became dangerous to him, he denounced her to the French and she found herself in front of a firing squad. Previous to this painful episode he had organized some successful sabotage on the American coast. Then he was captured by the Italians—who were in the Allied camp in that war—but escaped dressed in the cassock of the prison chaplain, whom he had strangled. After the war, Canaris was involved in the assassination of the German Communist leaders Rosa Luxemburg and Karl Liebknecht. He was also involved in General Kapp's attempted putsch, and helped the leaders to escape when it failed.

Such was the legend surrounding Admiral Canaris. It originated partly in the minds of British intelligence officers who, in 1942, organized a violent campaign against the head of the Abwehr, calling him an assassin, a "rat with a human face" and an "evil genius." The object was to divert the suspicions of the Gestapo from him, and to strengthen his position with the Nazi leaders. It was probably a maneuver without precedent in the annals of secret warfare.

Actually, Wilhelm Canaris had begun his intelligence career in 1915, when he was the intelligence officer of the cruiser *Dresden,* one of the German raiders which operated against Allied merchant shipping in the South Atlantic. Lieutenant Commander Canaris was highly successful at obtaining fuel and food supplies and in spreading false information about the position and course of the *Dresden.* When the raider was finally tracked down by British warships and took refuge in a Chilean port, the crew was interned. Canaris escaped and went to Spain, where he organized the meetings at sea between German submarines and their supply ships. At the end of the war he was in command of a submarine in the Adriatic. After the armistice he was executive officer of the training ship *Berlin.* One of the cadets under his command was Reinhard Heydrich. Canaris was finally transferred to the small naval base of Swinemünde, on the Baltic. It seemed likely that he was going to end his career there, in mediocrity and boredom, when, in January, 1935, he was made head of the Abwehr.

He was then forty-seven, a small man with a ruddy face and white hair who felt the cold even in summer and hardly ever took off his overcoat. He detested the military virtues and showed great disgust when told that some officer was the epitome of them. The sight of military decorations made him bristle, so anyone who had a favor to ask of him was careful to remove all medals and ribbons. He wore his uniform only when protocol forced him to. Leverkuehn, the officer in charge of the Abwehr office in Istanbul, described him thus: "Very brilliant and lively, and as talkative as an old lady." He was also an excellent cook.

He had a prodigious love for his dogs. When traveling he always reserved a room with two beds, so that his dogs would not have to sleep on the floor. If he was unable to take them with him, he telephoned to Berlin every evening to ask about them, even from the other end of Europe. These conversations about dogs and the state of their natural functions must have been puzzling to the secret police who tapped his line. His assistants had to endure long speeches on the faithfulness of dogs before being able to make their reports. The Abwehr chauffeurs lived in terror of running over an animal; they had all been told to exercise particular care in this respect. In general, it was understood among members of the Abwehr that if one did not like animals one might just as well give up all idea of promotion.

These peculiarities, which hardly fit the usual picture of a master spy, ought to have earned Admiral Canaris several ironic nicknames. But it is significant that he was never dubbed with one. On the other hand, Canaris is probably the only secret service chief in the world to have been called "the father of the persecuted." His mercy was never appealed to in vain. His assistants were continually boasting of his gentleness, while his enemies emphasized that his sentimentality was incompatible with his position.

For such a man to have been placed at the head of the Abwehr in Hitler's warlike Germany is a matter of constant amazement. In 1935 there was no lack of fanatical officers to choose from; if not a militant Nazi, some specialist who worried little about the ends so long as the means were abundant could have been found. But the extraordinary blindness shown in choosing Canaris inevitably cost Germany some serious setbacks.

Apart from the regrettable publicity given to the projected German invasions, the missed opportunities were many. Under the Nazi regime, the head of a secret service had unlimited resources at his disposal, complete freedom in the choice of means and the certainty that he would never be disowned. But Canaris, because of his humaneness and strict morality, took no advantage of this. The aims of the Nazis seemed wrong and senseless to him. He hated physical violence, and the furies of the Nazis were repugnant to him. So it was morally and physically impossible for him to make use of the carte blanche that was offered to him; he contemptuously let it drop. When the S.S. was preparing the false evidence of the Tukhachevski plot, Canaris refused to hand over the genuine documents, bearing the signatures of the Russian marshals, that were needed in order to imitate their handwriting. Himmler had to send men to rob the Abwehr offices. When Canaris was told to obtain Dutch army uniforms, to enable German soldiers to seize by trickery the strategic bridges in Holland, he vehemently refused. It took a personal order from the Führer to make him give in. And when he was ordered to have a bomb placed in the British plane from Stockholm he ostensibly set plans in motion but told his men to take no real action: "Unlike the S.S., the Abwehr is not a gang of murderers." Again it took an order from Hitler to overcome his resistance.

Exasperated, the Nazi leaders finally realized how unfortunate their choice had been. They had at their command an inexhaustible supply of adventurers who would stop at nothing, and yet a key post had been given to a type exceedingly rare in German official circles since Hitler had come to power: an honest man afflicted with a conscience and handicapped by scruples. "In many ways," wrote *Brigadenführer* Schellenberg, "he was what might be called a mystic."

*Brigadenführer* Walther Schellenberg worked up to seventeen hours a day, and his favorite relaxation was not so much riding as his collection of pornographic photos. He gave up an hour a day to riding in the Tiergarten early in the morning because it was connected with his work. Schellenberg, whose rank was equivalent to brigadier general, was head of the political intelligence division of the S.S. In 1944 he was thirty-four years old. The old militant Nazis did not like him; they called him *Märzveilchen*, "March violet," because he had not joined the Nazi Party until after it came to power in March, 1933. He was also called a "quibbling lawyer," because he had been completing his law studies when the S.S. leaders took an interest in him. He looked weak, with his puny body and sunken cheeks, but his consuming ambition was well served by undeniable intelligence, a great capacity for work, an absence of all scruples and a kind of genius for intrigue. He was no thug, like the average S.S. man, neither was he a bureaucrat of sadism like his chief, Himmler, nor a fanatic like all his colleagues. He might not even have been a patriot. He was an intellectual gangster whose undoubted abilities could be put to best use in Hitler's Germany. After ten years of rapid rise in the S.S. his appetite for power knew no limits.

Early every morning he left his house near the Kurfurstendam and went to meet Admiral Canaris at the riding stables in the Tiergarten. Knee to knee, the two rode along the leafy paths, then had breakfast together. Berliners on their way to work, whose sons were being slaughtered on the Russian front, must have felt bitter at the sight of the two officers jogging peacefully along under the trees. They did not know that the ruddy-faced old gentleman and the pale young man were, by the nature of things, mortal enemies. The head of the Abwehr had been struggling for the past ten years against the cancerous growth of the S.S. intelligence service. Schellenberg, who had been head of it since 1942, was scheming to absorb the Abwehr and so become chief of all the German secret services. He knew that he would succeed only over the admiral's dead body. Canaris knew it too. Each of their morning rides was a kind of stealthy duel; the two sounded each other out and tried to discover which way the next attack would come. For Schellenberg, who spent all day with the narrow-minded idiots at S.S. headquarters, these conversations had more than a practical value; they provided an opportunity for intellectual exercise with an opponent of his own level. That was the reason he never missed the morning ride with Canaris, not even when his house had been hit by a bomb the previous night and his son's bed had been covered with debris. Soon after dawn he had left his wife to clear away the rubble and had hurried off to meet the admiral. The latter had shown great emotion when he heard the story, and had reproached Schellenberg for not going down to the cellar with his family when the air-raid warning sounded. This was not, as might be thought, sheer hypocrisy; for nothing is ever simple and it happened that the two men had a liking for each other. Schellenberg admired Canaris's intelligence and class. The admiral appreciated Schellenberg's deference and liked his youthfulness. He called him "my young friend"; and, pointing to Seppl, his beloved dachshund, frolicking around the horses, he would say, "See how superior animals are, Schellenberg. My dog is discreet, he'll never betray me . . . I can't say as much about men!" Schellenberg would solemnly nod his head. The invasion was drawing near, and he considered that the Abwehr was too weakened by defeatism to be capable of winning the secret war that was both the prelude and the key to it. Schellenberg wanted to be the man to discover the Allies' great secret. He had put his bulky file on the Abwehr's underhanded maneuvers on Himmler's desk more than once. He wondered how much longer it would be before the S.S. leader decided to accuse Canaris of high treason.

# 8. The Santa Clauses versus the Blacks

CANARIS and his assistants did not believe themselves to be traitors. It was because they were convenced that Nazism would be the ruin of Germany that they had endeavored to thwart Hitler's plans. They had tried with all their might to prevent a war which seemed to them lost in advance. In warning the Norwegians and the Danes of imminent invasion, Colonel Oster had hoped that the British fleet, alerted in time, would put to sea and stop the operation. By informing the Dutch and the Belgians that their neutrality was about to be violated, Müller had hoped to cause a general outcry, a wave of solemn declarations which would make Hitler hesitate, unable for once to present the world with the accomplished fact. And the purpose of giving Churchill the plans for SEA LION had been to prevent Hitler from carrying out the decisive operation that would place all of Europe under his domination.

Then, when the Nazi war machine was fully under way, the men of the Abwehr tried to limit the disaster. When Hitler sent him to persuade Franco to enter the war, Canaris argued instead that Spain, which he loved, should remain neutral. In 1943 Canaris got warning of Italy's intention to defect to the Allies, but he abstained from informing the German high command, so that the unhappy country could have a chance of arranging its affairs. Similarly, when he warned the Swiss of a German invasion it was not to ensure a massacre of German soldiers but to prompt defensive measures by the Swiss which would cause the operation to be abandoned.

Canaris and his associates, all officers of the old school with a strict code of honor, therefore had clear consciences; traitors to the regime they might be, but not to their country.

This nuance naturally escaped the S.S.; to them, only hanging was good enough for the "Santa Clauses," as they called the aged Abwehr leaders. In the eyes of the S.S. they were traitors, which was serious, and rivals, which was unforgivable. Since 1933 Himmler and his men—"the Blacks," as they were called by the Abwehr, from the color of their uniform—had built up a police empire whose power stopped only at the door of Hitler's office. But there still remained the Abwehr, an irritating enclave which controlled military intelligence.

Heydrich, head of the Gestapo and Schellenberg's predecessor as the head of the S.S. intelligence service, soon crossed swords with Canaris. The Gestapo was ordered to keep watch on everything the "Santa Clauses" did. But this time they were up against professionals. It was in vain that they tried to infiltrate the Abwehr organization. Moreover, the great majority of the Abwehr agents knew nothing of their leaders' schemes and plots; and even the leaders were not working together in this respect. There was no morning conference to decide which German military secret should be passed to the Allies that evening. It was as a result of some personal initiative that warnings of German aggression had reached Copenhagen, Oslo, The Hague, Brussels, London, Belgrade and Geneva. And those responsible had not always been in agreement. Canaris had thought it proper to warn the Yugoslavs and the Swiss, but he considered that the information Oster had leaked to Sas was very close to treason. He covered it up, nevertheless, as he covered up burly Müller's leaks. Canaris, as an opponent of violence, rejected the idea of an attempt on Hitler's life. Yet when, in February, 1943, Canaris and some of his assistants flew to Smolensk, where Hitler then had his headquarters, he was not unaware that there were explosives and detonators taken from British saboteurs in his assistants' luggage.* He chose once again to close his eyes, for the leaders of the Abwehr were more united in their opposition to Nazism than in the means of destroy-

---

* A bomb was placed in Hitler's aircraft on March 13, 1943, but the detonator was affected by the extreme cold and the bomb failed to explode.

ing it. Thus, more than an organization for deliberate treason, the Abwehr was a mutual aid society in which men animated by a common ideal protected each other.

Heydrich tried all means of opening a breach in the Abwehr's defenses, and in time he was bound to succeed. Meanwhile he extended the political intelligence branch of the S.S. by placing its own agents in foreign countries. He thus placed it in competition with the Abwehr and prepared it to take over Canaris's duties. The outbreak of war in 1939, far from bringing a lull in the conflict between the two services, only aggravated it. When the tension became so acute that it was interfering with the proper functioning of each organization, a kind of truce was agreed upon. Canaris and the S.S. leaders had meetings throughout 1941, culminating in the Prague agreement of May, 1942, which was a compromise between the S.S. hunger for power and the Abwehr resistance against encroachment. But the opposition between the two was too violent for this truce to last for long. The struggle went far beyond the personal animosity of the leaders of the two organizations, and could only end when one was absorbed by the other.

Canaris was constantly in the forefront of this ruthless conflict. In his office at 74–76 Tirpitzufer ("the old fox's den," his men called it), in the heart of Berlin, he was under greater menace than any of his agents parachuted into enemy territory. They ran the risk of death; he ran the risk of torture and death. His hair went white from the constant nervous tension, his gentle face became deeply lined and his voice grew muffled. Until the spring of 1942 his direct enemy was Reinhard Heydrich, the "Angel of Evil," whom Hitler called "the man with a heart of iron."

A fascinating person if ever there was one, probably the most extraordinary that Nazi Germany produced, Heydrich was as handsome as a Nordic god. He had all gifts and all vices, being an accomplished violinist, obsessed with sex, a first-class fencer, an excellent rider, sailor and pilot, an assassin and a torturer; in fact he excelled at everything he undertook. Between two conferences in which he planned deportations and genocides, he would jump into his Messerschmitt and, in defiance of Hitler's strict orders, take part in a raid over Britain. As Himmler's righthand man he was, in Schellenberg's words, "the secret pivot on which the Nazi regime turned." He used his extensive powers with a kind of perfect cruelty, never being touched by any humane considerations or remorse. A beast of prey, magnificent and odious. The Nazi jungle contained a few others, but even there Heydrich stood out in one remarkable detail: all those who were in contact with him confessed that he aroused *physical* terror in them—"the Heydrich complex," said Schellenberg, who was not immune to it.

Such was the individual whom the dog-loving little admiral was opposing. "A fanatical barbarian," he said of Heydrich, "and by far the most intelligent of all those brutes." It was an opinion strangely like that expressed by Hitler years earlier: "An extremely gifted but extremely dangerous man." His mere presence upset the oversensitive Canaris, and for seven years a phone call from Heydrich was enough to make him shudder.

Canaris, however, did not burrow into his den and keep out of his enemy's way. Even if he had, their duel would have been fascinating. But it had an intensity and color which made it equal to some of the best episodes of the Italian Renaissance, because the two adversaries were constantly in each other's presence. They both lived on the Dullestrasse, and with their wives spent evenings at each other's houses. Heydrich and Frau Canaris played the violin, Haydn or Mozart usually, while Canaris, chin in hand, and Frau Heydrich sat and listened. What nice people! But then the Canarises moved to a small house at Schlachtensee. Was this to be the end of the musical evenings? Not at all, for Heydrich and his wife moved out to Schlachtensee too, only a few steps from the Canarises' house. On Sundays they played croquet together. Sometimes Schellenberg was invited to join them, and competitions were organized. Visitors to the Canarises' house were shown a large protrait in the entrance hall: Constantine Kanaris, a hero of the Greek War of Independence, wearing the national costume and grasping his scimitar. Admiral Canaris let it be understood that he was descended from this handsome warrior. His friends smiled. But when Germany was at war with Greece, Canaris took pains to point out that his family came originally from northern Italy and had no connection with Constantine. There were more smiles at this statement, which gently poked fun at the rigorous way in which the Nazis examined ancestries and stripped family trees. But the little joke had a special meaning for Canaris and Heydrich, for they both knew that in a secret safe the admiral had proof that there was Jewish blood in his croquet partner's veins.

Heydrich had done everything possible to wipe out all trace that his grandmother Sarah had ever existed, destroying the entries of her birth and marriage in the registers and even defacing her tombstone. But he had been unable to prevent his crafty enemy from gathering sufficient proof to denounce him, if need arose, as belonging to the race he reviled and persecuted. Canaris knew this was a weapon which kept the beast in check. Yet the feeling of security it gave him was not enough to overcome the terror that Heydrich could induce in him. Each time Canaris heard his voice on the telephone he feared that he had found a countermeasure that would tilt the balance of terror in his favor.

When Heydrich was assassinated by three Czech patriots in Prague on May 27, 1942, Canaris went to his funeral, and the "Blacks" were amazed to see real tears running down his face. "I've lost a friend," he said. No one thought he was sincere. But Canaris was weeping for himself, knowing that his most useful as well as his most dreaded enemy had disappeared.

It was then that Walther Schellenberg, who had long since guessed that the admiral had a hold over Heydrich, took the file on Canaris into Himmler's office for the first time. "Himmler bit his thumb nervously," Schellenberg wrote, "and said to me 'Leave it here, I'll show it to Hitler when an opportunity occurs.'" Schellenberg left the office believing that the fate of the Abwehr was sealed; the file held complete proof of all the many treacheries committed by Canaris and his associates. But months passed and nothing happened. Schellenberg raised the matter several times, only to receive vague replies from Himmler. He was finally forced to admit that he had underestimated the cunning old fox of the Abwehr: Canaris had a hold over Himmler himself! "Like Heydrich," wrote Schellenberg, "Himmler seemed incapable of taking any action against the admiral. I am practically certain that Canaris, at one time or another, had learned something about him, otherwise Himmler would never have sat on the file I had given him." Schellenberg did not know what secret hold Canaris had over Himmler. Twenty years later, it is still not known. Perhaps it concerned one of Himmler's cousins, of whom it was said in Nazi circles that there was "something odd about him." In 1933 he had called at S.S. Headquarters and asked to see Heinrich Himmler. When questioned as to his identity he had replied, "Just say it's his Cousin David." He died in a concentration camp eleven years later. It will probably never be known whether Canaris's safe held a card on Cousin David as well as a file on Grandmother Sarah.

In any case, the redoubtable little admiral continued to hold off the "Blacks," turning their own methods against them. He was unable to prevent the dismissal of a few of his assistants, Oster among them, in 1943, but on the whole the Abwehr remained impregnable. More proof of its treacherous activity piled up on Schellenberg's desk, but to no avail. Canaris was beginning to think he would survive the defeat and downfall of the Nazis, when one of the Führer's frenzies destroyed the protective network that had surrounded him. This thunderclap resulted from a very minor storm, and one in which Canaris, by bitter irony, had not been involved. It arose from the desertion to the Allies of the two Abwehr agents attached to the German consulate in Istanbul. Hitler was convulsed with rage. On February 18, 1944, he signed a decree which was a posthumous victory for Heydrich, the fulfillment of Schellenberg's desires and a triumph for the "Blacks": "I order the creation of a unified German Secret Service."

Canaris left the Abwehr. He was given a minor post at the Ministry of Economic Affairs. It was only after the July plot against Hitler that he was arrested, by Schellenberg in person; and even then he escaped the bloody reprisals. Not until final defeat was only a month away did Hitler order his execution. He and Oster were both hanged by the S.S. in the cold dawn of April 9. Canaris was stripped as naked as he was born, and to prolong his agony the "Blacks" used a piece of very thin piano wire.

So it was in February, 1944, that Schellenberg took over control of the Abwehr. With its sixteen thousand agents, it was an instrument that would at last enable him to show his capabilities. He intended to use it in his own way, which was not that of Canaris. This became obvious to the "Santa Clauses" the first time they were summoned to his headquarters; for, as in the admiral's case, the office revealed the man.

Canaris's "den" had been a small room on the top floor of

an old building whose elevator was always out of order. It was simply furnished with a desk, a few chairs, an iron bed, a safe and a filing cabinet whose bottom drawer was used by Seppl, the beloved dachshund. On the walls were photographs of General Franco, the Caudillo of Spain; of Colonel Nicolai, the legendary head of German intelligence during World War I; and Seppl, a dachshund. The office looked so shabby that Canaris's assistants felt slightly ashamed when he received important foreign visitors.

Walther Schellenberg received visitors in an immense room with mahogany furniture. The floor was covered with Oriental rugs. On his right was a battery of telephones and a microphone that kept him constantly in touch with Hitler's Chancellery. Highly sensitive microphones which picked up and recorded the slightest murmur were concealed in the walls, ceiling, and even the furniture. The windows were covered with iron grilles that were electrified at night. An electric warning system on the doors and windows was linked to the general alarm circuit. The desk, safe and filing cabinets were similarly protected. If an intruder approached them, an alarm automatically sounded, guards blocked all the exits and a company of S.S. surrounded the building. The large mahogany desk, outwardly like any other, had two submachine guns built into it. They were pointed at the visitors' chairs; if the visitors stood up and approached the desk, the guns automatically followed their movement. They could be fired by pressing a button.

Schellenberg had a car fitted with a short-wave transmitter which enabled him to remain in touch with his headquarters within a radius of twenty-five miles. He wore a ring with a large blue stone, and under the stone was a gold capsule of cyanide. When he had to travel outside Germany he had a false tooth fitted which contained another dose of poison.

However, the S.S. *Brigadenführer* hardly ever left his office-fortress. In March, 1944, when the secret services on both sides of the Channel were arranging their pawns for the final match, Walther Schellenberg was desperately trying to pick up the threads which had been broken or loosened by Hitler's decree the previous month. He had three months in which to discover the secret that was his Führer's obsession.

5

# APRIL

## 9.  Spies by the Thousand

WHEN the man came to you with his frightening proposition, it was like a flash of lightning in the gray drabness of those days. He wanted you to become a spy! What an idea! But, with pounding heart and dry lips, you agreed to do it. As you showed your visitor to the door of your farmhouse, or your rectory, or your bakery, you felt that you were embarking on a terrifying, exciting adventure. By evening you were already wondering whether it wasn't more terrifying than exciting. And with time you realized that it wasn't even an adventure. You were only a tiny spy, a microscopic spy! You were the spy of your meadow, or of the château where you went to hear the old dowager's confession, or of the requisitioned hotel where you went to deliver fifty loaves of bread every morning. You were asked only to report the weekly sickness rate among the soldiers manning the battery on the other side of the hedge, the identity of the headquarters staff installed in the château, the number of soldiers occupying the hotel.

Far from being exciting, it was dull and thankless work. Your disappointment would have been softened if you had known about Dominique Ponchardier, for example: he stood head and shoulders above you, he was the kind of resourceful, lion-hearted man you were likely to see only in the movies, but when it came to the battery in your meadow he couldn't hold a candle to you.

First of all, the whole coast was classified as a "prohibited zone" and anyone who went there had to have a special pass. Inside the zone the German military police had checkpoints on all the roads, and the paths were patrolled night and day. Even so, that diabolical Ponchardier was able to get into the zone when he had to. He had worked in a real estate agency before the war and was supposed to be there still: that was his "cover." Whenever he wanted to have a look at a certain section of the Wall, he would write to the local notary on the agency's letterhead and ask him if he knew of any country houses or building land for sale. This was always a wonderful surprise for the notary, because he was sure to know a whole multitude of people who were eager to get rid of country houses which they could no longer use and which might be demolished by the shells and bombs of the invasion. He would answer by return mail and set about getting the necessary passes. He would even go to the various properties with Monsieur Ponchardier and his assistant, a young man with a talent for drawing who was adept at making quick sketches of the landscape.

Cleverly done? Yes, but you were able to do better, because Dominique Ponchardier could never do more than take a quick glance at the battery. He might discover the caliber of its guns and his assistant might draw a plan of it, but you could report the names of its gunners, the number of their unit and whether their morale was good or bad. Because it was part of your life, because you saw it every day, perhaps because one of its noncoms was quartered in your house, in a requisitioned room. Unlike his soldiers, who were quarrelsome youngsters, the *Feldwebel* was a good-natured man with graying temples and a peaceful paunch. Before going up to bed at night he often had a glass or two of apple brandy with you. Sometimes he would show you pictures of his family and say, "War is bad. Terrible." And you would answer, "Yes, it's a filthy mess. It shouldn't ever happen." Perhaps you and the *Feldwebel* discovered that you had encountered each other thirty years earlier, at Verdun or Chemin-des-Dames. Actually, you liked him. You would have been greatly distressed if some vicious killer like Ponchardier or Pepe had suddenly opened the door and shot him in your living room. You didn't even hold it against him personally for living in your house without having been invited. There was a war on.

And because there was a war on, you repeated everything you had learned about the battery to the man who came every week to collect information. There was the gun that had finally been repaired; the fifteen soldiers who had just arrived from the Russian front with fingers so badly injured by frostbite that they were unable to handle the shells; the captain who was furious because he still hadn't received the rangefinder that had been promised to him. All this seemed so minor, so insignificant, that you didn't feel you were doing anything to get the *Feldwebel* out of your house. This conviction of being useless was your only certainty in the sea of uncertainties that formed your world in April, 1944. The Allies didn't need you. They had ways of getting the important information they needed. And anyway, they weren't going to land in Normandy. If they ever decided to come, it would be farther up the coast, in Pas-de-Calais.* It was a region that was used to war, and the crossing would be shorter. In either case, whether it was to be Normandy or Pas-de-Calais, you weren't doing anything useful. What possible connection could there be between the mood of a captain in the battery and the outcome of the enormous war?

Or the story of the roller coaster at Merville, for example —how could that have had any importance? You had gone to the Merville fair like everyone else, and you saw the commanding officer of the battery laughing uproariously as he got on the roller coaster. He was drunk of course. He was always drunk. The man in charge of the roller coaster set it going at full speed and forgot to stop it. Sick as a dog, the officer yelled and vomited on the seats. Some of the Russian soldiers serving on the German battery had to rescue him. Then, pretending to help him stay on his feet, they gave him punches that nearly broke his ribs. The incident had given everyone a good laugh, but how could it have been of any interest to the great generals in London?

You couldn't have understood. You didn't know that somewhere in the English countryside four steam shovels and six bulldozers had worked day and night to make an exact replica of the Merville battery. They had torn up woods and cultivated fields whose owners had been paid indemnities of fifteen thousand pounds. And now seven hundred paratroop-

---

* The French department whose coast is the eastern shore of the Strait of Dover.

ers and thirty-five officers were making practice attacks on the copy of the Merville battery while live ammunition was fired over their heads. Only volunteers had been taken, for the real attack was going to be something of a suicide operation. To preserve secrecy, the surrounding area had been declared a "prohibited zone." The men had sworn to say nothing whatever about what they were doing. As a test, the British security service sent pretty girls with instructions to do everything in their power to get information out of the soldiers, none of whom was over twenty-one. The soldiers succumbed, but in silence. It had been explained to them that the fate of the British invasion forces depended on them, and they knew it was true. For Merville was a powerfully equipped and fortified position. It had been little more than scratched by the heaviest bombings (only fifty bombs struck within the battery, of these only two struck the casemates, and neither of them burst through). The Merville battery, it was said, would sweep the beaches where the British were to land. It was one of the three or four major headaches of the Allied leaders. It is easy to understand what a relief it was to them to learn that the battery commander was a drunken lout and that many of his men were Russians who, on D-Day, would very likely prefer the white flag to the German swastika.

But even if you had known this, you still would not have understood entirely. You would have thought only of the strictly military consequences, of the fact that the position would be poorly defended. That was true. You, however, were used to the sight of the Germans stationed at Merville. You saw them every day and knew what they were like. Suppose you were one of the British paratroopers taking part in a mock attack on the battery position for the tenth time. The enemy he expected to be actually fighting before long seemed all the more formidable because he was unknown. The young Englishman had soon come to think of the defenders of the battery as ferocious warriors with nerves of steel who would fight to the death behind their machine guns. He said nothing to the others, but he had a hollow feeling in his stomach. But when, through you, he learned that most of the soldiers in the battery were Russians and that they were commanded by an alcoholic imbecile, everything looked different! Even if the commander had been a fanatical Nazi and his men all S.S. they would have seemed less formidable once you had reported who they were and where they came from, what they thought and what problems they had. *You had broken the awesome spell of the unknown.*

You had done even better: besides removing the Allied troops' anxiety, you had prepared the way for a breakdown of morale among the Germans, for every soldier is shattered to discover that an enemy of whom he knows nothing is aware of everything about him. Let us, for a moment, jump forward in time, from the freshness of April to the heat of late June—to the morning of June 28, 1944, and to the German stronghold Osteck a few miles from Cherbourg. The American VII Corps commanded by General "Lightning Joe" Collins had captured Cherbourg the previous day, but for the past three days had been knocking its head in vain against Osteck. Bombs and shells made no impression on it. Osteck repulsed the tanks and infantry sent against its walls. Osteck was the toughest morsel of concrete and steel that the Americans had been called upon to swallow since D-Day, a fabulous concentration of mines, automatic flame-throwers and tank traps, of blockhouses almost buried in the ground and connected by underground tunnels.

In the center bunker Major Küppers was fighting his battle through a periscope, like a submarine commander. He knew the American tide would eventually sweep over his fortifications one after the other. He knew he could not expect any help and that his situation was hopeless. But he fought on. When the elderly territorials defending one of the blockhouses had hung a white flag out of a loophole, he had fired on them until it was withdrawn. When the attacking infantry had forced a way into his bunker he had led a counterattack and driven them out. He had ordered his guns to fire on his own bunker to dislodge enemy troops on its roof. He had disdainfully rejected an offer to surrender, on the evening of the twenty-seventh.

The following morning, soon after eight, the lieutenant who was looking through the periscope reported several American jeeps approaching under a white flag. They were bringing the commander of the 4th Division himself, General Barton, and some of his staff. He entered the bunker with confident strides, spread his map out in front of Küppers, and showed him the strength he was bringing up for a final assault: two infantry regiments, a squadron of tanks and the whole of the Corps artillery. Any resistance was obviously futile. But Küppers remained unmoved. He glanced impassively at the map. Then he gave a sudden start as something caught his eye.

"Will you allow me to have a closer look?"

"Please do."

Küppers and his officers studied the map in detail and were amazed. Their dispositions were marked on it with more detail than on their own maps. Each gun was correctly shown with its field of fire and stock of ammunition; each blockhouse was marked with its strength in weapons and men, and even with the name of the officer in command. The Germans were flabbergasted. Everything was there. You had made only one error: Lieutenant Ralf Neste, shown on the map as commanding the Eleventh Battery of the 1709th Artillery Regiment, had met with an accident on May 5. He had been sent to a hospital and replaced. (Had the *Feldwebel* forgotten to mention the explosion of the antitank shell which had wounded Lieutenant Neste? More likely the information had reached London too late, after the maps were already printed and distributed.)

Küppers held a brief council with his officers and then, white-faced, informed General Barton that Osteck surrendered. Major Küppers was a broken man. Because of you. His gallant officers had the faces of defeated men for the first time in their lives. Because of you. They had stood up bravely to the deluge of bombs and shells, and had fought off repeated tank and infantry attacks. They might well have been prepared to face the terrific assault being mounted by the Americans. But they could not support the shattering revelation that the enemy knew all their secrets, their weapon strength and ammunition stocks and even their names; it was as though the reinforced concrete covering them were no more than transparent glass exposing them to the enemy's gaze.

Yet you would never have believed it if you had been told that when Osteck surrendered it would be partly into your hands. You were just a sweeper-up spy, as there are sweepers-up in factories—a collector of trifles that others ignored or cast aside. You kept your eyes fixed on the humble furrow that you had been asked to plow, and confined yourself to handing over your tiny harvest of information to the man who called once a week. Beyond was the unknown. England was a distant planet many light-years away. You could not even listen to the B.B.C.'s French Service any more, for on April 1 every *Kommandantur* in the coastal zone had ordered the local population to take all radios to the town hall. You no longer heard the sepulchral tones of the announcer advising people to move away from the Channel coast. These warnings had been given for weeks past; you had stopped believing in them. Back in the summer of 1943 the translation of one of Churchill's speeches had been read out in vibrant tones. The old lion had said: "Before the leaves fall the Germans will be attacked on new fronts, and the struggle will rage in the south, the west and the north." But the leaves had fallen, they had rotted on the ground, and there was still no second front.

During the winter the B.B.C. had trumpeted again that the decisive operation would take place in the spring. But the grass was high in the meadows and the *Feldwebel* was still drinking your apple brandy. There were times when you thought they would never come. The Wall frightened them. In that month of April, 1944, all was calm and peaceful. Occasionally there came the dull thuds of a railway junction being bombed, some miles inland. Now and then a lone airplane sped high above, leaving a white streak in the blue sky. Children picked up the strips of metallic paper, black on one side and shiny on the other. No one knew what they were. Children also picked up pamphlets and notices of all kinds, genuine and false. There was the one which announced that Normandy farmers would have to hand over their cattle without payment to the Anglo-American troops as the price of their liberation. It was signed "The Allied Commander-in-Chief." This stupidity of the Germans made you laugh. But the one about the fighting in Italy made you clench your teeth, because it struck home. It showed an Allied snail creeping slowly up the Italian boot—"It's a long way to . . . Rome!" True enough, there was no end to it; they would never come. They were abandoning you to the Gestapo, who would sooner or later come for you in their black Citroen and torture you before shooting you. That is, if the Germans did execute you by shooting. They sometimes sent condemned men to Germany, where the death sentence was carried out by beheading. And it was decreed that spies should be placed with the back of the neck on the block, so that they saw the axe fall.

You had more or less accepted the possibility of torture

and death when the man first called on you. But it had been with the thought that if you had to die you would have the satisfaction of work well done. By the spring of 1944, with the war seeming as if it would go on forever, you had become convinced that you were a useless pawn on the military chessboard. You were weighed down by the feeling of solitude. That was probably the most difficult to bear: the sense of loneliness.

You were mistaken. There were a thousand, ten thousand, fifty thousand of you, Norwegians, Danish, Dutch, Belgians and French. There were fifty thousand of you spying on the German armies, from the North Cape to the Pyrenees; fifty thousand pairs of ears always cocked. Individually you did not matter, that was true. But together, collectively, you were more effective than the major spies whose achievements were to astonish the world. They managed to get into headquarters offices and break open safes, steal orders of battle, filch maps of strategic defenses. But your exploit was without precedent in the annals of intelligence work: between you, you drew up a human map, the *living map of the enemy army*. The Allied airmen who photographed every yard of the coast were unable to do that. The commandos Scott-Bowden and Ogden Smith could not do it. Neither could Duchez, for all his cunning, nor Ponchardier, with all his courage. No one man could, for in order to see and hear everything fifty thousand pairs of eyes and ears were needed.

## 10. The Martians Are Submerged

WHEN there was no agent in a certain area to soak up all the available information, someone had to be sent there. There were always mailmen, railroad workers and meter-readers who belonged to the Resistance, but they were bound by more or less fixed itineraries. They picked up "letter drops" and gathered information on their way, but if a German patrol caught them on some remote dirt road or on the edge of a cliff, what excuse could they give? It was possible to send agents supplied with perfectly genuine-looking passes. For a well-organized Resistance group, official seals were no problem. Duchez's group, *Centurie*, had a hundred and fifty of them. They were hidden at the bottom of a laundry basket filled with old clothes so dirty and smelly that it was thought no Gestapo man would be heroic enough to search it. But although an official pass enabled one to enter the coastal area and travel on the main road, it could not justify being in out-of-the-way places where an honest man had no business to be. The difficulty, then, was to discover the rare pearl who would come and go freely without rousing the suspicions of German patrols.

There was Charles Douin, for instance. He was in his fifties, bearded, short, a sculptor and a martyr. Before the war, this ardent royalist had been obliged to earn his living by making busts of "Marianne," symbol of the French Republic, for the offices of mayors. And here was one of the leaders of the *Centurie* group asking him to spy for the British! He detested the British. By some complicated mental process he held them responsible for the French Revolution in 1789. Douin knew nothing about Britain or about the French Republic, and didn't want to know anything. If he took on the task, it would be for the King of France. Was that understood? Yes, understood. Thus reassured, Charles Douin slung his satchel over his shoulder and started going from church to church restoring statues and sculpture. During breaks in his work he chatted with the parish priest or the sexton and learned a few things. He went up into the tower or steeple and admired the view. He could pick out any barbed wire shining in the sun; he noted every interesting detail in the landscape with an accomplished sureness. Douin could remember happy Sundays in peacetime which he had devoted to his hobby: roaming the countryside with a military map in his hand. His happiness and been complete whenever he was able to find some slight error in the map and acrimoniously report it to the Minister of War of the Republic. And now Charles Douin, agent of the King of France, was ill-humoredly placing his cartographic passion at the service of the King of England.

There was also Cardron the fisherman. A timid man. He

did not like to venture far from the coast. He preferred casting his nets right under the mouths of the German guns. A clumsy man, too. Stretched on the deck of his boat, he wasted incredible amounts of time untangling his lines. Concealed in the tangle was his old Kodak.

Then there was Dr. Sustendal, who had a permit to be out even after curfew. He was gruff and taciturn by nature, but he forced himself to have endless conversations with his patients among the Todt workers.

There was Gilbert Michel, too. His spare-time occupation was being a hostage. A German troop train had been derailed at Moult-Argences, and since then a score of civilian hostages were put in the first car of every troop train. They traveled first class and were given the necessary passes. Michel always volunteered. Then he was successful in being appointed liaison agent for the Todt social services. That was more convenient.

And there was the inevitable Duchez. He recruited a dozen or so boys and girls, all with bicycles, and on Sundays took them cycling in a joyous group along the coast. The Germans approved; they were much in favor of healthy, athletic young people who had no concern with politics. The maps, tightly rolled, were concealed inside the handlebars.

There were also Arthur Poitevin and François Guérin. Arthur was blind, François was a boy who served as his guide. What harm could there be in letting them wander among the blockhouses? François whispered all he saw to Arthur. The blind often have an amazingly retentive memory.

And Duchez again, naturally. There were not enough men in the Civil Defense at Ouistreham, so Duchez and Henri Marigny joined it. They were on duty two nights a week. When the air-raid sirens sounded, they had the Allies over their heads, the Germans under their feet, and the harbor all to themselves.

There was La Bardonnie, a country gentleman from the Dordogne. He was sent to Cherbourg, where he disguised himself as a priest and gave some urchins a few coins to kick a ball about with him. They could often be seen along the waterfront and the nearby streets. The energetic priest and his yelling band made the German sentries laugh. They would willingly have joined in the game. La Bardonnie had almost finished his task when a priest, a real one, drew him aside and solemnly announced that he had been found out. By

the Gestapo? No, by some pious local ladies. From signs
known only to them, they had sensed that he was an im-
poster. A scandal was brewing. La Bardonnie took off his
cassock and hurried to Paris.

He had been sent to Cherbourg by Dominique Ponchardier,
head of the *Sosies* group. Ponchardier was obviously unaware that in the Cherbourg area alone the *Centurie* group
had a hundred and twenty agents who were able to go anywhere, without disguising themselves as priests. It frequently
happened that Resistance men took considerable risks to
discover something that was already known to others. In the
small coastal town of Port-en-Bessin there were seven agents
all unknown to each other. But this overlapping and duplica-
tion did not altogether displease headquarters in London, for
reports could thus be checked. Besides, Dominique Ponchardier realized that a fresh pair of eyes sometimes noticed what had escaped a person familiar with the scene or
caught up in the daily round. There had been the experience
of his brother Pierre when he visited the arsenal at Toulon
in 1943. Pierre had put on his handsome French naval
officer's uniform and simply walked into the arsenal, saluted
by the German sentries. It was an unwarranted folly. Pierre
Ponchardier was not expecting anything to result from his
visit, but like Dominique he considered that a leader should
sometimes startle his men; it bucked them up, it was excellent for the morale of the sweeper-up spy. He went through
the workshops where torpedoes were made. The daily output
was regularly reported to him by his agents there. They were
dumfounded to see their leader, who had the whole Gestapo
after him, calmly walk past them. He was intrigued by some
of the torpedoes being made. He said to himself that with
the addition of this and that they would become something
very different from torpedoes. Through him, London soon
learned that German engineers were constructing midget submarines at Toulon. Yet Pierre Ponchardier, naval officer
though he had been, was no armaments specialist like some
of his agents. But they had become so used to working
on torpedoes that they no longer saw them. La Bardonnie,
encumbered by his cassock and hustled around by his
urchins, may well have noticed something at Cherbourg that
the local people had looked at without seeing.

The Germans were doing their best. At the various headquarters in the west there were staff officers keeping double records of the army's strength. Real divisions were marked in red on the maps, imaginary ones in blue. In an effort to make the Resistance believe in the existence of the blue divisions, fictitious headquarters were constantly being created, the French railroads were inundated with false "troop movement orders," and advance detachments were sent to the coast without being followed by anything. If a division stationed near Marseilles was transferred to the Russian front it was sent by way of Normandy, to add to the confusion.

The troops had been duly lectured. They were given courses in counterespionage and made to sign a declaration that they had been warned. Long before 1944 the number of their units had been removed from their shoulder flaps, and all identification marks on trucks and other equipment had been obliterated.

But when a sick soldier died he had to be buried, and his grave in the local cemetery had to have a cross showing his name and regiment; it was indispensable for identifying the grave and having the body taken to Germany, after the victory. It often happened that the soldiers gave their dirty laundry and uniforms to civilians to be washed or cleaned. The jackets might not reveal anything, but the underclothes were usually still marked with the number of the unit. Then there was the postal number of each unit: the Resistance had only to discover it in order to keep track of the unit in all its movements. The soldiers' mail could certainly not be stopped. . . .

Nor could the fishermen be massacred! Before any coastal battery had a session of target practice, the local *Kommandantur* put up posters specifying the area that would be closed to all craft. Skipper Thomine of Port-en-Bessin was one of those who took down these posters. They revealed the field of fire of each battery to interested people in London.

Much more discretion was shown in sowing fields with mines. So how was the Resistance member to locate the mined areas, short of strolling around the countryside with a detector? By sitting in the local tax collector's waiting room! It was full of angry farmers who had come to demand a reduction in their land tax: they refused to pay it on this and that field which the Germans had just stuffed with mines.

It was a hopeless task. With all its security measures, the

German army in the west was like an elephant trying to hide behind a fan.

Unable to conceal themselves from the gaze of an army of spies, the Germans set about putting out their eyes. In the spring of 1944 the Gestapo struck with both hands in Normandy, and dozens of Resistance menbers went through its torture chambers. Arthur Poitevin and Dr. Sustendal had already been arrested. Gestapo men called at Duchez's house; he was not there. They found only Madame Duchez arguing with a customer who was complaining about some work that had been botched by the painter. The irate caller was thrown out—it was Duchez himself, of course—and, for lack of the husband, the Germans sent the wife to the Mauthausen concentration camp. By April the net was being spread so wide that the head of *Centurie,* Girard, received orders from London to break off all his contacts and disappear. His group had been decimated everywhere, from Cherbourg to Le Havre. At the same time the Gestapo had captured all the members of the Normandy section of the *Alliance* group, one of the most important underground organizations in France. These continued successes caused Colonel Giskes, who was in charge of German counterespionage in Holland, Belgium and Northern France, to write: "The reports of the heads of the services under my orders gave a picture of defensive measures which were most alert, energetic and truly productive."

The colonel meant to say that the Resistance was bleeding, and he was right. It was not difficult for the German professionals to cut deep into the organizations of amateurs, shakily built up and swollen in numbers beyond all rules of security (though this dangerous proliferation had enabled a close knowledge of German dispositions to be gained). Compartmentalization within each group was often inadequate. Worse still, some members worked for more than one group! Skipper Thomine, who sent German posters and other information to *Centurie,* also belonged to *Alliance,* each member of which had the name of an animal as his pseudonym. Thomine was known as "Sperm Whale." Charles Douin, the royalist sculptor recruited by *Centurie,* was "Civet Cat" to *Alliance.**

---

* Neither group was aware of this double membership. I was surprised to find, in the course of gathering material for this book, that Monsieur Jean Sainteny, the wartime head of *Alliance,* was still un-

Colonel Giskes's report continued: "But that made no difference in the catastrophic situation evident from the overall results. The wealth of minute detail in the many documents we seized proved how effective our adversaries' activities were. And we were well aware that what we seized here and there represented only a part of the mass of information reaching the enemy. In France and Belgium, the sacrifices accepted in order to help the Allied Secret Services had undeniably paid off. These Services had won the secret war."

The colonel was again right: the game was over. When the Caen Gestapo finally tracked down Robert Thomas it was too late. The man they forced to flee was ill and exhausted. As a cartographer for the *Centurie* group alone, Thomas had drawn or revised four thousand maps in eighteen months. With them, all of Normandy, down to the last inch, down to the last gun and soldier, had gone to London.

London was submerged.

At first there had been a group of experts known as "the Martians" in a basement office at Clive Steps, Whitehall. At a time when the world was ringing with German victories and Britain was fighting for survival, this group headed by John Austin, an Oxford don, was preparing an operation almost as unreal as a landing on Mars: an Allied invasion of the Continent. The task of these men was to gather as much information as possible about the European coastline; the map that Duchez had stolen from *Bauleiter* Schnedderer's office was their finest exhibit.

---

aware, twenty years afterwards, that Thomine and Douin had been working for *Centurie* at the same time as for *Alliance*. Monsieur Sainteny has a farm above Omaha Beach. He frequently went to stay there during the war for "professional" reasons, and was in close touch with both men.

A curious thing is that each group had a different and even contradictory idea of Douin, probably because of the role he played. He is remembered by members of *Centurie*, in which he had a secondary role, as an eccentric, ardent and vehement in his views. To members of *Alliance*, however, he was tranquillity itself. They do not seem to have been particularly struck by his monarchism and anglophobia—which were a joke among all the *Centurie* group—and in fact he was put in charge of the key sector of Caen because of his discretion and efficiency. It will never be known which was the real Charles Douin. With Thomine and ninety other Resistance members he was mowed down by machine guns in the courtyard of Caen prison of June 6 at six-thirty in the morning. H-Hour on D-Day was also the hour of their death. "God and my King!" cried Charles Douin as he fell.

But the Martians had disappeared, eliminated in a way by the full moon. For when the moon was full, R.A.F. Lysanders landed briefly in French fields marked out by the Resistance and took aboard more sacks of documents than there was room for in the basement office at Clive Steps. Each month French fishing vessels were braving the German patrol boats and making rendezvous with British submarines, to hand over more sacks of documents. Each day hundreds of secret transmitters were sending streams of messages to London. Most of this information eventually reached a building on Palace Street where 120 people headed by Colonel Rémy sorted it out. And what raw material they had to deal with! A professional would have been shaken out of his habitual calm by it.

There was, for instance, André Farine who took an interest in everything, passed judgment on everything and reported on everything. He had a restaurant near Grandcamp, and was very popular with the soldiers of the nearby coastal battery at Le Hoc. They came to the dance at his place on Sundays, against all regulations. He was very popular in London too, for that battery—like the one at Merville—was a great headache to the Allied commanders. From its position on the headland its guns could sweep both Omaha Beach and Utah Beach. The assault to silence this battery, which was to be carried out by American Rangers, looked like another suicide operation. "A dirty job," was all Lieutenant Colonel Terence Otway had said when the objective of his airborne battalion was revealed to him: to silence the Merville battery. When General Bradley explained to Colonel James Rudder that his Rangers would have to climb the steep cliff of Le Hoc—which is as high as a ten-story building—with the aid of rope ladders and under enemy fire, Rudder almost laughed: he thought the general was joking. A painful mistake. So it can be realized how anxiously Farine's reports were awaited in London; and with what bewilderment the following message was read, a message he had composed one Sunday afternoon after eating his lunch under the eyes of a group of German soldiers: "The morale of the troops is low. It is not true that the soldiers are well fed. They stared longingly at my plate of *rognons à la crème.*" Good old Normandy!

But the report on the kidneys with cream sauce, like the one on the caliber of the guns of the Le Hoc battery, like reports of all kinds sent by all the Farines in France, were received, sorted, reproduced and distributed by the Palace Street factory. Its average monthly output amounted to 200,-000 mimeographed sheets, 60,000 black-and-white copies of maps and sketches, and 10,000 photographic reproductions.

And only a part of the information received from France went to Palace Street: the part gathered by Resistance groups working for de Gaulle's Deuxième Bureau. The "Rommel document" stolen by Ponchardier had followed another channel, as the *Sosies* group worked directly with the British. Then there was the map fifty feet long, brought to London personally by Jean Sainteny of *Alliance*. It had been drawn by Charles Douin, and it showed every detail of the Wall from the mouth of the river Dives to the Cotentin Peninsula.

Whatever the route taken, this mountain of paper was eventually distributed among the different specialized units of the intelligence services, who analyzed, compared and assessed it. The terse reports they prepared could be used directly by staff officers, but Resistance members would have found in them none of the feverish anxiety that had gripped them as they wrote their messages.

They would have probably recognized their work better if they could have seen the huge model kept at the Duke of York's Barracks in London. It reproduced the invasion area and had all the "wealth of minute detail" that Colonel Giskes had mentioned. It symbolized the victory which he granted the Allied secret services. It represented—by the means employed, the sacrifices demanded and the results obtained—a rare accomplishment in the history of intelligence warfare.

Why, then, did the dozen British officers who kept it up to date look so glum?

## 11. The Real Problem

It was going to be a massacre. Anxiety reigned in the hundreds of Allied offices where operational plans for the invasion were being completed. London was full of pessimistic rumors and forecasts of disaster. There were certain known, unquestionable facts: for instance, German war production was still increasing despite the bombings; the morale of the German soldiers captured in Italy was still good and they had a fanatical belief in Germany's final victory; and the civilian population was standing up well to Allied air raids. There were all kinds of speculations about the secret weapons being prepared by Hitler. And there were the reports being sent by the French Resistance. They were unanimous: the Germans were building up their strength. At the beginning of the winter von Rundstedt had forty-six divisions under his command; by June he would have sixty—a quarter of the whole German Army. On April 2, Montgomery's chief intelligence officer, working from information supplied by the Resistance, made an analysis of German plans which could not have been more masterly if he had heard Hitler expounding his supreme gamble to his military leaders on March 20: "It would appear at the moment that the enemy is exposing himself to fresh disasters in the east, even more terrible than before, in order to retain all his chances in the west. It is a peculiar game from a military point of view, but becomes comprehensible when viewed from a political standpoint— with the hope of a compromise peace if this decision bears all its fruits. In short, more and more Stalingrads in the hope of a single Dunkirk."

In London, this last word opened an old wound and roused visions of a blood bath. Afterward, all those involved agreed that April had been the worst month. Inner fears had not yet been swept away by the rush of final preparations and OVERLORD was no longer that abstract operation which the "Martians" had viewed from afar, and which staff officers removed from the tumult of war had been working on for nearly two years. The stage of calculating the maximum loads of the assault craft had been passed; the job was now to prepare the cannon-fodder that would be packed into them and sent against the Wall.

On September 9, 1943, the Allies had landed at Salerno on a three-divisional front. Five days later Eisenhower had informed Washington: "We have been unable to advance and the enemy is preparing a major counterattack. . . . I am using everything we have bigger than a rowboat [to send reinforcements]. In the present situation our great hope is the Air Force." For three days the Allied planes were constantly in the air, bombing and machine-gunning everything that moved, and they saved the troops in the beachhead from disaster.

On January 22, 1944, an army corps had landed at Anzio without opposition, achieving complete tactical surprise. But a German counterattack first threatened to throw the Allies back into the sea, then pinned them down and blocked the beachhead for several months.

Neither at Salerno nor Anzio had there been any serious fortifications. But along the French coast there was the Wall. It was not exactly the rampart of concrete and steel which Goebbels had proclaimed to be impassable; it was, rather, the line of poorly constructed, inadequately armed blockhouses which the Resistance had reported. Nevertheless, with all its defects, it was the strongest line of coastal defenses ever known. A line that was too thin, and therefore fragile, but with some tough knots strung along it—such as Osteck, Le Hoc, the cliffs of Pas-de-Calais and the beach which was to be known as "Bloody Omaha." All the defenses of Salerno and Anzio combined would not have equaled those of Omaha alone: eight gun-casemates, thirty-five bunkers with light guns and automatic weapons, eighteen antitank guns, four big guns, six mortars, thirty-five four-barreled rocket-launchers and eighty-five machine-gun nests.

The Allied troops were fearful of the Wall and had every

right to be. The eight hundred Germans waiting at Omaha Beach were to kill or wound three thousand of them in a few hours.

The Allied High Command thought it could take the Wall in its stride, and was not far wrong. The mathematically minded generals had already fixed the price to be paid: ten thousand dead. This was more than necessary, for the German machine guns would jam or run out of ammunition before they reached that figure. Even if the stakes had had to be doubled, Eisenhower would have carried on; he could afford it. His General Bradley had a whole corps at his disposal in order to root out the eight hundred defenders of Omaha Beach. This enabled the shy, modest and prudent Bradley to tell war correspondents: "Getting ashore will be difficult, but we're not especially worried about it."

The longest day? When Eisenhower's aide-de-camp, Harry Butcher, tiptoed into the general's trailer early on the morning of June 6 he found him sitting up in bed reading a Western. There was no "longest day" for the Allies, because there is no instance in modern history of a large invasion force being thrown back into the sea in the first twenty-four hours. The attackers, striking when and where they choose, can always obtain an initial numerical superiority enabling them to get a grip on the landing area.

The real problem is to hang on under the hammer-blows which soon begin to rain down. The defenders can bring up reinforcements by road and rail (in 1944, the French railway system was the best in Europe); they are able to concentrate their forces with great speed. The invaders, however, have to send all reinforcements by sea, which is much slower, and problems of loading and unloading can cause delays. The invading force may soon lose its initial advantage; it has to build up its strength at a faster rate than the enemy can rush up troops to meet its assult, or it risks being thrown back—as at Salerno and Anzio. This was even more vital on the Normandy beaches, for the first assault troops had got ashore at Anzio without any real opposition, whereas in Normandy the attackers would have to fight their way past the defenders of the Wall. General Bradley had summed up the problem thus: "As soon as we land, this business becomes primarily a business of build-up. For you can almost always force an invasion—but you can't always make it stick."

So the Longest Day for the Allies was not going to be D-Day but D plus 3. By that time the enemy could theoretically throw eighteen to twenty divisions—eight of them armored—into the battle. Eisenhower would then have thirteen divisions, including armored elements of two divisions, to meet the German avalanche. There was, of course, the hope that pounding from the air and the action of Resistant groups would delay the regrouping of German forces. This hope was well founded. The German 275th Infantry Division stationed in Brittany took a week to cover one hundred and sixty miles; the 16th Division at The Hague had to make a wide detour to the south, through the Rhineland and eastern France, in order to reach the Normandy battle area; the 9th and 10th S.S. Armored Divisions transferred from the eastern front took more time to move from Strasbourg to Normandy than from Poland to the French border.

However, before D-Day it seemed that the balance of forces would be extremely precarious; Churchill, usually full of optimism, hoped for no more than a stubborn resistance which would enable the Allies to hold the beachhead. In April, 1944, he said to Eisenhower: "If by the coming winter you have established yourself with your thirty-six Allied divisions firmly on the Continent, and have the Cherbourg and Brittany peninsulas in your grasp, I will proclaim this operation to the world as one of the most successful of the war."

There was one possibility which was not even taken into account—though it was in everyone's mind. Close estimate had been made of the balance of forces in the battle area from D plus 3 to D plus 30. For instance, there was the German 16th Division, stationed at The Hague: the Allied Command knew the average rate of movement of a division of this kind; they knew that if a certain bridge were destroyed the division would have to make a certain detour, and that the bombing of a certain rail junction would hold up the division for a certain length of time. The harassing actions of the Resistance would also add to these delays. Altogether it was estimated that the 16th Division would not reach the battle area before D plus 15. But there was an important reservation to bear in mind: the 16th Division was not bound to remain stationed at The Hague. At any moment prior to D-Day the German Supreme Command might order it to move . . . perhaps to Caen. In that case it would miss the exciting game that the Allied air forces and the Resistance had prepared for it (bridge destroyed—go back three squares; rail junction blown up—miss a turn). The Allies' calculations would be thrown out, and the balance of forces would swing in the Germans' favor.

The detailed calculations on which OVERLORD depended would be completely useless if the Germans discovered the secret of the invasion area. They had no need to know the beaches; the name of the province or department would be enough (Brittany, Normandy, Pas-de-Calais). They could then concentrate their divisions in the right area, rush them to the vital part of the coast with minimum delay, counterattack the assault troops while they were still comparatively thin on the ground and overwhelm them by sheer weight. If OVERLORD were not postponed or called off entirely, Eisenhower would be sending his troops to be massacred.

It was an extraordinary situation. The Germans, because of their weakness, could hope to win only if they discovered the Allies' secret, and so delivered a quick knockout blow with the steel fist of their Panzers and shock troops. The Allies, despite their strength, could hope to triumph only if they kept the secret of OVERLORD until the very last, so that the troops holding the beachhead could survive the critical first ten days and enable the build-up to be made. By giving each side its chance and equalizing the advantages, surely the god of war had never before set up a conflict of such dramatic simplicity!

In London, General Thomas Batts was not prepared to bet a dollar on the Allies' chances. He was convinced that the enemy would discover Eisenhower's plan. And his opinion counted: as General Whiteley's adjutant, he was the man responsible for safeguarding the secret of OVERLORD.

## 12. When a Bigot Meets a Bigot

THE fact that Britain was an island simplified things. The fact that she was a democracy complicated them. So the great crusade against Hitler's dictatorship began with a skirmish against British liberal traditions. The generals wanted to clamp down on democratic freedom; they asked in particular for the south coast to be forbidden to civilian visitors. General Morgan, who had been in charge of the planning of OVERLORD for sixteen months, had told Churchill back in 1943 how easy it was for an enemy agent to deduce the general direction of the Allied invasion of the Continent. If the best units were seen to be concentrating in southeastern England, the invasion would be aimed at Pas-de-Calais; if in the southwest, at Normandy or Brittany. The reasoning was clear and simple; it had been that of Kliemann when briefing Lily Sergueiev.

Churchill and the Cabinet had rejected General Morgan's request in the name of democratic principles. Morgan replied that the government was merely trying to avoid irritating the population for political reasons. "If we fail," he said, "there won't be any more politics." The situation was still the same in March, 1944. All that had been done was to suspend civilian travel between Ireland and Great Britain as of February 9. This was a necessary measure, for Ireland was still neutral and the German embassy in Dublin had a large and active staff.

Montgomery returned to the attack and pressed Eisenhower to use his authority. He wrote to him: "It would go hard with our consciences if we were to feel, in later years, that by neglecting any security precaution, we had compromised the success of these vital operations or needlessly squandered men's lives." Eisenhower, with his friendly eyes and beaming smile, had a touching way of saying that if his requests were refused he would have to "go back home," as he put it. Four days after Montgomery's letter, the government decreed that after April 1, civilians would be prohibited from entering a coastal zone ten miles wide extending from the Wash to Cornwall; a similar zone was established round the Firth of Forth.

Hitler was shocked and annoyed by these undemocratic decisions. On April 6 he thundered to his General Staff: "These English demonstrations seem ludicrous to me—the latest reports on their unreasonable regulations, these security measures, and so on. Normally, such things aren't done when an operation of that kind is planned . . . I can't help thinking that it's just an impudent imposture after all, that it's all an insolent bluff!"

Hitler had a completely mistaken idea of General Batts, the watchdog of OVERLORD. Far from being an insolent bluffer, poor Thomas Batts—tall, stout and husky in a typically American way—was full of anxiety. He was wondering whether his iron curtain would succeed in stopping the German spies.

London was swarming with well-meaning but dangerous spies: the journalists. There were several hundred of them, all possessed by the demon of their species: the hunt for news. And in April, 1944, when the Allied army in Italy had been marking time for months, there was no more engrossing subject than the coming invasion.

Winston Churchill, himself a former reporter, knew this so well that he warned Eisenhower of the danger. There was obviously no fear that the secrets of OVERLORD would be spread across the front page. Censorship was alert. But there was a chance that reporters might put together scraps of information gathered here and there until they formed a fairly accurate general idea of the invasion plan. The Fleet Street bars in which these combined exercises in future Allied strategy usually took place were frequented by other customers than newspapermen—in particular, members of foreign diplomatic staffs. The duty of a diplomat being to inform his government, Churchill feared that revelations about OVERLORD might reach neutral capitals where German agents abounded.

Eisenhower hesitated. He knew that journalists were often more to be dreaded when restrictions were placed on them. After the Tunisian campaign he had cleverly neutralized the war correspondents by telling them about HUSKY, the planned invasion of Sicily. Once they had been given this momentous secret, they had to keep it. But Eisenhower could not repeat that stratagem now—OVERLORD was not HUSKY. He confined himself to asking the British and American journalists not to speculate about the forthcoming invasion in any way. At the same time he instructed his staff to treat them with great cordiality, but without giving them the slightest bit of information.

The fact remained that diplomats of neutral countries could pick up information in other places than Fleet Street pubs. This curiosity, it could be said on their behalf, resulted from a praiseworthy professional conscience. They were doing their job as informers. But there was a risk that the information they sent to their governments might be spread around; it might even fall into impure hands. British counterintelligence was convinced that two neutral officials, highly placed in the foreign ministry of their country, were working for the German secret service.

At the worst, a foreign diplomat in London might be an agent of Canaris or Schellenberg, and the privileges of his position would give him almost limitless freedom of action. In the early months of the war a Hungarian military attaché in London had thus been able to send information of great importance to Budapest, from where it was passed on to Berlin. His transmitter, hidden in an attic, was discovered, and that was his undoing. But a diplomat has a safer, simpler means of getting his secret messages to a "letter box": the diplomatic pouch.

General Morgan therefore asked the government to take the necessary measures. It was imperative to withdraw the privileges of the diplomatic pouch, and even to stop allowing embassies to send coded messages. This amounted to transforming each embassy into a ghetto isolated from the outside world. Morgan had caused a scandal. The Foreign Office considered his request absurd, and even in bad taste. Churchill was greatly shocked. There was consternation in London clubs, particularly as the members did not even have the consolation of Morgan being an American: he was English. In any case, there could be no question of placing restrictions on the diplomatic corps, and certainly not of suppressing its freedom of communications. It just wasn't done. England would lose face. In offices of the counterespionage services the files of the Tyler Kent and Menezes cases were perused with bitter remarks. . . .

Tyler Kent was the son of an American diplomat and had been educated at Princeton and the Sorbonne: he was a handsome, well-spoken young man, a gifted athlete and an accomplished linguist. He was twenty-seven and knew seven languages when, in October, 1939, he was appointed to the coding section of the American embassy in London. He soon found a welcome among Fascist-minded English socialites, and in next to no time he became anti-Semitic, anti-Communist, anti-plutocratic—and madly in love with Baroness Wolkoff.

Anna Wolkoff was a beautiful hussy of thirty-eight whose parents were Russian emigrants; instead of a dog, she led a large tomcat with a solid gold collar about with her everywhere. Tyler Kent was badly smitten. He had no idea such women as the Baroness existed. Between disconcerting caresses she revealed to him that he had a mission in the world: to shorten the war. To fulfill it, all he had to do was photograph the important documents that came into his hands at the embassy. She would then send the copies in the Italian diplomatic pouch—Mussolini had not yet entered the war—to pacifist-minded individuals devoted to the reconciliation of nations.

Six years later, at the Nuremberg trials, Admiral Raeder and Generals Jodl and Keitel admitted that German strategy between October, 1939, and May, 1940, had been based in part on information supplied by Tyler Kent. The Germans had received copies of all communications between London and Washington, and so knew the exact strength of the British army, the dispositions and needs of its forces, its reserve supplies, and its offensive and defensive plans. The Germans also knew all about Anglo-American political relationships.

This wonderful source eventually ran dry through crass stupidity. The baroness was being watched. The policeman keeping track of her movements became intrigued by the fact that meetings between her and her American lover nearly always ended up at a photographer's shop. When questioned the photographer admitted that the American embassy did him the honor of entrusting him with certain work. He showed the police the last roll of films given to him to develop. It was of course photographs of secret documents. The photographer's naïveté was great, but the stupidity of his two customers was even greater. By failing to take the precaution of setting up their own discreet darkroom, they spoiled their chances of becoming the spies of the century. Anna Wolkoff and Tyler Kent were arrested on May 18, 1940.

Nevertheless, they had done a great deal of damage. Copies of more than fifteen hundred secret documents had reached Berlin. And Kent had given the American diplomatic code to the Germans, thus enabling them to decipher messages between the State Department and its embassies over a period of eight months.*

Like Tyler Kent, Rogerio de Magalhaes Peixoto de Menezes was young and handsome, a diplomat, and stupid. He arrived in London in July, 1942, to take up his appointment at the Portuguese embassy, carrying in his luggage the invisible ink and the code given to him in Lisbon by agents of the German secret service. He was then twenty-six, and so lackadaisical that most of the items he sent to Lisbon were culled from the newspapers. He added some of the gossip he picked up in the bars where he spent his evenings. Menezes was obviously too lazy to make even a bad spy. After a time he neglected to use the diplomatic pouch and sent his messages by ordinary mail to the "letter boxes" which had been indicated to him. These addresses had been discovered by British intelligence in Lisbon and reported to the postal censors in London. Conse-

---

* The code obviously had to be changed, but six months passed before all the embassies were in possession of the new code. They were therefore almost reduced to silence at a time when France was collapsing and the balance of world power was being upset. American diplomacy suffered a hard blow. The reaction of Joseph Kennedy, the U. S. Ambassador to London at the time, was remarkable in its way. When confronted with his disloyal subordinate he said: "What do you imagine will be the effect of your treachery on your good mother?" Which is yet another indication that in 1940 Americans were not psychologically ready for war. Tyler Kent was given a seven-year sentence; he was released from prison in December, 1945. Anna Wolkoff was given ten years, and was released in June, 1946. In the early part of the war, spies were given comparatively mild sentences in Britain.

quently Menezes's correspondence led to his arrest, on February 22, 1943.*

The lesson to be drawn from these two cases was clear to the men responsible for the security of OVERLORD: a diplomat working for the Germans could not be discovered unless he gave himself away. Neither Kent nor Menezes had much talent for espionage, but that had not prevented the former from causing a disastrous amount of damage. If a cunning German agent was still active among the diplomatic staffs in London, the only means of neutralizing him was to cut his lines of communication with the outside world.

Eisenhower therefore took up the struggle which Morgan had lost. He declared that the possibility of diplomatic leak was "the most serious of the risks imperiling the security of the operation and the lives of our men." On April 9 he asked for strict measures to be taken as soon as possible after April 15.

On April 17 the British government withdrew the privileges of the diplomatic pouch, prohibited the sending of messages in code and informed foreign diplomats that neither they, their famiilies nor even their servants would be allowed to leave Britain before the end of June. These measures applied equally to the Allied governments from the occupied countries. The Belgians, Dutch, Poles, Norwegians and Czechs found themselves unable to communicate with their respective embassies. They were greatly shocked and, as a protest, decided not to pass on to the British the information they received from their Resistance groups. But Churchill held to his decision and refused to make any exceptions— apart, of course, from the Americans and the Russians.

There was, however, a problem with the Russians. To keep the secret of OVERLORD from them would deprive the Anglo-Americans of the supporting offensive in the east which Stalin had promised to deliver when the invasion began in in the west. The idea was impossible. Yet to reveal the invasion plan to Moscow was to increase the risk of a leak, and would give the Germans an extra chance of discovering the secret. It was not believed at all certain in London that

---

* He was condemned to death at the Old Bailey. His mother sent a heartrending appeal to King George VI and Winston Churchill, and both were said to have been affected by it. But his pardon was more likely due to the fact that he belonged to a very old Portuguese family and that, in 1943, the benevolent neutrality of Portugal was important to the Allies.

Moscow would be able to keep the plan secret. There were cynics who wondered if the Russians would even want to. A compromise was decided upon; the British and American military missions in Moscow were instructed to reveal the date but not the place of the invasion. Stalin was informed that D-Day would be two or three days before or after June 1, depending on weather conditions. He asked for further details, but the head of the British mission, General Burrows, was ordered to keep his lips sealed. He was forbidden to return to London or to send one of his assistants, thus enabling him to maintain that he had no knowledge of the details of the plan—and to spare the Russians' feelings. As for sending Stalin the marked map he was asking for, it was out of the question. London expressed regrets and pointed out the risks of the long journey.

There was also a problem with the French. The Allied military leaders had a feeling that the great secret would not be safe with the Free French. Because the French people were innately loquacious? Because de Gaulle's Deuxième Bureau would give in to the temptation to comfort its hard-pressed Resistance groups, who were constantly asking for at least a glimmer of hope? Whatever the reason, the Allied high command ordered Eisenhower to say nothing of OVERLORD to the Free French.

So by the middle of April the British people had been annoyed by restrictions on movement, the foreign diplomatic corps had been shocked, the refugee Allied governments alienated, the Russians offended and the Free French humiliated. But unfortunately all the Bigots could not be confined to a small desert island.

Every officer who knew the date and place of the invasion was a Bigot. He had a special pass to enter certain offices which a non-Bigot officer could not enter, no matter what his rank, just as he could not read documents marked "Bigot." When one Bigot spoke to another about OVERLORD over the telephone they used special green telephones equipped with "scramblers," so that their conversation was unintelligible to anyone who might be listening on the line.

General Thomas Batts watched over his Bigots like an anxious mother hen. But there were several hundred of them. How could he be sure an ugly duckling had not slipped into this large brood, in spite of the thorough screening by the security services? And how could he be sure that one drink too many might not lead to loose talk? Just before the North African landings, men in London bars had loudly asked about the best hotels in Algiers. And suppose the enemy came and snatched a Bigot from under the general's protecting wing. Since the Allies were making commando raids on the Continent, why couldn't the Germans do the same thing on the English coast? It would be less difficult for Otto Skorzeny than kidnapping Mussolini on the summit of the Gran Sasso. He could select a few S.S. men who spoke English and dress them in Allied uniform. Their guttural accent would arouse no suspicion, for Britain was swarming with soldiers of all nationalities who did not speak the purest of English, if they spoke it at all. Even if Skorzeny's uniforms did not quite meet regulations there would be no great danger. British Security had recently carried out a revealing test: an officer dressed in Luftwaffe uniform had walked around London for an hour without attracting any attention. The thought of that experiment troubled General Batts's sleep fairly often.

April 26 dawned at last; the day had been awaited with increasingly nervous impatience, for the American 4th Division was to carry out an important exercise: a rehearsal of its assault on Utah Beach. The place chosen was Slapton Sands, between Dartmouth and Plymouth, where for weeks past Engineers had been constructing a duplicate of the German fortified positions. After so many months of paperwork and planning, the day was greeted as joyfully as the exit from a long tunnel. There was also the importance of seeing how that huge abstraction OVERLORD would work out in the field.

That morning the Luftwaffe could have wiped out the Allied Command with a single bomb dropped on Landing Craft 495. Eisenhower had stepped aboard at six o'clock and was accompanied by so many American generals that it looked as though all the stars in the sky had dropped into the craft at dawn. For each of the generals it was like waiting to see his baby take its first steps. The naval bombardment was due to begin at seven o'clock, then the first wave of bombers would go in, to be followed shortly afterwards by the amphibious tanks, assault troops and Engineer units with the task of clearing the beach of obstacles. H-Hour was 7:30.

By 7:15 it was obvious that the exercise was off to a bad

start. The amphibious tanks were not yet in the water and were going to reach the beach behind schedule. The officers finally saw them come down the ramp of their LCT's and float on their big air-filled cushions. One sank almost immediately. Cheerfulness had already given way to uneasiness and this turned to desperation when H-Hour arrived and not a single soldier had set foot on the beach. The landing craft crammed with assault troops were going in circles instead of heading for shore. It was inexplicable. Something had gone wrong with the machine, but no one in LC–495 knew the reason. Finally, with appalling slowness, the first assault wave was landed on the beach and the exercise began. Eisenhower and Bradley found some consolation in the precision of the bombing. The planes were carpeting the ground 1500 yards ahead of the troops, an agreed margin of safety which now seemed overcautious. But just as Eisenhower was telling Bradley he would reduce the margin to 500 yards, a bomber dropped its load less than 500 yards from the leading troops. The two generals tacitly agreed to change the subject. Besides, what was happening on the beach deserved their whole attention. The Engineers were taking their time in blowing up the obstacles, and the tanks were rumbling slowly back and forth, waiting for the beach to be cleared. On the real D-Day it would be a delight for the German gunners to fire into those fat targets which were wandering across the sand like sleepy pachyderms.

As for the troops, they lacked spirit, initiative and cohesion, and their officers were clearly not up to their task. Harry Butcher, Eisenhower's naval aide, wrote in his diary that evening: "I am concerned over the absence of toughness and alertness of young American officers whom I saw on this trip. They seem to regard the war as one grand maneuver in which they are having a happy time. Many seem as green as growing corn. How will they act in battle and how will they look in three months' time? A good many of the full colonels also give me a pain. They are fat, gray and oldish."

At the end of the day Butcher joined the Allied commanders in the special train taking them back to London. His captain's braid had not been enough for a place in LC–495, and he was impatient to learn why the exercise had been such a fiasco. A heated discussion was going on between Eisenhower, Air Marshal Tedder, and the American generals

Bradley and Gerow, but they fell silent when Butcher entered the compartment. Then Eisenhower asked him anxiously if he knew who had given the order to put back H-Hour. Butcher was astounded and replied that he was about to ask the same question himself. None of them knew the answer to it. Nobody ever knew who had given the order, or even if one was given. The journey back to London was made in gloomy consternation. It was obvious that this exercise for a part of OVERLORD had escaped from the control of its planners. On paper, OVERLORD was the greatest and best conceived amphibious operation in military history. On Slapton Sands it had been a pitiful failure.

The hardest blow was still to come. That evening Eisenhower learned, seventeen hours after the event, that a convoy of landing craft on its way to Slapton Sands had been attacked by German motor torpedo boats. Two LST's* had been sunk and a third damaged. There were seven hundred men dead or missing. It had happened before dawn, in Lyme Bay, and none of the generals had been informed of it during the exercise. They were astounded by the audacity and success of the Germans. Their dismay was complete: if the enemy could break through the screen of escort ships and torpedo landing craft in an English bay, what would it be like off the coast of France!

For the Allied commanders, the day ended on this funereal note. For the security services, the day had only just begun. The Admiralty had ordered an immediate inquiry into the exact conditions under which the attack had occurred, and the report was expected before midnight. It was anxiously awaited, and was read with relief: the Germans had not been able to take prisoners. As soon as the torpedo boats had struck, they had come under fire from the escorting warships and had withdrawn at once. That settled the problem for everybody—except Montgomery. Suspicious and tenacious, he sent one of his staff officers, Ralph Ingersoll, to the port to which the damaged LST had been towed. Ingersoll questioned two tank officers who had been aboard her when the attack took place, and their story justified Montgomery's suspicions. There had not been any escorting ships; at least, not in the immediate area. The two officers said that after the

---

* Landing Ship Tank, able to carry 30 tanks and therefore much larger than a Landing Craft Tank.

two LST's had been sunk and the stern had been blown off their own, the German torpedo boats had approached to within a hundred yards. With great daring, they had turned on their searchlights. Survivors could be clearly seen bobbing in the water. The torpedo boats had cruised among them for a few minutes, then disappeared without being fired upon. The two officers did not know whether the enemy had taken any prisoners, but agreed that it was possible.

Any ordinary troops among survivors picked up by the Germans could not reveal details of the exercise, as their ships had been torpedoed before it began (if it had already taken place the soldiers would have known the layout of the fortifications on Slapton Sands, which were identical to those of Utah Beach). But ten "Bigot" officers were reported among the missing. Now the disaster was complete. The Germans, who knew how to loosen prisoners' tongues, were going to learn all about the invasion plans. The next day, the Allied high command considered abandoning OVERLORD.

General Batts and his men did not give up. They organized a vast fishing expedition for corpses. Lyme Bay was searched and dragged by dozens of craft. Since the currents were moving away from shore, it was clear from the start that most of the seven hundred dead would never be found. But only the ten missing officers were being sought. Rarely could human corpses have been pursued with such determination. Four were found, then five, then six. It was an unusual and distressing quest, for each macabre discovery aroused enthusiasm and revived hopes. Probably never before had men hooked corpses of their brothers-in-arms from the sea with such glad hearts. The seventh was found, then the eighth and the ninth. Was the invasion to be put off because of one man? Finally the sea gave up the tenth Bigot, already stiff in his lifebelt. Hundreds of soldiers were still missing and would never be found, but fate had ordained that Thomas Batts should recover his ten Bigots.

It was a battle won, but the secret war continued. General Batts lost much sleep. This placid giant of a man admitted twenty years later that the weeks before D-Day were a constant nightmare for him. How could the Germans fail, when they had so many opportunities? There were aerial reconnaissance flights, commando raids, seamen of neutral countries whose ships docked in British ports and who could observe the preparations, there were the inevitable indiscretions when a secret is shared by several hundred men . . .

And there were, of course, the German spies operating in Great Britain.

# 13. The Kamikaze Spies

THE Norwegian miner, the man from Oslo, having succeeded in extricating himself from the Junker–11, floated slowly down to Scottish soil. He landed on one foot, and fractured it. End of mission. The local police found him the next morning. A doctor set his broken bones, a court convicted him and a hangman executed him. Yet his instructor had told him it was essential to keep his feet together when he landed, to distribute his weight and take the shock better. The Norwegian had probably forgotten. He came down with his legs apart, and all his weight was on the foot that hit the ground first. This might not have happened if he had been made to do half a dozen practice jumps.

The training of spies in parachute jumping presented a difficult problem. If it was kept short, then a stupid accident occurred; if it was extended, then a detailed description of the spy might reach London before he jumped from a plane over Britain, for the Resistance kept a vigilant eye on airports and the training of parachutists. It had been thought that the Norwegian miner's strong muscles would compensate for his inadequate training. This had proved to be a mistake, and he would never help to settle the controversy over Berg and Klausen. The only positive result of his little outing was to prove how right were those in the German secret service who were agitating for a stop to such suicidal parachutings. The Norwegian was not the first agent to have gone to the gallows as a result of a clumsy parachute landing. Would he at any rate be the last?

Every night Joseph Jan Vanhove, the man from Stockholm and ex-waiter at the Hôtel Métropole, tried to fight down his terror of the Germans. The "little blitz" in 1944 was nothing like the Blitz in the summer of 1940; Goering was sending lone raiders over London rather than whole squadrons of bombers. But it was not very pleasant to hear bombs whistling down and exploding when locked between four walls and unable to get out. It could easily bring on claustrophobia. Vanhove was lodged in Pentonville prison. He couldn't understand it at all. His German masters—Schellenberg's S.S.—had been so proud of the cover story they had perfected for him. Armed with his newspaper clippings, Vanhove ought to have been greeted in London as a hero of the Resistance.

He had in fact been welcomed cordially, though without demonstrations of enthusiasm. Security officers had given him the usual interrogation, and then he had been allowed to go free. No more interest was shown in him. Vanhove had foolishly congratulated himself. He had not thought it strange that a man reputed to have handled the finances of the Belgian Resistance should be treated as of small concern. He wandered around London and did some spying, since that was what he had come for. But his heart was not in it. If he could, he would probably have confessed everything to the security officers. Spies were not hanged if they told everything they knew, right from the start. But the Germans had taken the precaution of ensuring that he had some blood on his hands, before despatching him to Britain: the blood of the French Resistance men he had betrayed. Whether he liked it or not, he had to carry on.

Not for long, though. He was arrested as soon as counter-espionage concluded he was a lone agent and would not lead them to any "contact." All that was found on him were a few notes on shipping movements and some rough diagrams situating recent bomb damage. None of that mattered. On the other hand, the fact that Vanhove's trips down the river had not aroused his interest in the huge caissons of steel and concrete moored near Tilbury was important and reassuring to General Batts. . . .

The trial of Joseph Jan Vanhove opened at the Old Bailey on May 23, 1944, and on the afternoon of the twenty-sixth the judge put on his black cap to pronounce sentence. Two months later Vanhove was hanged, still not knowing what mistake he had made. He would no doubt have been greatly astonished if told that he had made none, but that his fate had been sealed from the moment his German masters gave him the newspaper clippings. It was difficult for the hunter to put himself in the place of his quarry, and the Germans' idea that Resistance men had a feeling of power and self-confidence was far removed from reality. The British security officers were used to seeing hunted Resistance leaders who had managed to escape from occupied Europe; they arrived looking like men who had been close to death. No real Resistance leader would have been foolish enough to make the long journey across Europe that Vanhove had ostensibly made with papers in his pocket which meant arrest and execution if discovered.

German espionage in Britain had made a bad beginning. Two networks had been established by 1937. The first was composed only of minor agents, chiefly several hundred young German maids whose task was merely to snoop on their employers. These small fry would keep the British security services busy and divert them from the professionals in the second network, whose orders were to take no action until the outbreak of hostilities. There were then about three thousand agents in Britain, but only thirty-five of them belonged to the second network.

The security roundup of enemy aliens began on the night of September 3, 1939, and continued for several weeks. Two thousand police worked their way through a list of 73,235 names; 1004 were arrested and 6,000 had their movement restricted. This immediately eliminated the first network, which the Germans had expected, and nearly all the second network too, which they had not. For the professionals belonging to it had been carefully selected and then trained by the Abwehr at its school in Hamburg. Most of them, on reaching Britain, had scrupulously observed the lessons they had been taught, especially the very instructive ones given by Hans Stultz. This young instructor was an Oxford graduate, and his job was to teach the agents how to speak, dress, eat, drink and sleep in order to appear to be Englishmen. Some of his tips were quite ingenious. There was, for instance, the one about savings banks. Stultz told his students to deposit their money in a savings bank, then to go to the police and say they lost their bankbook. They would thus make an excellent impression on the police who, like all Englishmen—a nation of shopkeepers—judged a man's respectability by the size of his bank account. There was no reason why the German agents should not follow their instructor's advice. How were they to know that Hans Stultz was a very clever British agent? How could they have guessed that they had been carefully watched, and that all their contacts had been discovered ever since their visit to the police station about a lost bankbook?

After the massive sweep in September, London was convinced that the German spy network had been wiped out. Berlin was convinced that it had not, for a few agents were still in radio contact. But they were isolated, frightened and few. So in 1940 the Germans bravely started again from scratch, or almost, making use as much as possible of human material gathered from the conquered countries. With little preparation, they sent men to a country where the changed conditions due to the war could only be guessed at, a country the men had never set foot in before, and whose language most of them spoke badly. It was all wildly romantic; the suicide spies who tumbled into Britain had something of the tragic grandeur of the Japanese Kamikazes who crashed their planes on Allied warships, except that they did little or no harm.

Karl Meier and Rudolph Waldberg, a Dutchman and a German, were landed by boat on the south coast of England, near Romney Marsh, during the night of September 2, 1940. At nine in the morning Meier knocked at the door of a pub and asked for a bottle of cider. He was hanged on December 10. No one had told him that English pubs do not open until at least ten-thirty. Waldberg, arrested twenty-four hours after Meier, was hanged on the same day. He could not speak a single word of English, which limited his chances of survival.

Charles Albert Van den Kieboorn, a Dutchman, arrived on the same boat as Meier and Waldberg. He was hanged on December 17. He had landed on a beach occupied by a unit of the Somerset Light Infantry.

Another spy had a meal in a London restaurant and then offered the waitress some food coupons, with which the Germans had provided him. They did not know that food coupons were not required in British restaurants.

Karl Richter, a Czech, landed by parachute near St. Albans on the night of May 13, 1942. He hid in a forest for a day and a night, then ventured out to the road. A truck driver who was not sure of his way stopped and asked Richter for directions. Richter was hanged on December 10, 1942. His heavy accent would not have aroused the truck driver's suspicions if he had been in army uniform, for there were Czech troops in Britain, but the Germans had not thought of that.

Karl Theo Drueke, a German, Werner Waelti, a Swiss, and Vera Erikson, the daughter of Russian emigrants, landed on the Scottish coast after being brought to Moray Firth in a seaplane just before dawn on September 30, 1940. Not knowing exactly where they were, they walked to the nearest railroad station to find out. They had not been told that, as a security measure, all station names in Britain had been removed. "Where are we?" Vera Erikson naively asked a suspicious railroad worker. She saved her neck by agreeing to work for the British. Drueke and Waelti were hanged on August 6, 1941.

It was in a railroad station that another spy gave himself away. The ticket clerk told him that the price of his ticket was "ten and six"—meaning, of course, ten shillings and six pence, but the spy calmly handed over ten pounds and six shillings, which was far more than it would have cost to go from one end of Britain to the other. His instructors in Berlin had neglected to familiarize him with English money.

After this batch, which had given the hangman plenty of work, the Germans changed their tactics. Since the spirit of self-sacrifice carried to the point of suicide had not paid off, they would try to use more cunning. It was regrettable that, despite their tight controls, European Resistance fighters still managed to get to England, by boat or by way of Spain; but perhaps some good would come of this evil situation if a few German agents were slipped into the stream of escapees.

The idea was ingenious. But the Germans' almost total ignorance of life in wartime Britain meant that their agents still arrived there with no more assurance than astronauts taking their first steps on the moon. Many months passed before the Germans heard about a certain patriotic school, and it was even longer before they knew what it was. In the meantime, still more German agents had been caught and hanged.

For example, when Alphonse-Eugène Timmermans, a Belgian, reached London in April, 1942, he did not know he would be taken to the "Royal Victoria Patriotic School," where thirty-two counterespionage officers screened all new arrivals, or that his luggage and clothes would be spread out on a long table and examined under a magnifying glass for hours on end. If he had known this, the officers would not have found an envelope containing pyramidon powder in his wallet, together with some cotton wool and little sticks of wood, and instead of bringing these things which enabled him to write in invisible ink, he would have simply bought what he needed at any drugstore. Timmermans was hanged on July 7, 1942, and the counterespionage services had not even had to check on his Resistance story.

It may have been more plausible than that of his compatriot, Pierre Neukermann, who arrived in London on July 16, 1943, and was hanged on June 8, 1944. A short exchange of radio messages between London and the Belgian Resistance was enough to establish that, far from belonging to the Resistance, Neukermann was a notorious collaborator.

Dronkers, a Dutchman, was a more doubtful proposition. In his case, the Germans had used some of the inventive powers in which they had previously shown themselves to be so lamentably lacking. Dronkers reached England in a fishing boat on May 18, 1942, with two other Dutchmen who wanted to join the Dutch armed forces in Britain. But Dronkers admitted to his questioners at the Patriotic School that his ideals were not so high. His reason for escaping from Holland was that the German police were on his trail because of his black-market dealings. It was a clever story which relied on the benevolent contempt one feels for a man who frankly owns up to his dirty tricks. Dronkers was despised, but he felt sure he was going to be cleared. He was given a routine interrogation. How had he obtained his boat? He had bought it from a fisherman he met in Rotterdam. Where in Rotterdam? At the Atlanta café.

Mynheer Dronkers was hanged on January 1, 1943. Colonel Pinto, the Dutch intelligence officer who had questioned him, knew Rotterdam and its cafés, and knew that there was about as much chance of meeting a fisherman at the Atlanta as of sitting down beside a barge captain at Maxim's in

Paris. He was sure Dronkers was a spy, but he had to find proof of it. He found it after fifteen days and nights of exhausting work. While examining with a magnifying glass the 700-page Dutch-English dictionary found in Dronkers' luggage, Pinto had discovered there were tiny pinpricks under some of the letters. Put together in order, these letters formed two addresses, one in Lisbon and the other in Stockholm, where Dronkers was to send his reports.

On May 2, 1942, Sorensen and his team of four crossed the threshold of the Patriotic School. This time, the experts in detecting spies were up against experts in spying.

Hans Sorensen was the Abwehr's ace spy. In 1936 he had pulled off a minor "Cicero" exploit by photographing all the secret documents in the safe of the French consulate at Hamburg, where he worked as a doorman. He operated on Sundays, while the consul was at Mass. During a visit of the French ambassador, François-Poncet, Sorensen had succeeded in stealing a list of the Deuxième Bureau's agents in Germany. Soon after the outbreak of war he had sabotaged some British ships in the then neutral ports of Rotterdam and Antwerp, and had later operated successfully in the Balkans. The Abwehr had forgiven him for his only failure: he had not succeeded in blowing up the English plane that flew between Stockholm and Scotland, the one that Vanhove had taken on his way to the gallows.

Pedro was one of the two saboteurs who had crawled close to the Swedish soldiers guarding the plane. He had been born in Brazil but had German nationality. He was young, courageous, and had been working for the Abwehr for a long time. Braun, the second member of Sorensen's team, was particularly useful because he had lived in London before the war. Mewe and Koch were a couple of Hamburg toughs who gave weight and muscle to the team.

Their story was simple: they had deserted from the army. Sorensen had had enough of war; Braun had dug into his unit's funds; Pedro was homesick for Brazil; Mewe and Koch had been in charge of their regiment's canteen and had decided it would be better for them to be elsewhere when their accounts were checked.

The duel between the spies and the spy-hunters began. It lasted eight full months. The British called in some German refugees who had fled from Hitler before the war, and with their help prepared a questionnaire hundreds of pages in length. Sorensen was shown several kinds of German army underwear and asked when they were issued. The interrogating officers knew the answer; so did Sorensen. He said he had been in the 388th Regiment, stationed on an island in Oslo Fjord. He was shown an aerial photograph of the army camp on the island and asked to identify the huts and buildings. He was able to do so. Then he was handed another photograph, taken outside German army headquarters in Oslo. Did he recognize the man coming out of the building? No, he did not.

Hans Sorensen had just won his spurs as a master spy, for it was he himself who had been photographed by a member of the Norwegian Resistance. He remained unshaken by this knowledge that he and his men had been trailed and spied on while they were still preparing for their mission. His courage paid off. The photograph of him was slightly blurred, just enough to make identification uncertain. The security officers were convinced they were dealing with spies, but were unable to establish sufficient proof to bring the men before a court. In December they threw in the towel. But Sorensen, Braun, Mewe and Koch spent the rest of the war in an internment camp, and Pedro was sent to Brazil at the British government's expense. The Abwehr's best team was thus reduced to impotence.

The German organization could not even take credit for a negative success in having, for once, cheated the English hangman, for it was only by chance that Sorensen and his men had been able to give the right answers during their interrogation. The previous winter they had tried to land on the coast of Scotland, but a storm had forced them to turn back. Sorensen had at that time known nothing about German army underwear or the 388th Regiment and its island camp. If it had not been for the storm he would have been hanged. By delaying his mission until six months later, it had enabled him and the others to perfect their cover stories with a stay on the island in Oslo Fjord. Luck alone saved them from the gallows.*

---

* The better preparation of Allied agents sent into German-occupied countries owed much to the information supplied by the Resistance. In addition, between September, 1944, and April, 1945, the American O.S.S. parachuted 84 agents into Germany dressed in German army uniform. By passing themselves off as German soldiers they had more freedom of movement, but their preparation had necessitated the

Furthermore, the whole operation was based on a false assumption. Its organizers had hoped that Sorensen's team would be able to enlist in one of the special units of the British army in which anti-Nazi Germans were serving. But they did not know that these units were open only to refugees who had come to England before 1939. Sorensen and his men would not have been accepted into any of them even if they had walked out of the Patriotic School with their heads high.

Yet suppose they had been—what freedom would they have had to carry out espionage and sabotage? Sorensen had put that very question to his superiors, and they had told him that he could act during his weekend leaves. The Abwehr was creating a new kind of secret agent: the weekend spy.

## 14. Lily Has a Message for the Abwehr

HANS Schmidt could be little else than a weekend spy. The young Dane, whom Vanhove had once waited on at the Hôtel Métropole, was naturally the pride of the Abwehr, which regarded him as the rare bird that had evaded the snares of the counterespionage for four years, as the spy who had carried the policy of integration to the point of marrying an Englishwoman and becoming the father of a British subject.

---

greatest attention to detail. For instance, each agent's military paybook showed the units in which he was supposed to have served since 1939, the places where they had been stationed, and the signatures—perfectly forged—of the units' pay-officers. In spite of the many checks being made by German military police in their search for deserters, only two of the 84 agents were betrayed by their documents. Another had a narrow escape from the firing squad: his paybook was so well prepared that it aroused the suspicions of the German police: they had never seen such a perfect book. However, they finally let him go.

But was not loss of efficiency the price paid for this security? By taking on the protective coloration of the English masses, the spy had become indistinguishable to the eye of the spy-hunters; but in so doing he lost sight of the enemy's movements. How could Hans Schmidt, farmhand, find out what was being hatched in London offices? During the week he worked with his tractor; on Saturdays he pushed his English son in his stroller. It was only on Sundays and holidays that he could get away from the fields and take a worm's-eye view of the big world. Troop concentrations? The famous alternative: southeast means Pas-de-Calais, southwest means Normandy? Yes, but it wasn't so simple. England was crammed with troops. From the south coast all the way to Scotland, it was impossible to walk for an hour without bumping into the barbed-wire fencing of an army camp. In February, 1944, the Engineers had declared that there was not a single site left in the whole of Great Britain which could be turned into an airfield, and a standard joke among airmen stated that it was possible to go from one end of the island to the other in an airplane without ever taking off.

Even if the invasion were planned for Pas-de-Calais, southwestern England would still be packed with troops. And so would the southeast, if Normandy had been chosen. There were so many troops that there was a problem of where to put them. To discover the Allies' intentions, an enemy agent would need to know the whereabouts of the best generals, the best equipped and most experienced divisions, and the specially trained units for the initial assault.

This was within the bounds of possibility, and was certainly not so difficult as obtaining a Bigot pass to enter a Bigot office and take out Bigot documents. But Hans Schmidt could not do it, and the other German spies could not have done it either, even if they had not thrown themselves into the hangman's arms. All they could have done would have been to note the number of tanks, trucks and soldiers going past the windows of their hideouts. The German agents were on a par with the sweeper-up spies of the French Resistance. But there was only a handful of the former, and an army of the others. The tiny fragments of information gathered by each member of the Resistance added up to a complete and detailed picture of the German forces along the Atlantic Wall, whereas the information which the solitary

Hans Schmidt was able to acquire was far too fragmentary to give Berlin even an approximate idea of Allied strength and dispositions.

At least, that was how it should have been. But by some amazing ingenuity which dazzled his Berlin masters, Schmidt had overcome all the disadvantages that, theoretically, went with his job as a farmhand. He was succeeding where an ordinary sweeper-up spy would not even have tried: he was sending full and precise information on Allied troop concentrations. He knew the whereabouts of the best generals, the specialized units and the armored divisions. Perhaps, after all, Hans Schmidt would be able to discover the secret of the invasion plan. . . .

However, Berlin was mainly counting on Lily Sergueiev for this crucial task. She worked in a British ministry. Through her cousin she had entry into London society and met Allied staff officers, some of whom were Bigots. She was pretty, vivacious and resourceful. In April, 1944, after the wholesale elimination of German agents by British counterespionage, all the hopes of the German secret service rested on Lily Sergueiev.

She got out of the car with the other three. It was April 16, a cold, cheerless night. She knew she was in Hampstead, but Marya had not told her the exact address. Marya never said anything unnecessary. She seemed to delight in living up to her cold appearance. She was ungainly and hard-faced, with almond-shaped gray eyes, and wore her hair in an untidy bun. Her name was of course Mary, but Lily preferred the softer-sounding Marya.

The two men walked away from the car, into the total darkness of the blackout, closely followed by the women. Lily had taken Marya's arm; she felt her fur coat under her fingers and wondered whether it was ocelot or real leopard. She had been wanting to ask her for months, but it was not the kind of question one asked Marya. A moment later Russell and Ronnie stopped and pushed open a creaking old gate. The four of them crossed the garden by a gravel path. The beam from Russell's flashlight slid rapidly over the gray front of a large house.

"That's it," said Russell, turning off his flashlight. He was a calm, neat and meticulous young man, with a good-humored round face, round eyes, a snub nose and lots of pimples. An intellectual with a spring rash. Ronnie, on the other hand, was thin and short, with a pale face, a long nose, and blond hair that almost touched his collar. Neither of them was more than thirty.

Russell pushed the button, and they heard the doorbell ringing in the hall. Then there was silence. No one came to the door.

"What's happened?" said Marya.

"I don't know," Russell murmured. "He said he'd be here." They stepped back and looked up at the house.

"Listen!"

They could hear someone snoring in a room on the second floor. Russell dashed back to the door and kept his finger on the bell. When he took it off, the man was still snoring. Ronnie picked up a handful of gravel and threw it up at the window. It clattered against the pane, but did not disturb the sleeper.

"We're wasting time," said Marya. "It'll soon be too late."

"Wait here," Russell told them. "I'll try to find a telephone booth and call him."

He hurried off. Before long, the other three heard the telephone ringing in the house. They went close to the door, but when the ringing stopped the snoring was still continuing.

"We could break in one of the ground-floor windows," suggested Lily.

The other two curtly answered that such things were not done in England. She had clearly shocked them, but she was too tired to care. She shivered as she leaned against the stone wall. She had not been free from pain for several weeks, and she thought she was going blind. The slightest effort was unbearable to her. While the others were anxiously awaiting Russell's return she was thinking that they were not very fair to her, that they might have spared her the agony of such an evening.

Russell arrived, hot and breathless. He hammered on the door. When he was out of breath, Ronnie took over. Marya watched his vain efforts, then said:

"That's enough. There's no point in rousing the whole neighborhood. In any case, our time will soon be up."

They turned away, after a last glance at the house, and had almost reached the gate when something unexpected and funny happened. A window opened and a hoarse voice called down:

"Who's there? What's all that whispering?"

Russell gave a name. The man came down to let them in. Pulled by Ronnie and pushed by Marya, Lily did not even catch a glimpse of him. They hurried up the stairs and into a room on the left. It was small and sparsely furnished. On the table was a radio transmitter.

"Quick!" said Russell.

Lily sat down, put on the headphones, plugged the crystal into the set and began tapping out her call sign: AK—AK— AK . . . Marya sat down beside her, eyes fixed on the stop-watch. They she said: "Now! Go ahead!" Russell held out the text that was to be Lily's first message since her return to London. She tapped away at the key. She had sent half the message when her face twisted with pain and her eyes closed.

"What is it?" Marya asked anxiously. "Are you all right?"

"It's my eyes. I can't see very well."

"Don't worry. Take your time."

The two men were pacing up and down the room. Lily started tapping again, then shut her eyes.

"You don't think you're going to faint, do you?"

"No. I'm sorry."

She tapped the last letter of the message, tore off the head-phones and threw herself on to the bed, sobbing. She was overwrought, and no wonder: it had taken three years of hard work to achieve that radio message, and she had only two months to live, according to the doctors.

Marya, Russell and Ronnie put away the transmitter. The evening had been an ordinary one for them. It was not the first time that they, as members of British intelligence, had been in radio contact with the Abwehr.

Hans Schmidt, for instance, had been sending messages for three years under the supervision of the British officers who had caught him and put him to work for the Allies. The young Dane had taken no part in the British agri-cultural effort. He had never set foot on the farm in the southwest. He led an uneventful life with his wife and son in a small house in a London suburb, his sole occupation being the transmission of messages carefully designed by intelligence officers to mislead Berlin.

Schmidt's survival was entirely due to the fact that a recording of his transmitting style was kept in the Abwehr files. Each radio operator has his own particular rhythm and touch—his "signature." By comparing a spy's transmissions with the recording made before his departure, the Abwehr was assured that he himself was sending the message. It would have been useless for the English to hang Hans Schmidt discreetly and have someone else operate his transmitter. All the spies rounded up in September, 1939, all the hapless pupils of Hans Stultz, could not be sent to the gallows if the Germans were to be duped with false information. The toughest of them had been disposed of, but the more amenable had become double agents. Why, then, was poor Vanhove hanged, since he was quite willing to become a double or even a quadruple agent? Alas, many are called but few are chosen in the doubtful paradise of double agents. Vanhove had no transmitter; he had to send his information to a "letter box" in Portugal—too slow and complicated a method. Yet even radio operators were not always immune. When the British caught Meier, who was so fond of cider, the papers published the news of his capture, with photographs of his transmitting apparatus. This was primarily to sustain the "spy fever" in Britain, which added to the difficulties of German agents. It was also intended to boost the value of double agents whose duplicity was still unknown to the Germans. It succeeded beyond all expectation. Berlin had been depressed by the great proportion of spies captured, and therefore tended to regard as supermen those they thought to have evaded the counterespionage measures. There was no surprise at the amount and variety of information supplied by the farm laborer Hans Schmidt. He would almost have had to announce that he had been received at Buckingham Palace before any uneasiness would have been felt.

However, this paradise sometimes turned out to be only an uncertain purgatory. The British made one double agent send messages saying that he had obtained some sensational documents but had no means of getting them to Germany. The Germans sent a submarine. Two British destroyers lay in wait for it and sank it. The double agent, now unmasked, was sent to hell.

This would not happen to Lily Sergueiev. In 1943, when crossing Spain on her way to England, she had secretly called at the British consulate in Madrid. She had explained to the intelligence officer there that she had been wanting to get to London since 1940, to help the Allied cause, but had not wished to arrive empty-handed. Now she could put the Abwehr's confidence in her at the service of British intelligence.*

It was a handsome present, and would have been even better if she had had a transmitter, which was essential for feeding false information to the Germans with speed and efficiency. Hence her journey to Lisbon in March, after she had written to Kliemann telling him that she must have a transmitter.

It was with some trepidation that she had gone to the rendezvous in the Plaza Pombal. The Germans might have set a trap, might have guessed what she was doing and decided to eliminate her. She had been terrified by the way she was dragged into the car. For a few seconds, before recognizing the good captain of the *Adel Traber,* she felt sure she was being taken to her death. She had no idea that she was the pride of her German employers, that they were astounded to see her traveling between England and the Continent, and regarded her as their main hope of winning the secret war. Kliemann had been only too pleased to deliver a transmitter to such an exceptional agent. As for the reserved British intelligence officers, they had drawn considerable satisfaction from the thought that the Germans themselves had provided the instrument for their own duping. Lily had been able to savor the soft Portuguese spring, so it could be said that the rendezvous in Lisbon had given complete satisfaction to everyone concerned.

Berg and Klausen, on the other hand, were still a headache for the German secret service. It was known in Berlin that the parachutist sent to spy on them had broken his leg on landing and had been captured. The information had been sent by the two Norwegians themselves. They were furious, and had threatened to throw up everything if another agent were sent to their area. Berlin, although puzzled and embarrassed, had to admit that they were right. If the parachutist had talked, the two Norwegians would have been in great danger.

---

* From the very beginning Lily had kept a diary. In view of the work she was doing, this was most imprudent and endangered her life. However, no harm came from it; the diary has survived, and makes that rarest of all documents: the memoirs of a double agent.

However, their detractors were now more vehement than ever. In the first place, how did Berg and Klausen find out that the parachutist had been caught? British newspapers reached Berlin through neutral countries; there had been no mention in them of the capture of a spy in Scotland. Not a word. So the Norwegians must have been told by British intelligence, which proved their treachery.

It was possible, but not certain. Why should the British make their double agents send a message of protest? There was no reason for it. If they had wanted to take advantage of the capture, it would have been cleverer to make the parachutist into a double agent and have him send a message assuring Berlin that Berg and Klausen were loyal. As for the way in which those two had learned of his capture, it was probably quite simple. The man had dropped not far from where they were. His arrest must have caused quite a stir among the local population, and it was not surprising that they had heard about it.

So were they single or double agents? Nobody knew.

Twenty years later, it is still a mystery. If Berg and Klausen really did escape detection for four whole years, they did not boast about it after the war. And if they were caught and made into double agents, the British kept the secret well. But statistics are against the Norwegians. Other spies hardly set foot in England before they were caught and either put to work for the Allies or hanged. It is hard to believe that these two could have survived for four years. But there is one detail which supports the possibility, although it would also have limited their spying activities. During the whole of 1944 they were wandering around Scotland; they could hardly have expected to find out much about the invasion plans up there, but it was safer for them and they refused to go to southern England. That has a ring of truth. Furthermore, it seems natural to assume that if they had been caught and "doubled," they would have been made to tell Berlin that they were leaving Scotland for the south coast of England. If they had been used to mislead the Germans, it would seem that they would have had to be in a region where the Germans believed they could best obtain information on the forthcoming invasion.

And the British would have done it if they had been able. In April, 1944, they began their biggest attempts at duping the enemy. Lily Sergueiev and Hans Schmidt took

the leading roles, but the whole wretched band of spies who had been "doubled" since 1940 also played a part. Even fictitious spies were used—spies who existed only in the Berlin files. There was, for instance, a highly placed British civil servant who sent copious messages full of false information to "Aloysius," a Hungarian military attaché in a neutral country and a German agent.

The whole operation was based upon the well-proven maxim that a good offense is the best defense. The work of the Bigots was defensive, for it consisted in guarding the secrets of OVERLORD. But complete success could hardly be expected; so instead of passively noting any German triumphs, a counteroffensive was undertaken. The object was to flood the enemy with false information, to deceive him about the date of the invasion, and especially to convince him that it would take place not in Normandy but in Pas-de-Calais.

This operation was called FORTITUDE, an apt name. The Allied commanders were haunted by the possibility of a sudden concentration of German divisions in Normandy, and it was a comforting thought that FORTITUDE was endeavoring to keep the best German units two hundred miles away from the landing beaches.

Leonard Cheshire could almost drop a bomb in your pocket. At twenty-five, he was the youngest colonel in the R. A. F. His group of bombers, the 617th Squadron, was reserved for special missions. On May 16, 1943, it had performed the terrible feat of bombing the Ruhr dams, freeing 330 million tons of water which swept down in a huge tidal wave over towns and villages, flooded coal mines within a radius of fifty miles, submerged airports, destroyed 125 factories, carried away 25 bridges and drowned 1300 people. To set off this catastrophe, the British pilots had to make their run in at a height of only sixty feet and keep straight at the target, thus presenting an easy mark for the antiaircraft guns. A deviation of only a few feet would have made the special bombs lose much of their effect. Eleven of the nineteen bombers failed to return, but the drop in German production due to the lack of electric power was the equivalent of six months' work by a hundred thousand men.

The next mission of the 617th had been to perfect the

dropping of incendiary bombs on a target to guide the following night bombers. It meant hurtling down to 500 feet in a heavy four-engined bomber before pulling out of the dive. The pilot never knew whether he would be able to pull out or not. Each dive was a gamble. But even if it was lost the sacrifice paid off because the blaze made by the bombs marked the target far better than flares.

In the spring of 1944 the Allied air forces began hammering away at France. Eisenhower wanted to seal off the northwest by destroying bridges and railroads, to prevent the Germans from bringing up reinforcements after D-Day. Harris and Spaatz, the British and American bomber commanders, had opposed the project. First of all, they felt they could win the war by simply crushing Germany under a rain of bombs. France was a waste of time. And they were skeptical about the effectiveness of attacks on lines of communication: bridges, viaducts and railways were narrow, difficult targets. But Eisenhower overruled their objections; he knew how essential it was for Normandy to be sealed off from the rest of France.

It should have been just the job for the 617th Squadron: Leonard Cheshire's sharpshooters were the best at precision bombing by day and "marking" by night.

But on April 29, at the outset of the air offensive over France, Cheshire was summoned to group headquarters and told that his squadron would not be operational during the next few weeks. It was being put back in training. He was mystified—the 617th in training! He was informed that his squadron was to prepare for a special mission in connection with the Normandy invasion. On D-Day the crack 617th Squadron would have the most important of all the tasks assigned to the air forces. And it would not have to drop a single bomb!

## 15. A Shrewd Crew

POOR Walther Schellenberg. When he was a student at Bonn University he had enjoyed immersing himself in the Italian Renaissance. The period had fascinated him, with its brutal vitality and intrigues, and its colorful personalities. Ten years later, the pasty-faced, skinny student had become head of the combined secret service of the Third Reich, yet it seemed to him that he had left the Italian Renaissance only to plunge into a ludicrous world which had all the former's inconveniencies but none of its beauty, and he was fed up with bizarre personalities.

There was the visit he had made to *Reichsmarschall* Goering, for instance. Schellenberg had gone to ask that the research institute which bore Goering's name should come under the control of the intelligence services instead of the Luftwaffe. This seemed a logical transfer, because the Hermann Goering Research Institute was in fact the most modern "listening post" in the world. It could record any telephone conversation that took place in German-occupied Europe, and could pick up radio transmissions at a considerable distance. The Luftwaffe did not know what to do with this very useful intelligence instrument, and the conscientious Schellenberg wanted to remedy the situation.

He was kept waiting for a good half-hour at Karinhall, Goering's sumptuous summer residence, and was admiring the antique furniture and splendid carpets in the entrance hall when a door slid open and a fat man disguised as a Roman patrician came in. It was Goering. Schellenberg gaped at the toga and sandals and the incongruous marshal's baton that Goering was carrying, then followed him into one of the rooms. Perched on a kind of throne, Schellenberg did his best to explain the object of his visit, while Goering kept dipping his hands into a bowl filled with diamonds and pearls, watching with an enraptured eye as they trickled between his fingers. The interview soon came to an end, and the research institute remained under Luftwaffe control.

Ernst Kaltenbrunner was another uncommon individual. He had succeeded Heydrich at the head of the police and espionage services, and was Schellenberg's immediate superior. He was a giant of a man, over six feet tall, with shoulders like the deck of an aircraft carrier, a bull neck and turned-up chin, tiny eyes with a venomous stare and a face marked by livid scars. This exterior concealed a remarkable vacuity.

At eleven every morning Schellenberg took his courage in both hands and went to make his report. He found Kaltenbrunner barely awake, for the giant rarely got up before half-past ten. No sooner had Schellenberg entered his office than Kaltenbrunner reached eagerly into a drawer of his desk for a bottle of brandy and two glasses. Schellenberg had no liking for alcohol at eleven in the morning, but he could not refuse a drink with his chief. This was a crucial moment of the day for the head of the intelligence services of the Third Reich: he was going to try to empty his glass on the carpet without Kaltenbrunner noticing. He broke out in a cold sweat, but he managed it. Then followed his report on matters in hand. Kaltenbrunner listened with the distant look of a drunkard while trying to focus on Schellenberg, and his set features expressed nothing but the placidity of a self-satisfied imbecile. When a question was put to him, a long silence followed, then he smashed his fist down on the desk. Kaltenbrunner's hands were in proportion to his build—"real assassin's paws," Canaris used to call them. A layer of nicotine coated Kaltenbrunner's fingers, residue of the hundred or so cigarettes he smoked every day. Having brought down his fist, he started to speak. Schellenberg was all ears, for his superior's speech was hindered by rotting teeth which, besides making him difficult to understand, gave him a powerfully foul-smelling breath. Made even worse by musty smells of tobacco and alcohol, it darkened the lives of all his associates. But everyone had given up hope of persuading him to go to a dentist. Even Himmler had not succeeded, despite stern ultimatums. It would have taken an order from Hitler. Kaltenbrunner had never been known to disobey an order from his living god.

Schellenberg did not necessarily have to take orders from Kaltenbrunner. He could bypass the drunken sot and go to Himmler, who called Schellenberg his favorite and allowed him direct access. And *Reichsführer* Himmler, Minister of the Interior and head of the S.S., was the most powerful man in Germany after Hitler.

Gentle with animals and good Aryans, Himmler had his head full of romantic ideas while wading in the blood-bath prepared in accordance with his orders. He believed he was the reincarnation of King Heinrich I, who had ruled over the Germanic peoples in the eleventh century, and whom he made the S.S. worship. His crude but imaginative brain seethed with unusual plans. Thus he had a plan all ready for Russia, after the final victory. The lords of the S.S. would live there in military communities based on the ancient Teutonic order of chivalry. Modern technology, which was vulgar and softening, would be banned from these communities. Airplanes, cars and trains would be replaced by a breed of horses specially adapted to the climate: the "steppes horse." A renowned biologist, Professor Schaeffer, had been given the task of breeding the ideal "steppes horse." He had been supplied with thoroughbreds from all over the world. In 1944, when the Red Army was far from being forced back to the Urals, Heinrich Himmler still made regular visits to the Professor's stud farm in the Austrian Alps.

These harmless crazes were less of an obstruction to Schellenberg than Himmler's fanatical faith in magicians, spiritualists, fortune-tellers, astrologers and conjurers of all kinds. These professionals had had their ups and downs. Held responsible for their client Rudolf Hess's trip to Britain, they had been thrown into a concentration camp in 1941. Himmler got them out in 1943, so that they could determine where Mussolini was being held prisoner by the Badoglio Government.

The forty best charlatans in Germany, astounded by this change in fortune which their occult powers had not foreseen, found themselves installed in a luxurious villa normally reserved for important foreign visitors. Still clad in rags, they were served a wonderful meal accompanied by the best wines available in Europe. The first to succeed in discovering where Mussolini was being held would be given his freedom and a reward of a hundred thousand marks. By a common accord they decided to proceed with wise slowness.

Schellenberg's agents had in the meantime picked up Mussolini's tracks, helped by the fact that they were able to pay a fortune for the slightest bit of information (the British banknotes they handed out so generously were counterfeit.) It was relatively easy to discover that Mussolini was being held prisoner on the small island of Maddalena; the real difficulty lay in accouncing it to Himmler. Since he had confidence only in his magicians, a séance had to be carefully prepared. Himmler finally received the revelation from the mouth of a bald, pot-bellied old soothsayer who had gone into an impressive trance.*

This incident was by no means exceptional. More than once Schellenberg had to produce some frightened astrologer in order to overcome Himmler's reluctance to make a decision. These additional complications were a loss of time and energy, and brought on general gloom. As for the secret of D-Day, Schellenberg would not have been surprised if Himmler had ordered him to assemble a council of magicians to discover it.

Kaltenbrunner would have been more inclined to send a detachment of S.S. spies to Britain under the command of an officer. Believing that the main strength of spies lay in discipline, Kaltenbrunner greatly preferred missions of the PASTORIUS kind.

PASTORIUS had been organized in 1942, when Hitler, obsessed by sabotage, had demanded large-scale action against American industry. Canaris, whose network of agents in the United States had just been broken up by the F.B.I., protested that he did not have the necessary men available there and that any attempt to introduce agents into the States was bound to fail. When the admiral's enemies heard of this disagreement they saw it as a chance to show that he and his Abwehr were corroded by defeatism. They produced eight magnificent fellows of iron fanaticism, all volunteers for the United States.

The Abwehr leaders, feeling sorry for them, trained them as best they could, then sent them, by way of Paris, to the

---

* Otto Skorzeny's raid on the island came too late; Mussolini had already been moved to a mountaintop. Schellenberg's men discovered his new prison on the Gran Sasso.

submarine base at Lorient. The stay of the PASTORIUS group in Paris was marked by several embarrassing incidents. On their first night the eight volunteers brought some women back with them to their requisitioned hotel, quarreled with them and, carried away with enthusiasm for their mission, began shouting in English. The German officers in the hotel thought an attack was being made by British parachutists and came rushing in, brandishing their pistols. The PASTORIUS mission almost came to a premature end, but the men managed to explain in time.

The next day they had a fight in a bar. Since they had openly announced that they were on their way to America, it is safe to assume that, between the hotel and the bar, a large number of people had at least a general idea of the PASTORIUS operations by the time the volunteers left Paris. Only seven of them reached Lorient: the eighth had picked up a venereal disease.

They were a little disconcerted at Lorient when they found that most of the dollar bills given to them were overprinted in Japanese; this was particularly unfortunate because the attack on Pearl Harbor had occurred some months previously. Some of the other bills were no longer legal tender in the United States. The bad dollars were taken from the men and, after being promised that better ones would be sent to them, they were packed into a submarine. They were all arrested within a few days after setting foot on American soil. Two of them, less fanatical than had been thought, gave themselves up and denounced their companions. No one is perfect. Another had gone into a drugstore to buy a razor and succumbed to a conditioned reflex: he clicked his heels, gave the Nazi salute and cried *"Heil Hitler!"* to the astonished salesclerks.

Kaltenbrunner never heard this story, but it would probably have touched his heart. He would undoubtedly have preferred that fanatical agent to the Jewish spy whom Schellenberg was striving desperately to save from the gas chamber. The man was mysterious; he refused to reveal his sources of information, but he was believed to have a well-organized intelligence network in Russia and to be in contact with some Russian staff officers. He was able in any case to give the Germans several weeks' warning of the Red Army's strategical plans, and in important cases he divulged their

tactical intentions down to divisional level. Kaltenbrunner
cared nothing about the fact that the German high command
said the man was indispensable: he was a Jew, and Schellenberg, who had inherited him from the Abwehr, had to "fight
like a lion"—to use Schellenberg's own phrase—to keep him
out of the gas chamber.

Schellenberg's position was already difficult and disagree-
able, with the mad Himmler on one side of him and the
idiotic Kaltenbrunner on the other. But it was made un-
tenable by the ghost of an honest man: Admiral Canaris.

Perhaps he had been too honest. Colonel Giskes, head of
German counterespionage in Holland, Belgium and northern
France, was devoted to Canaris. But he had a vivid recol-
lection of a conference with the Abwehr officers serving in
the west which the admiral had held in Paris in 1942. The
outcome of the secret war was still uncertain—it was not
until two years later, in March, 1944, that Giskes wrote that
his counterespionage services had lost the fight against the
Resistance. During this conference an officer had pointed
out that it was impossible to keep enemy agents from learning all about the Atlantic Wall. The labor force could not be
relied upon. There were, for example, thousands of Spanish
Republicans working for the Todt organization, men who
had become refugees in France after Franco's victory. Giskes
knew there was truth in what this officer said. He himself,
in 1940, had found a complete copy of the plans of the port
of Saint-Nazaire in the possession of a Frenchman who had
been arrested. When Giskes had ordered the Abwehr representative at Saint-Nazaire to report to him, the agent simply
replied that he had no more than half a dozen men, who
could speak only German, to keep watch on twenty thousand
foreign workers, many of them Spanish, Scandinavians or
Poles.

Giskes had wondered what solution his colleague at the
Paris conference would offer for this problem of the Spanish
Republicans, who were all convinced anti-Fascists. "The concentration camp," the officer had said. Canaris had leaned
forward and murmured, "I didn't quite hear you. What did
you say?" The officer repeated, "Concentration camp."
Canaris, with a stony stare, asked him to say it again. The
officer grew red in the face and did not utter another word.
The other officers present felt prouder than ever to serve

under a man like the admiral and the Spanish Republicans were able to continue sabotaging the Wall and giving information about it to Allied agents.

It was true, however, that harshness and terror were effective: the whip that the Gestapo held over the German people helped to keep them going in their world struggle. But beyond a certain point the drawbacks of cruelty became almost as great as its advantages, for it aroused horror in the strong, panic in the weak, and made them both act in undesirable ways. There was, for instance, the disappearance of the map from the Todt office in Caen. The officers in charge knew quite well that by not reporting the matter they were failing in their duty and that it might have disastrous consequences. Because of them, fortifications would be built whose every detail was known to the enemy. To avert this catastrophe, they had only to report the theft. They said nothing. Were they traitors? No—just faint-hearted. There was no reason to doubt their patriotism. They would probably have accepted severe disciplinary measures or even being transferred to the Russian front. But what would the Gestapo do to them? This fear was so great that they preferred to betray their duty rather than risk falling into the clutches of the Gestapo.

Shortly before D-Day a young British officer was reported to Allied counterintelligence by his parents: he had told them the date of the invasion. They felt that their talkative son was a danger to the country. They knew he would be demoted to the rank of private, but that nothing worse would happen to him. If those parents had been German, they would have known that denouncing their son to the Gestapo meant sending him to his death. Would they have done it?

Stout-hearted Canaris had been deterred not by fear but by horror. He knew better than anyone else how dangerous the Spanish workmen were. But if he reported it, the measures taken against them would be atrocious, for the German repressive machine had gone mad and dealt out nothing but torture, executions and deportations. Canaris preferred to keep quiet rather than supply it with another batch of victims. Even in his personal actions he instinctively refrained from procedures which might align him with the Nazi brutes. To keep his distance from the "Blacks" he tried to be whiter than he really was, while the head of an intelligence service must necessarily resign himself to being more or less gray.

This almost excessive morality may have reduced the Abwehr's efficiency, but what difference does a flat tire make when the engine is failing? The poor state of German intelligence was caused less by Canaris's scruples than by his profound disagreement with Hitler's policies. How could the sixteen thousand Abwehr agents have been given any decisive driving force by their leaders when Canaris and his assistants were opposed to the Nazi adventure and had finally come to dread the thought of a German victory that would place Europe under Hitler's yoke? The Abwehr machine continued to function, of course, but at a sluggish pace. Its planning did not bear the mark of the deep belief in its own cause which animated Allied intelligence. Its activities and missions in enemy countries were badly conceived, as was proved by the fate of Abwehr agents in Britain.

Yet how could it be otherwise, when Canaris and his associates had, by their own admission, devoted more care and energy to their struggle with the "Blacks" than to the war against the Allies? Internal strife among competing secret services within a country has always been a highly respected tradition. A defeat inflicted on a rival service is more enjoyable than a victory over the enemy. The many Anglo-American services—O.S.S., G2, S.O.E., M.I.6, and others—did not escape the rule. They had vigilant hatred for one another. But the struggle between the Abwehr and the "Blacks" had one important peculiarity: it ended on the scaffold. Such warfare necessarily occupies a man's attention, and eventually it wears him down.

But that was all in the past, and Walther Schellenberg wanted nothing to do with it. He knew that when he took possession of Maibach Two he would have to do a major job of housecleaning. Maibach Two was a concrete fortress at Zossen, south of Berlin, where Abwehr headquarters had been installed in 1943. It was a counterpart of Maibach One, which sheltered the German supreme command. It was a six-story building, three above ground and three below, all exactly alike. In the event of air raids the staff moved down below and work continued; even the telephones were transferable and could be reconnected in the underground offices.

Schellenberg had thought that once Canaris had been got rid of, it would be easy enough to take over Maibach Two, its staff and the thousands of agents attached to it by the invisible threads of a great web. He had not foreseen that the dismissed admiral would exercise an even greater influence over Maibach Two than when he had been head of the Abwehr. As the chief Abwehr officer in Istanbul, Paul Leverkuehn, wrote: "He *was* the Abwehr. As soon as he was dismissed, the Abwehr began to disintegrate." And Richard Protze, who was in charge of the Abwehr's Amsterdam office, said: "When the admiral had gone, I stopped sending reports to Berlin. Without him, we had no confidence in the Service." Hundreds of officers resigned from the Abwehr and volunteered for the Russian front. In the west, to avoid being absorbed by the S.S. intelligence service, the Abwehr men formed themselves into mobile units directly under the orders of the Wehrmacht, on the pretext that the danger of an invasion called for close liaison between intelligence agents and the army.

Colonel Giskes, from his headquarters on the Hôtel Métropole in Brussels (obviously a popular place with German intelligence), directed one of these units—No. 307—and took orders only from the Wehrmacht. Like many of his colleagues, he was ready to ask for a transfer rather than serve under the Himmler-Kaltenbrunner-Schellenberg trio. Like all Abwehr officers, he had been greatly influenced by the character of Canaris, who was to them a leader, an example and a symbol. The admiral may have sometimes exasperated them by his excessive scruples, but they were grateful to him for having been able to keep their hands clean amid the tide of blood and mud which was sweeping through Germany. Thanks to him, the Abwehr had not been compromised. After him, there was no possibility of working with the "Blacks."

The S.S. countered this instinctive antipathy with their own mistrust. They had no intention of using the men of the Brandenburg Division. The Abwehr had created this special unit in 1939, and it had grown in size as its successes increased. It had begun as a company, then reached the strength of a regiment, and by 1942 was organized as a division. It specialized in activities behind the enemy lines, and had been particularly successful in Holland, Rumania and Russia.

One of the regiments was made up of Germans who spoke English and was intended for use against Britain. From Pas-de-Calais and the Channel Islands, they could make raids on the southern coast of England and bring back information and prisoners who might be persuaded to talk. However, the S.S. did not trust the Brandenburg men. Soon after the unit had been created, Heydrich had firmly opposed the idea of turning it into a parachute unit—it might be dropped on the Führer's headquarters. Heydrich was not wrong: in many of the plots fomented by Canaris and his assistants, the Brandenburg Division was intended to be the spearhead. Confidence in it diminished as suspicion of the Abwehr increased. It was finally sent to the Russian front. So great was the fear of its being used against the Nazis that it was wasted in the fighting against the Russians, when it might have thrown the English into turmoil.

By April, 1944, *Brigadenführer* Walther Schellenberg knew that his victory over Canaris was an empty one. He had replaced the admiral at the helm of the Abwehr, but many of the crew had deserted the old ship and the remainder were reluctant to sail it. At a time when the secret war had reached its height the Abwehr was like a phantom vessel, completely unfit for battle.

# 16. A Fiasco and a Hope

THERE was still the S.S. intelligence service. Poor thing. It was still a bumbling child and it was expected to take on crafty giants like the British Intelligence Service and the Russian N.K.V.D. This was absurd, and Schellenberg knew it. In 1938, when he was only twenty-eight, he had written: "An intelligence network has to be built up gradually. In alien soil it must be fed like a plant and be given plenty of time to take root. Only then will it have a healthy growth and bear fruit in abundance . . . Useful contacts should be maintained for years if necessary, and only be exploited when the time is ripe . . . In intelligence work, one must never be in a hurry." A year later, the outbreak of war made him discard these wise principles and plunge into hasty action.

But even if Schellenberg had had the time to build up his organization, its success would have been by no means certain. The Himmlers and the Kaltenbrunners had, like bad fairies, given the newborn service poisoned gifts such as fanaticism, a rigid outlook, and the primacy of courage over intelligence. These are traditional German characteristics. They make excellent soldiers and bad spies. Knowing his compatriots, the shrewd Canaris preferred to use foreign agents whenever he could. But the S.S. leaders were unaware that the qualities necessary for a secret agent are not the same as those of a soldier in the front line; they thought that a spy went into action as a soldier did. Even their courage lacked imagination. They were incapable of the sublime madness of a Churchill. When France capitulated on June 22, 1940, Hitler had proclaimed: "The English have been driven from the Continent forever." That very evening Churchill had sent a commando force of a hundred and twenty men across the Channel; they went ashore near Boulogne and killed a few Germans. Several days later, in the depths of disaster, when no one would have bet much on the old lion's chances of survival, he set up Combined Operations and ordered it to make raids on the coast for the purpose of harassing the enemy and gathering information.

Four years later the situation was reversed, but the "Blacks" continued to sit on their backsides. They never considered making commando raids on the English coast, although the trained men and the vessels were available. Apart from the Brandenburg Division, there were the special units of Skorzeny, who was becoming unbearable with his continual bragging of his kidnapping of Mussolini, the *Kampftruppen,* or shock troops, and the *Kostenjäger Kompanie,* or "coastal hunters," who had been trained by Rommel's Afrika Korps in commando operations behind the enemy lines. To carry the men across the Channel there were submarines and torpedo boats such as those which attacked the convoy making for Slapton Sands.

Much was possible, but nothing was done; imagination and initiative were lacking. The "Blacks," trapped by their own propaganda, had the "fortress complex." They were prepared to fight to the last to defend "Fortress Europe," as ordered, but they never thought of leaving it in order to surprise the enemy at his preparations. Confined within their own narrow little world, the S.S. leaders were unfit for the subtle intelligence game. It was much more complicated than organizing a commando raid.* Himmler and Kaltenbrunner, with their bloodstained hands and vile deeds, were no match for the British Intelligence Service. Their naïveté was their undoing. They lacked the pragmatism, the "perverse" turn of mind and the macabre sense of humor of the gentlemen graduated from Oxford and Cambridge. Those German giants of crime were pygmies in espionage. Even so, they hardly deserved the "Cicero" fiasco.

Elyesa Bazna was the most opportune of agents. At a time when the German espionage services were doing everything they could to get their agents into Britain, Cicero fell from heaven with his bundles of documents from the British ambassador's safe. He was obviously better placed than any German agent to discover the Allies' secrets. He was a godsend. The S.S. intelligence service had undoubtedly realized all that, because the mistakes it made were not marked by its usual startling imbecility. Clearly, it was trying hard to show competence. It did, however, take the foolish risk of paying the spy in counterfeit pound notes, thus chancing an abortive end to the business if one imperfect note was refused by a bank. Nothing was done about sending experts to help the secret service man in Ankara, Ludwig Moyzisch, to "handle" Cicero; all Moyzisch received was a large crate filled with spy novels and treatises on espionage, so that he could improve himself. These were venial errors. Kaltenbrunner remembered to take the essential step: Moyzisch received strict orders not to show the microfilms of documents he obtained from Cicero to the German Ambassador to Turkey, Franz von Papen. He was to send them straight to

---

* Hitler himself, when he heard of the early end to the PASTORIUS mission, exclaimed to Canaris: "Poor boys! And all loyal members of the Party! That must never happen again. In the future, you will use Jews or criminals for missions of that kind." Canaris seized the opportunity to get a number of Jews out of Germany. "Special orders from the Führer" was his reply to the Gestapo's indignant protests.

Berlin. This was a simple security measure to protect Cicero, such as any other secret service would have imposed.

But the unbelievable happened: Moyzisch disobeyed. For reasons which he never explained, he continued to show von Papen copies of secret documents received from Cicero. The German ambassador was thus able to read the record of talks between the British ambassador and the Turkish government. At the time, Turkey was preparing to abandon her neutrality in favor of the Allies. She had already agreed to the "clandestine" use of her territory by Allied forces. The Cicero documents even specified figures.

Pompous little von Papen, armed with this information, asked for an audience with the Turkish Foreign Minister and threatened him with massive reprisals. No sooner had von Papen left than the minister informed Knatchbull-Hugessen of the disaster. That evening a cable reached London: "Von Papen obviously knows more than he should." A few days later some members of British counterintelligence arrived in Ankara; a new alarm system was fitted to the ambassador's safe, and security measures at the embassy were thoroughly checked and tightened. Cicero was no longer able to get at important documents. From then on, all that Moyzisch received from him were papers of no great value, such as the invoices of office furniture bought by the embassy . . .

Von Papen had sacrificed the most effective spy in the Germans' pay for a diplomatic move which did not prevent Turkey from supporting the Allied cause. But the blunder would not have occurred if Moyzisch had obeyed orders. Considering that one of the gravest defects of the S.S. intelligence service was an excessive emphasis on discipline, it would seem rather unjust that the disobedience of one man should have had such dire consequences for the whole service. At the very least, it was a stroke of bad luck.

Schellenberg still had some hopes of discovering the secret of OVERLORD. Not all his cards had been wasted. He still had a few trumps that might enable him to win the game. He was counting on agents introduced into Britain by the Abwehr or his own organization, not knowing they had been captured and hanged or "doubled." All of them? It was not certain; a last-minute miracle was still possible.

Even if he had no more ears in Britain, he had many along the Dutch, Belgian and French coast—at the radio-interception stations. These were powerful enough to pick up radio communications between the various headquarters in England and even radio messages exchanged by troops and tanks on an exercise. The Dutch station had once succeeded in picking up conversations on the London–New York radiotelephone link, by listening in on the same wavelength as the Allies' "scramble" system. Schellenberg had thus received a recording of several talks between Roosevelt and Churchill. One of them had caused a sensation among the Nazi leaders, confirming their belief that war was much too serious a business to be left to democracies. Roosevelt, having given an opinion on several matters of high strategy, had ended with the words: "Well, we'll do our best . . . And now I'm going fishing!" Nothing had been picked up concerning OVERLORD. But that might still happen.

If it came to the worst, there was still the Luftwaffe. Its reconnaissance planes could report on the concentrations of invasion craft, when D-Day became imminent, and the location of the bulk of these craft would show whether the assault was aimed at Pas-de-Calais or Normandy. But that would be almost too late. Something better was still possible. German counterintelligence might succeed where its espionage services had apparently failed. Some success had already been obtained among the Resistance groups: in addition to capturing a high proportion of members, a good many German informers and double agents had successfully penetrated underground organizations, sometimes to the point of obtaining control. The real object was to get in contact with London via Resistance channels.

Colonel Giskes, back in 1942, had realized the importance of this method; he had few illusions about the chances of German spies in Britain. "The discovery of the date and place of the invasion had become the chief objective of the German secret services operating in the west," he wrote later. "All else was subordinate to that. . . . The heart and brain of the Allied forces were in London. To send our own agents to the island to try to penetrate to the center of the enemy services carried so many risks and uncertainties, and meant such a loss of time, that the possibility was practically ruled out." However, when Giskes was in Amsterdam and in charge of counterespionage in Holland, he made a worthy effort to make up for the deficiencies of German spies by mounting Operation NORTH POLE.

On March 6, 1942, he had "doubled" a Dutch radio operator who had been captured after being parachuted into Holland by the Allies; through him, Giskes was in contact with London. The British replied to the Dutchman's messages and gave details of other agents and radio operators to be dropped into Holland. Giskes had them all captured on landing, "doubled" the radio operators and duped the British with false messages more than ever. After a few months of this game—an exciting one for Giskes—he had fifty-three parachuted agents in prison and eighteen transmitters in regular contact with the enemy. The British were jubilant—Operation HOLLAND was showing every sign of success. An underground army recruited and trained by the parachuted agents was waiting to rise on a signal to be given when the invasion was launched. In the meantime, arms and supplies were being dropped to it. Giskes thus received 30,000 pounds of explosives, 3000 submachine guns, 5000 pistols, 300 automatic rifles, 2000 grenades, 75 transmitters and half a million clips of ammunition, as well as a large amount of money. However, the end came before he received what he wanted more than anything: the answer to the question "When and where?" On November 23, 1943, twenty months after the capture of the first radio operator, three of the imprisoned agents managed to escape, and succeeded in informing London of the disaster. Operation NORTH POLE was over.

It was repeated elsewhere, on a minor scale and in slightly different forms. Partly due to information received during NORTH POLE, the Germans were able to break up the sabotage groups organized by British agents in northwestern France. There were ten "doubled" radio operators in touch with London. The British apparently suspected nothing; at the end of April they sent over a Canadian radio operator, Lieutenant Leonard, who dropped right into a German reception committee.

In fact the number of Resistance groups penetrated or watched by the Germans was continually increasing. Unable to wipe out the Resistance movement, the German counterespionage services had at least succeeded in contaminating it. There was the *Carte* network, organized by the British to carry out sabotage and guerilla warfare; the leader of its group in Normandy, Michel, was a double agent in the pay of the Gestapo. The *Mithridate* group, which was under Gaullist control, had been penetrated by the Germans; they had succeeded in introducing into it a Russian spy whom they had captured and "doubled," a Lieutenant Sukulov. None of the members of *Mithridate* suspected him. But he had set up three radio operators, at Dreux, Poitiers and Le Mans, who were in contact with London.

In order to launch the Resistance into guerilla warfare and sabotage when the invasion began, the Allies had prepared a series of code messages that would be broadcast by the B.B.C. at the right time. Certain phrases would mean that invasion was coming within the next two weeks. There were the "A" messages. They would be followed by the "B" messages, which would indicate that the time for action was imminent. And within forty-eight hours after the "B" messages, London would broadcast the personal messages that would send previously selected groups into battle.

Schellenberg knew more than two dozen of these phrases, through his double agents in the Resistance. They sounded innocent—"The flowers are turning very red"; "The long sobs of the violins of autumn"; "Thérèse is still sleepy"— but they would announce the imminent launching of the military operation on which the outcome of the war depended. And since the messages were different for each Resistance group, Schellenberg thought it would be possible to discover which part of the coast the enemy intended to land on, for he knew the territory covered by each group, and could note those which had messages sent to them. If, for instance, Michel heard the message arranged for the *Carte* group in Normandy it would indicate that the invasion was going to be on the Normandy beaches.

Besides the cards he already held, Schellenberg still had the hope of receiving an unexpected trump such as luck sometimes deals: a miraculous spy like Cicero, a prophetic item of information dropping like manna from heaven; a wink from fate.

# MAY

## 17. The Great Panic

"ROMMEL's asparagus" had been a false alarm. In mid-April Allied reconnaissance planes had photographed the stakes which the Germans were erecting in meadows. There were trip wires running between them, said messages from the Resistance, which when touched would set off mines or shells. Parachutists would be blown to pieces and gliders would be ripped open by the stakes, as well as being damaged by exploding mines. And the stakes had first appeared in meadows by the river Orne, just where the parachutists and gliders of the British 6th Airborne Division were going to land . . .

The anxiety was soon dispelled, for more "asparagus" sprang up all along the coast from Normandy to Pas-de-Calais. This dispersion proved that the Germans had neither guessed nor discovered the secret of the landing. The Allied commanders breathed more freely again.

But not for long. There was more anxiety in the first week of May, when reconnaissance aircraft reported intense troop movements by rail in the region between the Loire and the Seine. Then reports came in from the Resistance, which gave the worst pessimists a bitter feeling of triumph. The secret of OVERLORD had leaked out. The Germans knew everything. Their best armored division, the Panzer Lehr, had been moved back from Hungary to France, and instead of returning to its old quarters in Verdun it had been sent to the area between Chartres and Le Mans—from where it could reach Caen in twenty-four hours. Moreover, the 21st Armored Division had moved from Rennes to Caen—from where its tanks could reach the British landing beaches in half an hour.

Allied anticipations were completely upset. It had been expected that on D-Day the enemy would have only one armored division available to throw into the battle: the 12th S.S., centered on Lisieux. But now there were three, and they were the best equipped and trained of all the armored divisions in the west. This was probably only a beginning, for the move of the 21st Division was highly significant: it was the first time since 1940 that the Germans had stationed an armored division in the Caen area. For them to do so now must surely mean that they had good reason, or rather information.

Had it come to them by way of the Chicago package?

It was a strange affair. The security services in Washington had informed Eisenhower about it in mid-March. It began with a commonplace incident: some post office employees in Chicago opened a badly wrapped package. In it was a bundle of military documents marked "Bigot." These were taken to Sixth Army headquarters in Chicago, where four officers examined them and found that they revealed the invasion beaches, the military strength to be employed and the approximate date of the assault. Counterintelligence took over, and their investigation began on a grim note: the address of the package, Division Street, was in a neighborhood where many German immigrants lived.

The addressee was questioned. She recognized the writing on the package as her brother's. He was found to be a sergeant who worked in Eisenhower's headquarters. He was put under great pressure, but he tirelessly repeated the same explanation. He was supposed to send the documents to the Transportation Division in Washington, but he was overworked and also worried about his sister's ill health, so he must have written her address on the package without realizing what he was doing.

He and his sister were of German origin; but so were eleven million other American citizens. If he were a spy, he would surely have taken the trouble to wrap the documents more securely. Wrapping them so carelessly was just the kind of thing an overworked and worried man might do.

The case was left at that. But there were a dozen people in Chicago who knew the great secret: eight post office workers and four officers at Sixth Army headquarters. The F.B.I. checked on them and was satisfied. They were all warned that any indiscretion on their part would have tragic consequences for their country. A watch was kept on their movements.

What more could be done? How could a Chicago post office worker be prevented from indulging in idle talk when there were senior officers in London guilty of almost criminal negligence?

London was like a pot coming to the boil. The invasion fever which had the whole world in its grip was at its height in this city packed with military staffs. A dozen fresh rumors were born and died each day. Any small indiscretion was greeted with excitement, discussed and analyzed. When Major O'Brien, one of the heads of the American O.S.S., arrived at a reception given by the Free French Deuxième Bureau wearing jump boots, everyone concluded that the invasion was due to begin the following night.

Above all the agitation, but stirring it up by their mere presence, were the Bigots with their slightly condescending air. Their days were hard, but at evening parties they had the subtle pleasure of being the ones who knew, were known to know, but could not even be questioned. This inner satisfaction was not enough for one U.S. Air Force general, who had been a classmate of Eisenhower's at West Point. He was at an afternoon party at Claridge's when some of the ladies complained about the poor quality of the pastry. He gravely pointed out to them that Allied freighters were carrying war supplies and that foodstuffs would start to reach Britain again after the invasion, so there ought to be good pastry to eat again after June 15. He was demoted and sent back to the States. Another time, a British colonel told people that his men had been training for months to carry out an attack on a fortified position which was in Normandy. He, too, was demoted and removed from his command.

Not long afterward, an American naval officer revealed the place and date of the invasion to some of his friends, at another of these decidedly unfortunate parties. He was demoted and transferred. This time, Eisenhower really had a fright. Until then his even temperament had saved him from great anxiety and nervous tension. His considerable confidence had not been shaken when Churchill had said to him after they had lunched together on May 8: "I'm in this thing with you to the end, and if it fails we'll go down together." After the naval officer's indiscretion, Eisenhower began to think it might fail. "This breach of security is so serious that it practically gives me the shakes," he said.

There were more shakes to come.

Reports from the French Resistance: On May 6, the German Seventh Army received orders from Rommel to reinforce the troops in the Cotentin peninsula. The 6th Parachute Regiment, commanded by Colonel von der Heydte, a veteran of Crete, Libya, Russia and Italy, was now stationed in the area between Lessay and Périers. The 206th Tank Battalion was in position in the northwestern part of the peninsula, between the Cap de La Hague and Carteret. The shock battalion of the Seventh Army, trained in hand-to-hand fighting, was moved first to La Haye-du-Puits and then to Saint-Vaast on the east coast. The 17th Panzer Division had been shifted from Poitiers to Normandy.

On a wet, gusty May morning in London a window of the War Office suddenly blew open and twelve copies of a report summarizing OVERLORD were whisked out into the street. Officers dashed downstairs and recovered eleven copies at once, but the other one could not be found. Two hours later, after much inquiring and searching, the missing copy was discovered. It had been picked up by a civilian and handed to a sentry on the other side of Whitehall. The civilian wore thick glasses and had said to the sentry that the print on the copy was difficult to read. It was impossible to trace the civilian. Had he taken the trouble to read all the text? And if so, would he hold his tongue?

In Exeter one May evening a railway employee found a briefcase in an empty compartment. It contained a complete plan of OVERLORD. The employee handed it to the stationmaster, who locked it in a cupboard and had it guarded by some men of the Home Guard. Next morning, a security officer came and took it away.

In addition to these incidents there was a rather odd puzzle—a crossword puzzle, to be exact. Was a spy ingeniously using the *Daily Telegraph* crossword puzzle to transmit his information? In the May 2 issue the clue for 17 Across was:

"One of the U.S.," and the answer given next day was "Utah." On May 22 the clue for 3 Down was: "Red Indian on the Missouri"; the answer appeared as "Omaha." Was it just a coincidence that these two clues should give the code names of the two American landing beaches? Perhaps. But discreet inquiries were made about Leonard Dawe and Melville Jones, the two schoolteachers who were joint compilers of the *Daily Telegraph* crosswords.

For one leak that was plugged, how many were not even detected? With secrets of OVERLORD blowing along London pavements, being left in trains and displayed in crossword puzzles, the catastrophic troop movements made by the enemy were hardly surprising.

Reports from the French Resistance: The 91st Division was being moved from Germany to southern Brittany, but as the troop trains were nearing the Loire a last-minute order sent them to the Cotentin peninsula instead. The division was now at La Haye-du-Puits, in the heart of the peninsula. The 101st Regiment, equipped with flamethrowers, was spread out along the coast. The 17th Machine Gun Battalion, composed of young, well-trained men, was stationed near the Cap de La Hague. In the Carentan area, the 795th Georgian Battalion had been joined by the 100th Armored Battalion.

All these units were ordered to prepare to meet an enemy airborne assault. They were in the exact area where the American paratroopers were to land.

This information caused consternation in England. The commanders of the American 82nd and 101st Airborne Divisions, Generals Matthew Ridgway and Maxwell Taylor, were hurriedly summoned to headquarters, where they learned that their long-planned missions had become impracticable. They would be heading straight for disaster. Opponents of the airborne operation pressed for it to be called off. General Bradley flatly declared that he could not make his assault on Utah Beach without the support of the airborne divisions. A compromise solution was reached. The 82nd, instead of dropping in the area of Saint-Sauveur-le-Vicomte, to the west of the peninsula—with the object of isolating it and preventing the enemy from reinforcing his troops to the north—would now drop in the area of Sainte-Mère-Eglise in the center of the peninsula.

However, although it was still possible to modify the airborne operation, the assault on the beaches could not be changed in any way. The British would have to attack almost under the guns of the 21st Panzer Division, on the alert just south of Caen. So vast was the concept of OVERLORD, with its thousands of ships and aircraft, its hundreds of thousands of troops, with the timing of different phases dependent upon one another, that the slightest alteration would mean a general readjustment. It was too late for that; OVERLORD could still be held back—at least, until June 5—but it could no longer be modified.

The operation had been planned to break through the thin crust of concrete and human flesh which the enemy had laid along the coast. Now that the Germans knew, it would crash against the steel of the Panzer Divisions which they were about to concentrate in Normandy.

## 18. The Field Marshal and the Spies

AT Saint-Germain-en-Laye, where his headquarters building was a huge, three-floored underground blockhouse, one hundred yards long and sixty feet deep, Field Marshal von Rundstedt was waiting for the Allied invasion. He had been expecting it for more than two years. In the past, in a third of that time he had forced two nations to capitulate and had driven a third to the brink. He was one of the most outstanding commanders in the German army. He had planned and carried out the lightning campaign against Poland, had overrun France after his breakthrough at Sedan, and had led his armies across Russia as far as Rostov. In November, 1941, when he was at the very gates to the Caucasus, he had resigned his command rather than obey Hitler's stupid orders, thereby gaining immense prestige among the German officer corps. Von Rundstedt was respected. Hitler, who respected nothing and nobody, was nevertheless not the man to leave this paragon of prestige and military science lying idle. He recalled him in March, 1942, and put him in command of the German armies in the west.

So Gerd von Rundstedt was now learning the virtues of patience after having tasted the delights of the Blitzkrieg. He was doing quite well. Laden with years and honors, he did not exert himself overmuch, but left his junior, Rommel—whom he called "The Boy Marshal"—to hurry from one end of the Wall to the other, to inspect damp blockhouses and to make rousing speeches to the troops. The old gentleman suffered from insomnia and only fell asleep, helped a little by alcohol, in the early hours of the morning; and he rarely got up before ten-thirty. He often lunched at his favorite restaurant, the Coq Hardi at nearby Bougival. While Rommel's face, bronzed by the desert sun, became weather-beaten by the sea breezes, von Rundstedt's was consistently pale. The blood hardly seemed to flow through that hard, expressionless face. Like a stone statue in his concrete den, he seemed to be awaiting the Allied assault with a serenity that strongly resembled fatalism.

A less lofty commander would have long since lost his calm. Not only did von Rundstedt have some fourteen hundred miles of coastline to defend, but the German intelligence services were constantly sounding false alarms at all the gateways to "Fortress Europe." As far back as May, 1942, they had given warnings of landings in Denmark. At the beginning of June they had believed the Cotentin peninsula and the area around La Rochelle to be threatened, but by the end of the month they had thought the target was Belgium. In July, after an engagement between British and German torpedo boats, a waterproof bag had been washed ashore on the French coast. It contained documents relating to landings in Norway, with a diversionary attack in the Bay of Biscay. Appropriate defense measures were taken. On August 19 came the Dieppe raid. After that, the Abwehr began studying the geographical distribution of Allied commando raids with the object of discovering the area to be invaded next. The report made at the beginning of 1943 gave the following areas as being in the greatest danger of attack: Pas-de-Calais, the Seine estuary, Bordeaux, western Brittany and the south coast between Sète and Marseilles. By spring, however, the danger zones had been narrowed down to Pas-de-Calais and the Cotentin Peninsula. It seemed certain that the Allies would invade there. Summer passed and nothing happened.

A few months later, Canaris's organization gave warning that the enemy was preparing to land in Spain or Portugal. This information had come from agents in Vichy and Madrid, and from sympathizers among Spanish officers. Three possible landing areas were mentioned: Lisbon, the Balearic Islands and Barcelona. Operation ILONA was hastily planned, to be put in motion on confirmation of an Allied landing. Five divisions were ready to head for Barcelona, and five others for Valladolid and Salamanca.

No sooner was ILONA planned than the pendulum swung towards the north: Denmark and Norway. But it soon swung back again, for at the beginning of 1944 came numerous reports from agents operating in North Africa that Allied landings could be expected in the Rhone delta and near the French-Spanish border. It was considered likely that there would be a supporting landing in the Bordeaux region, and that the two forces would make a pincer movement in the direction of Toulouse. This threat was taken so seriously by Berlin that three divisions, including the 9th Panzer S.S., were ordered to the south of France and two others to the southwest.

In March the pendulum became more stable. The prime danger zones were Pas-de-Calais, Normandy and Brittany.

Von Rundstedt had known it would come back to that. He had been little concerned by all the false alarms, and had treated Operation ILONA as an excellent opportunity for a map exercise—one of those *Kriegsspielen* that were his speciality. All these scares only served to confirm him in his scorn for intelligence services in general, and those of his own country in particular.

He came of an aristocratic Prussian military family, and as such despised everything to do with espionage, counter-espionage and the ignoble arithmetic of double, triple and quadruple agents. A proud officer should not soil his hands with such dirty work. The S.S. manual issued to its intelligence service stated regretfully: "The Germans consider espionage to be work for criminals and adventurers." Schellenberg used to say: "If you ever told an ordinary German officer—to say nothing of a high-ranking one—that you were working for an intelligence service, you were at once regarded as a suspicious character or even a common adventurer."

The manual and Schellenberg both erred. It was not quite accurate that Canaris's officers were so scorned by their Wehrmacht colleagues. It was not true to say that the "Blacks" of the S.S. intelligence service were held in suspicion by the army; they were just considered downright scoundrels. The Wehrmacht had not forgotten the von Fritsch tragedy. The Gestapo had fabricated an accusation of corrupt morals against von Fritsch, the commander-in-chief of the Wehrmacht, which had obliged him to resign his command. He was acquitted by a court-martial but reduced to the rank of colonel. He was shattered by his humiliating ordeal, and on the eve of the Polish campaign he wrote: "In this war I shall accompany my regiment as a target, because I cannot stay at home." He kept his word. On the outskirts of Warsaw he went ahead, alone and unarmed, and met the "suicide" he sought.

But if von Rundstedt as a man differentiated between Canaris's officers and those of Schellenberg, as a field marshal he condemned them all equally: inefficient, unfailingly duped by the enemy, and incapable of discovering his plans.

They had been completely discredited by the corpse of Major Martin.

The story of William Martin* is comical, macabre and perverse. Only the British could have thought up such a ploy. There was no William Martin. He was invented by Ewen Montagu, who had been a King's Counsel at the outbreak of the war, when he joined the R.N.V.R. before appointment to Naval Intelligence.

He persuaded two eminent men to adopt the creature he had fathered: Sir Archibald Nye, Vice Chief of the Imperial General Staff, and Lord Louis Mountbatten, head of Combined Operations. This was in April, 1943. The Allies had cleared the enemy from North Africa, and their next objective would obviously be Sicily. "Anyone but a damned fool would know it is Sicily," Churchill gloomily remarked. The Germans and the Italians were convinced of it. Their certainty was annoying.

Montagu was looking for a corpse. After a tiring search

---

* Described in full in *The Man Who Never Was*, by Ewen Montagu (Lippincott, 1954).

he found one. The man had died of pneumonia; Montagu put the body in cold storage while he compiled its life story. Name: William Martin. Occupation: officer in the Royal Marines. He was provided with an old father who wrote to him in Victorian style: "I cannot say that this Hotel is any longer as comfortable as I remember it to have been in pre-war days . . . Your cousin Priscilla has asked to be remembered to you . . . I cannot say that her work for the Land Army has done much to improve her looks." He was also given a fiancée, Pamela, who wrote to him: "I do think dearest that seeing people like you off at railways stations is one of the poorer forms of sport." He was put into uniform (a difficult undertaking—they had to thaw his feet with an electric radiator in order to get the shoes on). In the pockets of his battledress and his trench coat they put his officer's identity card and personal letters, some money, several receipts and bills—including one for an engagement ring—pencil stub, two bus tickets, a pack of cigarettes, a bunch of keys and a letter from his bank manager informing him of an overdraft. But the most precious thing he was given was a briefcase, attached to him by a thin chain.

He was then put aboard the submarine *Seraph,* and was cast into the sea off the coast of Spain, on April 30, 1943. He was wearing a Mae West, so that those who found his body would think he had died in a plane crash on his way to Algiers. British experts had calculated that the currents which flow parallel to the coast in that area would not prevent the corpse being driven by the wind towards the small town of Huelva, where a German agent was known to be particularly active. In any case, the Spanish and German secret services were on such good terms that the three letters in the briefcase could not fail to reach the right hands.

One letter, signed by Sir Archibald Nye, was to General Alexander, Deputy Commander-in-Chief in North Africa. It was a personal letter, but Archie took the opportunity to give Alex a few details about the forthcoming landings in Greece, in the Peloponnese. Archie was optimistic: "We stand a very good chance of making [the enemy] think we will go for Sicily." He indicated that Sicily had been chosen as a "cover target" for another operation which was being planned.

The second letter, signed by Lord Mountbatten and addressed to Admiral Cunningham, contained a joking allusion to that operation. Mountbatten asked that Martin should be sent back to him as soon as it was completed, and added: "He might bring some sardines with him. They are 'on points' here."

The third letter was not directly intended, like the others, to deceive the Germans, but showed an attention to detail such as might have saved the lives of a few German spies if their masters had been equally meticulous. It would have been risky to slip the first two letters into one of Martin's pockets: the Spaniards might have neglected to search it. Hence the briefcase. But a briefcase just for two private letters might have aroused the suspicions of the Germans. So page proofs and illustrations of a book on the history of the Commandos were inserted, thus providing a good reason for its use. Everything had been carefully studied down to the smallest detail. But while William Martin was drifting towards the Spanish coast, Montagu was worried by one small mistake. The receipt for the shirt on the body had been slipped into a pocket of the raincoat, and it was of course in Major Martin's name. But the officer who had bought the shirt at Gieves', tailors to the Royal Navy, was not himself a Naval officer and had paid cash—but no Navy or Royal officer ever paid cash at Gieves'! They all had accounts. Montagu's thoroughness would have amazed his German opposite numbers, but he himself was wondering whether the whole affair might fail because of this oversight . . .

But he had worried unnecessarily. On May 14, Admiral Doenitz wrote: "The Führer does not agree with Duce that the most likely invasion point is Sicily. Furthermore, he believes that the discovered Anglo-Saxon order confirms the assumption that the planned attack will be mainly against Sardinia and the Peloponnesus." In the meantime the Martin documents had arrived in Berlin and the German intelligence serivices had decided that they were genuine.

Hitler reacted quickly. He sent the 1st Panzer Division halfway across Europe, from France to Greece; he had defense works increased in Greece and Sardinia, sent more guns and had mine fields laid. At the beginning of June, some German torpedo boats were sent from Sicily to Greece. And on July 23, thriteen days after the invasion of Sicily had begun, Hitler still thought it was only the "cover target" mentioned by Sir Archibald Nye; and he sent his best general, Erwin Rommel, to take command of the troops stationed in Greece!

Meanwhile, in Huelva cemetery, solemn-faced British officers had placed a wreath from the sorrowing Pamela on the grave of William Martin, watched by the ever-alert Abwehr agent . . .

So the Allies had attacked in the center, in Sicily, when they were expected in Sardinia and Greece on the flanks. The Germans had been taken in on that occasion—but what about the landings in North Africa, which had occurred eight months earlier? A whole armada had sailed from Britain, crossed the Bay of Biscay, and calmly landed its divisions on Moroccan and Algerian beaches. There had been hundreds of ships and thousands of men. They had come like thieves in the night, and the blow was dealt while Berlin slept. Yet it should have been easy enough to spot the convoys heading for Oran and Algiers as they passed through the Straits of Gibraltar.

Quite easy—and, even better than that, the invasion armada had been reported while still in Scotland. Berg and Klausen, the two will-o'-the-wisps, had noted the large concentration of ships in the Clyde estuary as early as October, 1942. Later in the month they reported invasion exercises being held on nearby beaches. Then the troops were confined to the ships; but the two Norwegians learned from drunken sailors that arctic clothing had been issued to the troops. "Our fate is to be decided in Norway," Hitler declared to Admiral Raeder. "We must defend that country at all costs." The battle cruisers *Scharnhorst* and *Gneisenau* and the heavy cruiser *Prinz Eugen* were ordered from Brest to the Baltic, and successfully ran the gauntlet up the English Channel. At the end of the month Berg and Klausen sent a brief message: "The fleet has sailed." Luftwaffe reconnaissance planes took off and searched the North Sea from Scotland to Norway. But the armada was nowhere to be seen.*

It was discovered heading south. Raeder could have cut it to pieces. His U-boat packs were sinking Allied shipping at the rate of 700,000 tons a month—more than could be replaced by the shipyards of Britain and North America working at full pressure. All that was needed was to know where the convoys were bound. Berlin was positive—Dakar. So

---

* This should not be taken as proof that Berg and Klausen had been "doubled": artic clothing had indeed been issued.

Raeder placed his U-boats off Dakar, like a nest of deadly vipers. And the armada swung into the Straits of Gibraltar.

It could not avoid having its presence noted by the enemy. At Algeciras, right opposite the Rock, the Abwehr had an observation post with instruments which could detect shipping even at night. Berlin was informed. Reports had been received for several days past that Allied landings were expected in North Africa. But other reports indicated that the convoys were headed for Malta. Which was it to be—North Africa or Malta? Berlin decided on Malta, with a third possibility in mind: that landings might be made near Tripoli or Benghazi, in the rear of Rommel's positions.

A sad affair . . .

After North Africa there was Sicily. And after Sicily, Anzio. It was as though fate had decreed that the Allied landings should always have the benefit of complete surprise. Apparently German intelligence found it impossible to discover anything about enemy intentions. A few days before the Anzio landings, General Westphal had asked Canaris if he knew the whereabouts of the British naval force. "We're keeping an eye on it, don't worry," Canaris replied. Incompetence or treachery? Canaris carried his secret to the grave. But too much credence should not be given to treachery, for all the admiral's professional failures could not have been premeditated. There was at least one that he would have wished to avoid, one whose consequences affected von Rundstedt personally.

"No nation embarked upon a war with so much information about the enemy as we had about the Russians," Canaris stated to his senior officers soon after Operation BARBAROSSA had launched the Panzer divisions across the Eastern plains. He was sincere on that occasion. Strongly anti-Communist, he had not been torn by that war, though with his usual clearsightedness he considered it an act of folly.

He was sincere, but mistaken. He had given Hitler the Russian order of battle on the frontier; but beyond this screen all was mystery. Some time before the offensive, Canaris and Schellenberg had compared notes during one of their morning rides. Canaris contended that the great Russian industrial centers were linked by single-track railroads, but Schellenberg insisted that there were double tracks. The Russian economic potential would vary a great deal according to which of the two was right. An amazing spectacle, this—the heads of the two German intelligence services riding under the trees and unable to agree on such a vital point!

Tragedy was the result. On August 10, the chief of the German General Staff, Colonel-General Franz Halder, wrote: "Our calculations were based on the enemy having a force of about two hundred divisions. After three months' fighting we have already identified three hundred and sixty! No sooner are a dozen or so wiped out than another dozen take their place." Von Rundstedt reported: "Soon after the outset of the fighting I realized that everything we had been told about Russia was nonsense. The maps we had been provided with were incorrect. The roads indicated by thick red lines turned out to be only tracks, while those marked as tracks were in fact main roads. And the railways that we were supposed to use for our advance did not even exist. Where a map showed an empty region we sometimes came upon American-type towns with factories and everything!"

It was not until eighteen months later that German intelligence found that the statistics published by the Russians in Russia itself were false, and that an institute had the responsibility of collecting economic, scientific and technical data, and then falsifying certain important aspects. The correct figures and information were given only to authorized officials.

So since 1942 there had been a constant succession of failures to give advance warnings. Von Rundstedt was quite convinced it would be madness to place any confidence in intelligence services which could only give warning of imaginary landings and never predict the real ones. It was by calling on his great experience of strategy and tactics that he, the only German field marshal still unbeaten, sought to solve the riddle of the invasion. Deep in his den at Saint-Germain, he asked his maps to tell him the secret of D-Day.

They answered him.

## 19. The Sixth Commandment

PAS-DE-CALAIS.

It was obvious, clear as daylight, practically irrefutable. Every time von Rundstedt studied the map his finger inevitably jabbed at the coastal strip between Dunkirk and the mouth of the Somme. "If I were Montgomery," he often said to his staff officers, "that is where I would attack." Somewhere between Dunkirk and Saint-Valéry, probably in the Calais-Boulogne sector. The staff officers agreed. They could have recited by heart the litany of arguments which their chief had so often propounded, and which could have been called "The Five Commandments of the Perfect Invader."

*One—Choose the shortest crossing.* Obviously Dover—Calais. The crossing to Normandy is three times as long, to Brittany four or five times. By invading across the Straits, landing craft and ships could make more journeys and so speed up reinforcements and supplies.

*Two—Obtain the greatest air support.* Since Pas-de-Calais was close to the English air bases, the Allies could give the best air cover to their invading forces. Whereas Normandy—and Brittany even more so—would raise problems of refueling, and fighter aircraft could remain over the landing areas for only a limited time.

*Three—Seek the greatest gain.* The shortest route to the Ruhr and its heavy industries, which were indispensable to the German war effort, passed through Pas-de-Calais. Once the beachhead had been established, the Allied armies could reach the Rhineland in four days. A thrust at the heart, and the Third Reich would collapse. But an invasion of the Cotentin penisula might be sealed off. Similarly with Brittany. Even if the Allies succeeded in breaking out, they would still have to fight their way across France.

*Four—Capture a port.* This was essential for the build-up. Without a port and its installations how were the Allies to land their tanks, trucks and heavy artillery? Normandy had no suitable port, apart from Le Havre or Cherbourg, and both of these were heavily fortified and strongly defended. Whereas a landing in Pas-de-Calais might quickly lead to the capture of Calais, Boulogne or Dunkirk.

*Five—Destroy the enemy.* The V-1 and V-2 launching sites were in Pas-de-Calais. A race had been going on for months between the Todt organization and Allied Bomber Command. During the winter, British bombers—including Cheshire's 617th Squadron—had destroyed seventy-three of the ninety-six launching platforms which were ready to send the terrible new weapons over England. The sites had been repaired and made less vulnerable to air attack; in particular, they were much more carefully camouflaged.* Hitler had given orders for a supply of missiles to be at hand in the area. He was waiting for the invasion to begin before starting his V-2 offensive, for the Allied air forces would then be concentrating on tactical objectives and have little strength to spare to attack the launching sites. But all these preparations were known to the Allies, through reports from the Resistance. Surely they would not let such a deadly menace hang over London; surely they would attack the area where Germany's reprisal weapons were concentrated.

Merciful von Rundstedt! He seemed to be trying to console the French generals he had defeated in 1940. His "Five Commandments" implied that it was their defensive attitude rather than their incompetence which had lost them the battle. They had reasoned in 1940 as von Rundstedt was doing in 1944, and had decided that the enemy was bound to attack across the Belgian plain—certainly not through the Ardennes, with its forests and winding, hilly roads. In 1944, as in 1940, the army on the defensive was forgetting the "Sixth Com-

---

* The unit to launch the V-1's and V-2's was the 155th Anti-Aircraft Regiment, commanded by Colonel Wachtel. He endeavored to keep its role secret by first eliminating all non-Germans from its ranks and then hiding its identity under cover of the Todt Organization. These precautions were not unreasonable, but his officers were probably somewhat surprised when he insisted that they move to the new headquarters in requisitioned taxis and on a dark night. His next step was to change his name to Wolf, and finally he took to wearing a false beard.

mandment," the most important of all: *Take the enemy by surprise.*

The leaders of the German army in the west were trying to guess the enemy's intentions by putting themselves in his place, or rather by considering what they would do in his place. By sheer reason they arrived at the logical direction of the assault. It did not seem to occur to them that the enemy might disregard logic and decide to attack in one direction for the good reason that he was expected in another. This did not necessarily mean that they were lacking in imagination. The von Rundstedt who was expecting the enemy in Pas-de-Calais was the same man who had conceived the bold plan to crush Poland and who had tricked the French by his breakthrough in the Ardennes. He had not changed. It was his situation which had changed. He was no longer the cat, but the mouse—a transition which is bound to have some psychological consequences.

On the other hand, the deductions drawn from von Rundstedt's "Fifth Commandment" were due to a chronic weakness of the Prussian military caste: it had always underestimated the moral strength of the enemy. Even after four years of war the Germans had still not realized Churchill's bulldog qualities. The threat of the V-1's? Churchill had told Eisenhower that it must on no account lead him to modify his invasion plans. The Londoners had already shown that they could take it. London would die if necessary in order that OVERLORD might live. But Churchill's rousing phrases could not have been heard or understood properly in the blockhouse at Saint-Germain.

As for the "Fourth Commandment," von Rundstedt could hardly be blamed for including it. The Allies had always known they would need a port soon after D-Day. So had the Germans. Hitler's generals had told him, back in 1942: "As long as we hold the ports, we hold Europe." The Führer, convinced, had reacted in his usual manner, which resembled Churchill's in its sense of the dramatic, but differed from it by an interest in detail of bad taste. He had the main ports fortified and dignified them with the name of "fortresses." Each fortress was ordered to resist the enemy "to the last drop of blood," and the officer in command had to sign this oath: "I swear to hold and defend the fortified position under my command to the end of my life and that of the last soldier under my orders." Before that last soldier fell he had to set off all the demolition charges and blow up the port installations.

Wise old von Rundstedt had crossed out from Hitler's decree the words "last drop of blood" and replaced them with "last cartridge." But the guns defending the "fortresses" were more to be feared than words. The Allies had learned at Dieppe what a frontal assault could cost: of the 5000 Canadians who took part in that attack, 2900 had not returned. The defenses had been strengthened even more since then, and Montgomery was quite explicit: a port could not be captured from the sea.

The problem remained:

a) A suitable port was indispensable for the success of OVERLORD.

b) Its facilities had to be ready for use again three weeks after D-Day.

c) It was practically impossible to capture a port in such a short time.

d) Even if this could be done, the mines laid by the enemy and his destruction of the port's facilities would make it unusable for at least two months.

Lord Mountbatten found the answer at the end of a frustrating conference. "Well, if we can't capture a port," he concluded with a sigh, "we must take one with us." The idea was greeted with laughter. Then came reflection. Two years later there were twenty thousand men working on the artificial harbors known as "Mulberries." Von Rundstedt's "Fourth Commandment" had lost its significance.

He knew nothing about the "Mulberry" project, but he should have. The project was, admittedly, surrounded by security measures that were even more stringent than those for the rest of OVERLORD. The room in which the models were kept was never cleaned. The only people allowed to enter it were a handful of high-ranking officers whose dignity precluded their wielding a cleaning rag, so they worked in a constant cloud of dust. But there were the twenty thousand workmen, and the blocks of concrete and steel as high as six-story buildings. Yet all this escaped the notice of German agents! When Vanhove had gone down the river to Tilbury, the caissons moored there had meant nothing to him.

German reconnaissance planes eventually sighted them, but they were at first thought to be silos. Then the Germans concluded they were to replace jetties or pierheads blasted out of use in an assault—which meant the Allies intended to seize a port. The idea that these caissons themselves might be a port never crossed the German mind. How could the problem of tides be overcome? Churchill's imagination protected the secret of the "Mulberries" better than any security measures. He had thought of floating jetties which would rise and fall with the tides, enabling cargo ships to unload at any time. The idea had seemed difficult to put into effect; Churchill had written in the margin of the memorandum he sent to Mountbatten: "Don't argue about it. The difficulties will argue themselves."

Such inventiveness was lacking in Berlin. The Germans did not believe in the "Mulberries" until weeks *after* D-Day. How was von Rundstedt, weeks before, to suspect that his "Fourth Commandment" was not as imperative as he thought?

The first three—short crossing, air support and maximum gain—still justified von Rundstedt's concentration on Pas-de-Calais. In 1942 it had been allocated four times as much cement as Normandy, and this favorable ratio continued into 1943 and 1944. The Fifteenth Army had thus been able to build reinforced concrete casemates for 93 of the 132 big guns along the coast between Dunkirk and Boulogne. But in Normandy only 27 out of 47 had been similarly protected. There were two and a half times as many troops stationed in Pas-de-Calais as in Normandy. During the winter of 1943 the strength of the Fifteenth Army was increased from ten to fifteen divisions. The Wall between Dunkirk and Saint-Valéry was backed up by troop concentrations some miles inland. If the Atlantic Wall anywhere resembled the ferocious image popularized by Goebbels, it was in the segment where von Rundstedt was expecting the Allies.

His obstinacy was superb. Even if his initial guess had been correct, he should have realized that his massive fortifications and troop concentrations were enough to make the enemy decide to attack elsewhere. But he fiercely clung to his idea. Was it because Admiral Krancke had assured him that landings were impossible on the coast of Lower Normandy because of the offshore reefs? Or because he considered that the flooded areas at the base of the Cotentin peninsula were sufficient to halt the movements of an invading force? Or simply because he could not bring himself to believe that all his efforts in Pas-de-Calais might have been in vain? In any case, the Commander-in-Chief of the German armies in the west gratified the most ardent wishes of the Allies: he was sure the attack would come in Pas-de-Calais.

Why, then, was there a sudden movement of units to reinforce the troops in Normandy—the 21st Panzer Division to Caen, the 91st Division to the Cotentin peninsula, and the 6th Parachute Battalion to Périers? Von Rundstedt had given the orders reluctantly and on specific instruction from an amateur strategist who was scorned by all the best military minds in Germany, from the man von Rundstedt disdainfully referred to as "the Bohemian corporal": Adolf Hitler.

# 20. The Führer Is Always Right

THE scene is Hitler's headquarters, any morning. The Master is still asleep. He went to bed at four in the morning, as usual, and will only get up in time for the staff conference at noon. In the map room, Vice Admiral Bürckner of the Abwehr is completing his report on the situation on the eastern front. His assistants are shifting little flags around on the operations map. There are red flags to represent Russian divisions and blue ones to represent German divisions. Bürckner frowns as he watches them. Now and then he grunts: "Ach! Don't put so much red on the map!" And his men, either from discipline or indifference, put a few Russian divisions into their pockets. It would not do to upset the Führer, and a rash of red flags always throws him into a rage.

General Gehlen, head of intelligence for the German armies in Russia, was not such a good psychologist as Vice Admiral Bürckner. When he was summoned by Hitler he gave a detailed report of the Russian divisions held in reserve. The Führer grew red in the face, rushed at Gehlen as though he were going to strangle him, and shouted, "Do you dare to tell me that I'm losing my war?" Gehlen, completely taken aback, stammered that he was only giving the latest information he had received. He was dismissed.

Even Walther Schellenberg was not exempt from these mishaps. In 1942 he drew up a detailed report of American war potential. The astute Heydrich turned pale as he read it. Goering returned it with the comment: "Everything you've written is pure nonsense. You'd better see a psychiatrist." As for Hitler, he said curtly, "I don't believe a single word of it." A year later, Schellenberg made the same mistake over Russia. His experts made a close estimate of Soviet industrial and military potential. "Very good work, on the whole," was Schellenberg's own opinion. But when Hitler read the report he ordered that all the experts be arrested and charged with defeatism. Panic-stricken, Schellenberg turned to Himmler, who at first declared that the experts must be "agents of the Russian N. K. V. D." However, after two hours of pleading by Schellenberg, he agreed not to hand them over to the Gestapo. Schellenberg had saved his men, and would not be caught again sending "defeatist" reports to a higher level. He wrote bitterly: "Hitler automatically rejected any unfavorable information, even if it was founded on actual fact or common sense."

Was Hitler mad? Yes, he was. But who drove him mad? Canaris, among others.

Canaris had wanted peace in 1938. The chiefs of the Wehrmacht feared a war that they considered Germany was unprepared for, and so they looked with approval on the admiral's attempts to deceive Hitler.

When the invasion of Czechoslovakia was being planned, Canaris produced pessimistic reports on the strength of the Czech fortifications. They had been built on the same principle as the Maginot Line, and were indeed a strong barrier. But Canaris made them out to be very formidable obstacles. The occupation of Czechoslovakia showed exactly how much of an obstacle they were.

During the Polish campaign Canaris was summoned by Hitler to his special train at Ilnau on September 12, 1939, when the fighting was at its height. The admiral brought the worst possible news: "The French are massing troops and artillery, especially in the Saarbrücken area, and are preparing a great offensive." This was the nightmare that haunted the German generals. Hitler had left only a thin screen of twenty-three divisions facing the one hundred and ten British and French divisions. "During the Polish campaign," Keitel said later, "we soldiers expected to hear every day of a French offensive, and were very surprised that nothing happened . . . A French attack would have encountered only a covering screen, not a real defense." Hitler listened to Canaris's report and merely said that he did not believe there would be a French offensive. He was right.

The Wehrmacht had disapproved of the plans to invade Denmark and Norway, and desperately tried to hold Hitler back. Canaris set to work as soon as he heard of the preparations. As late as April 3 he told his chief assistants, Oster and Liedig: "It is the Abwehr's duty to provide as many alarmist reports as possible on British countermeasures." Hitler was inundated with bad news, and was warned that the British navy would sink his troop transports, but he obstinately carried on with his plans. He was right.

The German generals had been gloomy about the outcome of the attack on the Low Countries and France. They were convinced that they were in for a severe beating. Von Rundstedt was pessimistic. Halder, chief of staff at supreme headquarters, noted in his diary: "No one among the staff thinks that the offensive has the slightest chance of success." In an effort to dissuade Hitler from embarking on it, von Brauchitsch, commander-in-chief of the German army, went so far as to invent stories of mutinies and desertions among the troops. Hitler icily asked how many death sentences had been passed. "Nothing can stop me!" he raged, "I'll destroy everyone who opposes me! I'm going to crush the enemy!" And he did.

Apparently the Führer was always right.

A Führer is always more or less convinced that he is always right; it is one of the peculiarities of the breed. He has his own personal star to guide him toward his destiny. He has revelations, he knows the secrets of the gods. Fortune is on his side, ready to tip the scales if necessary. He is surprised if the Red Sea does not divide to let his army cross. Hitler, for example, could not admit that it was bad weather which had forced him to postpone his offensive fourteen times between November, 1939, and May, 1940. It was abnormal. He was the man of sunlight. When he was to speak at an open-air meeting, the heaviest downpours would cease a few minutes before his arrival. This was so well known in Germany that clear days were called "Hitler's weather." His plans were upset by rain in the winter of 1939–1940, and by snow two years later. From then on he had a physical horror of snow. He could not bear to see or touch it. It had caused the death of thousands of Germans. He would not forgive it. A Führer does not compromise with the elements: they must fall in with his plans, as men do.

But a Führer is not necessarily mad. And even if he seems certain to end up a megalomaniac, history shows that although this form of madness may bring disaster upon others it does not always prevent him from having an acute sense of his own interest. Stalin was extremely wary to the end of his days. Hitler showed an extraordinarily wily caution until 1939, but this changed completely after 1940. He had been right too often, and it had gone to his head.

At this point the strange fate of Wilhelm Canaris verges on the tragic. In making his alarmist reports, he was surely acting from morally commendable motives. But intelligence work has its own moral code, which has nothing to do with common morality. It overlooks many minor sins, but never condones the major one of manipulating information for political ends. Canaris was guilty of this when he invented or distorted his reports to influence German policy. He was implacably punished for it. Hitler stopped taking notice of any unfavorable reports that were sent to him, even, as Schellenberg has said, when they were based on actual fact or common sense. Hitler became convinced that he was surrounded by weak, spineless creatures who got cold shivers at the mere suggestion of danger, and from then on no advice or appeal had any effect on his plans. He had rightly disregarded the Abwehr's frights, and now he refused to see the real dangers that were pointed out to him.

After his triumphs in 1940 it is quite possible that, even without Canaris, he would sooner or later have embarked on the course that led to Germany's downfall. But because of Canaris the man who rushed into it was blind and deaf; he could not see the abyss at his feet or hear the warning shouts. Canaris, by trying to spare his country the horrors of war, only helped to plunge it into the bloodiest and most disastrous conflict of its whole history. The Führer was so puffed up with vanity that he believed only in his intuition;

and the Abwehr's constant failures and the political plots it fomented were not calculated to restore his faith in his intelligence service. Not even the counsels of his best generals or the reports submitted by the loyal S.S. could prevail against this intuition, which had reigned over the battles of 1940. Nor could stark facts do anything against it. Hitler still had faith in it after Stalingrad, where thanks to his intuition he lost a quarter of a million men. He still had faith in it after the Tunisian campaign, where he lost as many again. For two years he was unshaken by the disasters which his intuition heaped upon him.

From 1943 on, there were no more chances for strategic gambles; "the greatest military leader of all time" was no longer able to spring surprises on the world. Having poured the Wehrmacht into the bottomless Russian pit, he had to keep on plugging regiments into the gaps that the powerful hands of the Red Army tore in the eastern front. It was piecemeal work for the man who had been cavorting all over Europe two years previously. With his intuition thus left dormant, one might have expected his sense of reality to awaken. But Hitler remained blind and deaf—because otherwise he would have been obliged to admit that his situation was hopeless. If he had believed the figures on American and Russian war potential compiled by Schellenberg's experts, there would have been nothing left for him to do but surrender. Instead, he rejected the experts. He stubbornly ignored or swept aside everything which might extinguish his faith in his destiny and his confidence in his intuitive powers. Gehlen was dismissed. Bürckner kept his post only by pocketing handfuls of little red flags. Unfavorable information, inevitably considered inaccurate, was automatically rejected.

Even, and especially, the documents from Cicero.

"The study of these documents positively took your breath away," wrote Schellenberg. Just as the hangman's rope does. The strength of the Allies lay revealed to the masters of the Third Reich. They saw the figures on American war materiel sent to Russia, promising further disasters in the east. They read that the three Allied powers were so certain of victory that they had already begun to divide the world among themselves, a world in which Germany would have no place. Between the lines, the German leaders read their own death sentences, for the documents left no doubt as to Allied intentions on that score.

Fortunately the documents were forged. Von Ribbentrop was quite convinced of that, and he had no difficulty in getting others to agree. The German leaders had not recovered from being duped over the Sicily invasion. These documents were therefore another British attempt to mislead, and Cicero must be a double agent. Yet there were many indications of his good faith. Thanks to him, German cipher experts had succeeded in breaking the British diplomatic code. Whenever Schellenberg had been able to check his documents with information obtained from other sources, they had been found to be accurate. A final proof of his loyalty was the copy of a document concerning air attacks that the Allies were preparing to make on the capitals of Balkan countries. The first raid was to be on Sofia on January 14, 1944. Berlin decided to make this a test of Cicero's reliability. On January 14 Moyzisch, in Ankara, tried to telephone the German legation at Sofia, but was told that communications were cut. He got through the following morning, when an official told him: "We've had a terrible air raid. The whole town is in flames. There are heavy casualties." Berlin had its proof; several hundred corpses had vouched for Cicero's good faith.

Nevertheless, if the documents were genuine the promise of the gallows implicit in them was not to von Ribbentrop's liking. And the German Foreign Minister was adept at ostrich-like policy. Before 1939 he had made up his mind to believe—and to make others believe—that Britain would never go to war against Germany. He had issued a directive to all members of his staff which ended with this vigorous warning: "If it came to my notice that anyone had expressed a contrary opinion I would kill him myself in his office, and take responsibility before the Führer for it."

Ludwig Moyzisch, who thought he had pulled off the coup of the century, was driven to bitter despair. Even when he discovered that OVERLORD was the code name for the Allied invasion, Berlin refused to give much credence to it. The only comment Moyzisch received was: "Possible, but not very likely." It may well be that this discouragement was the reason for his disobedience. Von Papen, at least, believed the documents were genuine—and wanted to make use of them. With them, he caused a considerable flutter in Ankara diplomatic circles. It was better than nothing, though very little compared to what could have been done.

Schellenberg was sure that something had to be done. As head of an intelligence service he could not shut his eyes to the facts. He exchanged his S.S. boots for Canaris's slippers and, sliding into the defeatism he had found so reprehensible in the admiral, he entered into contact with Sweden and Switzerland. His object was to obtain a compromise peace which would save what was still left to be saved. He wrote later: "My work had brought me face to face with reality. . . . From that moment, my problem was to make our leaders aware of the painful facts, when they absolutely refused even to consider the possibility that they might be true . . ." A tricky problem indeed. Alarm was growing in enlightened German circles at the Führer's obstinate refusal to recognize the facts. Would he ever see reason? But they should not have chosen Hitler as Chancellor if they wanted someone reasonable. They should have retained cunning little von Papen, for example, instead of raising to power a man who, unemployed in Vienna, went without food in order to go and hear *Götterdämmerung*. Hitler could not and would not negotiate.

He could not, first of all because the Allies would refuse to recognize him as a valid spokesman, and also because he was concerned with his biography. A Führer does not stoop to salvage the furniture: he dies under the ruins.

He would not, because he still had hope. The bright intuition which had brought Europe prostate before him in the splendid days of 1940 had dwindled to a mere flicker, but it needed only a favorable opportunity to flare up again. This opportunity was not to be found in the east, where the only thing to do was to resist the patient, steady pounding of the Russian colossus. But in the west, when the Anglo-American champion lunged forward he might throw himself off balance and leave his guard open.

When Hitler had told his western commanders-in-chief, on March 20, 1944, that final victory would come with the defeat of the Allied invasion, he had also given them the benefit of his intution:

"The areas most favorable to the enemy, and consequently the most threatened, are the Cotentin peninsula and Brittany. Both are equally tempting, for they provide the greatest possibility of establishing a beachhead, which could be gradually extended by using aircraft and armor in great strength."

The Führer had not based his opinion on specific information any more than von Rundstedt had done when he put his finger on Pas-de-Calais. Involuntarily combining their efforts, the German and Allied secret services had achieved this prodigious result: the two men on whom the fate of the German armies in the west depended had lost all confidence in intelligence reports. Hitler relied only on his intuition, von Rundstedt on his reasoning. Neither could provide the slightest proof in support of his contentions. They had left the bleak world of facts for the higher plane of fantasy or the almost equally unreal domain of abstract logic carried to extremes.

And intuition won. Hitler even declared a few weeks later that the Cotentin peninsula was the most likely scene of the invasion. He had succeeded where German intelligence had failed over the months, rendering useless the thousand and one security precautions surrounding OVERLORD.

It was a poisoned success, for the Führer had disdained intelligence, and intelligence, in its own tortuous way, would have its revenge. In the course of his conference Hitler had declared: "We must take example from Dieppe." Dieppe —with landing craft blazing on the gray water, with hundreds of corpses lying on the beaches, with Canadian prisoners marched through the streets stripped to their underwear. The Führer dreamed of another Dieppe, and thought he had made it possible. Neither he nor anyone else then knew that in winning the battle on the Dieppe beaches he had lost the secret war.

Von Rundstedt left the conference without having raised a single objection to what Hitler had said. One did not converse with the Führer, one listened to his monologue. In any case, von Rundstedt despised him too much to enter into a discussion with him. His conviction was not shaken in any way. He went back to Saint-Germain-en-Laye still certain that the Allied landing would be made in Pas-de-Calais. It was up to him to organize troop movements. Nothing moved.

But five weeks after the conference the Berlin oracle handed down another message which reached Saint-Germain on May 2: "The Führer thinks that landings will not be made along a 300-mile front, but that the attack will first be on Normandy and then on Brittany."

This time the oracle was heeded. Reinforcements were sent to Normandy, much to London's alarm. Not that von Rundstedt had discarded his "Five Commandments"; he still thought the attack would come in Pas-de-Calais. But the "Bohemian corporal" had found a disciple: the "Boy Marshal."

## 21. Rommel Listens to the B.B.C.

AT seven in the morning of May 10, 1944, Field Marshal Erwin Rommel left the headquarters of the 84th Corps at Saint-Lô and headed for the east coast of the Cotentin peninsula. Since the beginning of the year he had been running up and down the Dutch, Belgian and French coasts, shaking up the staffs and exhorting the troops. Hitler had first entrusted him with this mission of inspection, then given him command of Army Group B, which was guarding the ramparts of "Fortress Europe" from the Zuider Zee to the mouth of the Loire. The troops in Pas-de-Calais, Normandy and Brittany were therefore under Rommel's command, though he was under the distant authority of von Rundstedt.

On this particular morning, Rommel's Horch convertible, driven by the faithful Daniel, was making for the coastal battery at Morsalines. Four months earlier, during his first inspection, Rommel had examined its six French 155-millimeter guns installed in open concrete emplacements. From their hill, the 155's covered a considerable portion of the Bay of the Seine, particularly the approaches to a long, pretty beach which a few men in London had named Utah Beach. The battery was an old one. Its emplacements had been completed in 1941, long before anyone had ever spoken of an Atlantic Wall. In three years it had become, so to speak, absorbed into the Normandy countryside. Brambles and bushes had sprawled over the air-raid shelters and the ammunition magazines. Grass had been planted along the paths linking the various elements, then they had been covered with latticework. When the grass had grown through the latticework, the paths had become indiscernible from the air. Above the emplacements were camouflage nets that were changed in accordance with the seasons.

That first visit to Morsalines had been a real joy to Rommel. During the first few weeks of inspecting defenses he had seen only too many batteries "camouflaged" with white netting against a background of green fields, and dummy minefields which were designed to catch the attention of enemy reconnaissance aircraft, but which the local commanders allowed cattle to graze on. So Morsalines had given Rommel every satisfaction; and he had said as much to Rear Admiral Hennecke, who was accompanying him. Hennecke's comment had been disconcerting. He had said that since the local people knew about the battery, the Allies must know about it too, and so the camouflage had no real use; it could not even prevent the battery from being spotted by enemy bombers, for the local people had undoubtedly given its position in relation to the church and the road. The six guns should therefore be placed under concrete turrets as soon as possible.

Such problems were new to Rommel, who was far more used to a war of movement. In June, 1940, the Panzer Division he commanded had advanced so swiftly that it had been nicknamed the "Phantom Division." When it went through French villages at night, the old women had cheered and cried out, "*Vive les Anglais!*" In 1942, in the empty wastes of the African desert, his duel with Montgomery had no civilian onlookers except for a few Bedouins who robbed the dead and picked up the abandoned weapons.

And although he was a remarkable warrior, Rommel had no understanding of the Norman soul. The local commanders had informed him soon after his arrival in the region that the civilians pressed into service to help build "Fortress Europe" were showing extreme inertia. Rommel issued instructions of a psychological nature which he apparently believed would lead to the work being done with enthusiasm. The instructions ended with the words: "And make them sing in chorus on their way to work." For dealing with Norman peasants, this was rather inadequate. Rommel particularly wanted the civilian population to understand that the more strongly the region was fortified the less chance there was that the horrors of war would descend upon it. This seemed to him a powerful argument, yet Rear Admiral Hennecke had assured him that the people of Morsalines had been foolish enough to send information which would sooner or later cause the battery to be bombed by enemy aircraft, whose accuracy was not always outstanding. And the village was only a few hundred yards from the battery.

Rommel had told Hennecke that putting the guns under turrets was out of the question. Skilled workmen and materials were lacking. If it ever became possible to fortify gun emplacements, a start would be made on batteries in a more exposed position than the one at Morsalines, which was so well camouflaged.

Daniel was probably driving at full speed that morning; he usually did. Admiral Friedrich Ruge's old Mercury must have been gasping for breath as it tried to keep within sight of the Horch. It is also probable that the admiral, who had been assigned to Rommel's staff, was urging his driver, Seaman Hatzinger, to keep up with the other car, and that Hatzinger replied as usual that he could catch up only on downhill stretches. Hills are rare between Saint-Lô and Morsalines.

The mist had cleared by the time they reached Morsalines and the hill overlooking the bay. The battery commander reported that the previous night enemy bombers had made a low-level attack, after dropping flares which were so bright that it had seemed like day. Two of the guns had been destroyed and all the others damaged. The shelters and magazines had not been hit, and there were no casualties.

Rommel showed no surprise. Since his first visit, six months earlier, he had had time to appreciate the work of the Resistance. He gave orders that the four damaged guns were to be moved three hundred yards inland, and were to remain in their new positions even after being repaired. It was obvious to every officer present that the guns would then be unable to fire on moving ships. But it was also certain that the R.A.F. would return, and that it was necessary to save what could be saved. In any case, only a confirmed pessimist could believe that the enemy would achieve complete surprise. Sea and air reconnaissance were bound to sight the convoys on their way across the Channel. There would be at least twenty-four hours' warning, which would give time for the guns to be brought forward to their old emplacements.

When would it be?

From the top of the Morsalines hill, now bathed in sunshine, Rommel could see the yellow sand of Utah Beach. The high rocky spur of La Pointe du Hoc hid Omaha Beach from his sight. Further on lay the beaches of Le Bessin. Rommel did not know *when* it would be, but he was convinced that this was *where* it would be. He had not always thought so. Like everyone else, he had first thought of Pas-de-Calais. After his tour of inspection he had written to Hitler on December 31, 1943:

"The center of gravity of the enemy landings will probably be the sector held by the Fifteenth Army (Pas-de-Calais) . . . It is quite likely that the enemy's main effort will be directed against the sector between Boulogne and the mouth of the Somme, and on either side of Calais, where he will derive maximum advantage from the support of his long-range guns, from the shortest crossing for the assault and later supply operations, and from the best utilization of his air power. His chief objective will almost certainly be to obtain possession as quickly as possible of ports capable of accommodating large numbers of ships. Moreover, he can be expected to try to gain rapid control of the area from which our long-range missiles (V-1 and V-2) are launched."

It was practically a repetition of von Rundstedt's "Five Commandments." Rommel had joined the chorus of generals who sheepishly bleated their strategic catechism. They would go on doing so until D-Day, and even later, like General Warlimont, who said after the war: "We generals had based our planning on the rules of our regular military training"—a peevish statement with more than a hint of a professional's disgust for an adversary who had ignored his theoretical handbooks and landed in the wrong place.

But Rommel was not very strong on theory. He was out of tune with the traditionalists on the General Staff, who in any case did not consider him their equal. In three years he had risen from the rank of colonel to the dignity of Field Marshal—a rapid promotion that carried a strong whiff of favoritism. One stood at attention before him because he had the rank, but that did not prevent one from thinking he was an upstart. There was no surprise when he tip-toed out of the "Pas-de-Calais Chorus" and began pointing to Normandy with his marshal's baton.

Rommel, the "Desert Fox," may not have been a great strategist, but he was sure of his common sense. "From the Allied point of view," he wrote, "the number one objective is to get firmly ashore . . . This is improbable on the Pas-de-Calais coast, which is strongly defended, but possible on the Normandy coast, which is barely fortified."

So it was to be Normandy. Before leaving his own head-quarters at La Roche-Guyon the previous day, Rommel had written in his diary: "Tour of inspection in the Cotentin peninsula, which would seem to be the main objective of an enemy invasion." Since the beginning of the month he had been moving to the Normandy coast all the units that von Rundstedt left under his orders. He had asked Goering for the 3rd Antiaircraft Corps, which was scattered all over France. Its twenty-four batteries, all equipped with the most modern guns, would make an airborne assault on the Cotentin peninsula either disastrous or impossible. He also requested the transfer of the Panzer Lehr Division from Le Mans to Bayeux. Two days later, on May 12, he was to ask for the 12th S.S. Armored Division, the Hitler Jugend, to be moved up from Lisieux to Carentan, which would put it only half an hour from Utah Beach, and an hour from Omaha. The Panzer Lehr would also cover Omaha Beach and would be within close range of the beaches where the Canadians were to land. The 21st Panzer Division was already at Caen, half an hour away from the beaches where the British were to land.

Rommel obviously did not know to what extent his beliefs would be confirmed by events, but so strong was his conviction that this part of Normandy had been chosen by the Allies that he was determined to have his way. If the High Command showed reluctance he would appeal to the Führer himself.

With three armored divisions lined up along the coast, and twenty-four antiaircraft batteries in the Cotentin peninsula, he would be able to defend the whole area that lay before his eyes. But would he have time to put his plans into effect? When would this gray, smooth sea be covered with enemy ships? When should the Morsalines battery be moved back to its original position, and when should the Tiger tanks go rumbling towards the beaches? Berlin had been announcing ever since April that the invasion would be on the following night. The troops had been put on the alert so often that it had lost all meaning. It was almost permanent, with the unfortunate result that the men were no longer on their toes. After so many false alarms they felt safe again; when the attack did come, they would not react quickly or energetically enough.

Rommel was convinced he knew "where"; he only wished someone would tell him "when."

Rommel continued northward from Morsalines, and at one o'clock he stopped for lunch at Saint-Pierre-Église, a small town that straggles along the main road east of Cherbourg. During the meal he and his staff listened to the B.B.C.'s German service. This was not bravado or for a laugh, but was an old habit that had sprung from a real desire for information. Ever since Hitler had issued his "Order of Principle No. 1" on January 13, 1940, German staff officers had taken to listening to enemy and neutral radio stations.

On that January 13, Hitler had flown into a justified rage, caused by an incident that had occurred three days earlier. On his way to Cologne, a Luftwaffe staff officer, Major Helmut Reinberger, had stopped at Münster to see some friends who were with Fourth Army headquarters. The party went on for so long that Reinberger missed the train to Cologne, so he was taken by plane; but the pilot encountered fog, lost his bearings, and when he was almost out of gas he made a forced landing near Mechelen-sur-Meuse—in Belgium. The "phony war" was still on and Belgium was neutral. But in Major Reinberger's briefcase were papers putting an end to that neutrality: the plans of the German offensive, and marked maps. At the time, the Germans had not yet decided on a thrust into the Ardennes. The attack was scheduled for January 17, in a week's time—through Belgium, as in 1914. Reinberger, panic-stricken, got behind a hedge and began trying to burn the documents. A Belgian patrol came galloping up, and a quick-witted soldier snatched the documents from Reinberger. They were damp and had only smoldered. The Germans were taken to the nearest military post, where the bundle of charred documents was handed to an officer. Reinberger grabbed them and threw them in the stove, but the officer managed to get them out in time.

The problem for the German General Staff was: were the documents still readable? Inquiries led to the conclusion that they were not. But the Belgians called up their reserves and began massing troops along the border. And the Belgian Foreign Minister summoned the German ambassador and asked for an explanation of "this grave and extraordinary document which contains proof of aggressive intentions."

Hitler called off the attack planned for the seventeenth and issued his "Order of Principle No. 1." In the future, no German officer was to have any knowledge of an operation in which he was not directly concerned. Luftwaffe majors would no longer be allowed to carry around the complete plans of a great offensive. Hitler was thinking of military security at that time, and he was right. Four years later, when he had his "Principle No. 1" applied with the utmost strictness, he was thinking politically, and he was again right. It was not enough for him to become deaf and blind; the German people, especially the officers, must be prevented from seeing and hearing too well, otherwise they would start dreaming of white flags. They were given blinkers and earplugs. They were to see only the enemy directly opposed to them, and were not to hear the ominous din of enemy forces assailing the Germans elsewhere.

It was a simple policy, and largely effective. When the news of the July Plot reached General Alfred Schlemm he was most indignant. How dare they! What criminals! And fools too—trying to assassinate the Führer just when Germany was winning the war! General Schlemm, who commanded the First Parachute Army, saw the military situation through Goebbels's eyes: the Russians were near the end of their rope; the English and Americans were being bled white in Normandy, and Kesselring was holding them in check in Italy; Germany had masses of divisions in reserve, which would be thrown into the battle at any moment and bring final victory.

In practice, Hitler's "Principle No. 1" had its drawbacks. Since the Wehrmacht was not informed in advance of the Luftwaffe's tactical operations, it sometimes happened that German aircraft were shot down by German gunners. Divisional commanders attacked without knowledge of the movements being carried out on their flanks, which led to disastrous mixups. Orders had to be rigidly adhered to; if plans were upset by enemy tactics, as is not unknown in war, unit commanders were unable to adapt themselves to the changed situation, for they had no overall view of the operation in which they were involved.

At the highest level, von Rundstedt, who had a quarter of the whole German army under his command, did not know how many divisions were fighting on the Russian front, nor did he know the strength of Kesselring's forces in Italy; he was unaware of what reserves he could count upon if needed, or even if any existed. He learned about the war on other fronts only by listening to foreign broadcasts and talking with officers who had served in other commands. It was the same with Rommel, whose chief of staff, Major General Hans Speidel, wrote: "Military as well as political information had to be obtained by roundabout means. Rommel was not officially kept informed of the evolution of operations in Italy and in the east. It was only through 'good relations' that he was able to keep himself informed."

Or through the B.B.C.'s foreign-language broadcasts, as at Saint-Pierre-Église . . .

On that May 10, after reading a summary of the news, which ended with a report on the bombing of the Morsalines battery, the B.B.C. announcer added ironically, "Well, Herr Rommel, you've finally managed to discover your battery at Morsalines—the one you didn't see on your last inspection trip because it was so well camouflaged!"

It was amazing; it was even diabolical, for the visit to Morsalines had been included in the busy day's schedule only at the last minute. Rommel had planned to go to Cherbourg, but the previous evening he had been told that the B.B.C.'s German service had just announced that he would be inspecting the troops at Cherbourg the next day. So the schedule had been changed, with Morsalines being substituted for Cherbourg. The B.B.C.'s German service had many listeners among the troops, and here was a chance to demonstrate its inaccuracy. But the trick had not come off. Rommel had listened to the enemy broadcast to find out how the war was going in Russia and the Pacific, and had learned that the enemy knew he had been in Morsalines three hours earlier. It was humiliating—and alarming.

In the afternoon Rommel inspected batteries at the Cap

de La Hague and along the west coast of the peninsula. He found everything in good order, and that his anti-invasion obstacles were being erected on the beaches at a satisfactory rate. As was his custom, he distributed accordions to the units who had made the best progress. He always took a number with him, piled on the back seat of the Horch, when he went on a tour of inspection. The soldiers who received these instruments did not always know how to play them, but coming from the famous field marshal the gesture mattered more than the gift, for he was almost as popular with German troops as he was with British troops. The latter regarded him as the most formidable military leader they had had to face since Napoleon. And in Germany Goebbels's propaganda had trumpeted his glory on the radio and in the press until he had become the Third Reich's most illustrious soldier. He had already decided to lend his prestige to the plot that was to culminate in the attempt to assassinate Hitler on July 20. He knew all about it. And on his way back to Saint-Lô he passed through the area in which the 6th Parachute Regiment was stationed, between Lessay and Périers, at the base of the peninsula. Its commander, Lieutenant Colonel von der Heydte, had fought under Rommel in North Africa. With his paratroopers, he had covered the Afrika Korps' long retreat from El Alamein to Tunisia. Rommel knew he could count on him and on his unit. Von der Heydte was in the plot too. His men were as loyal to him as a clan to its chief.

But although Rommel had become anti-Hitler he still remained intensely patriotic. When the Führer had been eliminated, negotiations could be opened with the Western Allies; and in order to obtain honorable peace conditions the best means was to break up their attack on the Normandy beaches.

There was a message waiting for Rommel at Saint-Lô. It had been sent by the supreme command of the Wehrmacht, the O.K.W.:

"1. The O.K.W. anticipates the enemy attack for the middle of May. The eighteenth seems highly probable, although there is, of course, no sure indication. Main effort in Normandy, with secondary attack in Brittany.

"It is thought that the enemy will attack land targets with very heavy bombs, concentrating on small areas, and will try to silence coastal defenses in the same way, combined with heavy naval bombardment and attacks from the sea. The use of new weapons cannot be excluded. Large-scale parachute drops may be made after nightfall.

"2. Units should be dispersed and camouflaged with great care, and everything not protected by concrete should be dug in. Inside the Cotentin peninsula, troops must be particularly on the alert against airborne landings. Keep a watch on the skies!"

The O.K.W. has based this message on reports received from the naval high command, which gave May 18 as the "certain date" of the invasion.

This date was too early for Rommel. He had not completed his defensive measures. More than half a million of his lethal underwater obstacles stretched along the coastline, but he wanted as many again. There were five million mines of all kinds infesting the coast, but he wanted twenty million planted before the attack came. He was being deprived of time, but in return he had been given the date of the attack. The exchange might work to his advantage. He would speed up the work, put the troops on the alert. The date was "highly probable" according to the army high command, "certain" according to the navy. May 18.

## 22. The Lull

ON the morning of May 18, the German radio's first news broadcast announced that the invasion might come at any moment.

That same morning, Londoners read in their newspapers that the hospitals were sending home all patients except the critically ill. The beds had to be available. The papers also announced that when the invasion began all laundries would have to give priority to hospital linen.

The most significant event of the day occurred at Eisenhower's headquarters. He met a five-man delegation of American war correspondents and heard from them that some British and American journalists believed there would be no invasion and that all the preparations were part of a gigantic bluff.

The journalists were mistaken, as sometimes happens, but as always they were correctly conveying the mood of public opinion. The feverish excitement of the first two weeks in May had died down. It had reached its peak with Exercise FABIUS, a rehearsal for the attack on Omaha Beach. The worst had been feared, for the convoys of landing craft had to go well out to sea and presented an easy target for enemy torpedo boats. On the other hand, it was hoped that the enemy would sight the large force being employed and so believe that the great day had arrived. If he took any action it would reveal something of his intentions on the real day. But except for one soldier collapsing with pneumonia and an officer being accidentally shot in the behind, everything went smoothly. The absence of enemy reaction was, to some optimists, proof of his blindness, but most observers felt that he had been perfectly informed and had not wanted to show his hand over a mere exercise.

Then the British carried out their rehearsal. The only odd thing about it passed unnoticed: the presence among Montgomery's staff of an English sergeant who watched his every move with extraordinary attention.

When the exercises were over the troops went into their barbed-wire assembly areas. Their activity was followed by a period of inaction and uncertainty. D-Day was drawing near, obviously, but just how near no one knew. They were all sure of one thing: the sooner the better. Get it over with . . .

The American troops were ordered to send home all their personal belongings, at government expense. They kept only their combat equipment. Their mail to the States was held back in Britain, and they were forbidden to cable or telephone across the Atlantic. The British troops had their letters rigorously censored. The waiting troops were hemmed in by barbed wire, barriers, patrols and prohibitions. There was doubt and anxiety everywhere. After months of frenzied activity, England was sinking into lethargy.

It was, of course, only the calm before the storm. On May 8—two days before Rommel was informed by the O.K.W. that the invasion would probably begin on May 18—

Eisenhower had decided to attack on Y plus 4, that is, June 5. The chips were down.

Across the Channel, in pillboxes along the Wall, at Rommel's headquarters and in von Rundstedt's underground bunker, the nervous tension had almost reached the breaking point by May 18. Since April the Germans had been like sprinters waiting for the starter's gun. A dozen times they had thought they heard it, and each time they had made a false start. The one on May 18 had drained away what little nervous energy they had left. After that, forecasts about the invasion suddenly became reassuring, as though from an unconscious reaction. The navy announced that no attempt was to be feared before August: the weather and tide experts guaranteed it. The O.K.W. now maintained that before making their landing the western Allies would surely wait for the Russian offensive, which would give them powerful indirect support; and since the thaw in the east had come much later than usual, the Russians would not move before the end of June.

There were, then, some German leaders who thought the invasion would not come any time soon. There were others—and they were increasingly numerous—who thought it would not come at all. Admiral Kranke, for example, commander of the western naval forces, and General Günther Blumentritt, von Rundstedt's jovial chief of staff. They had not always thought so, but the successive false alarms had finally convinced them that the enemy was bluffing. The Allies were afraid of the Wall. They were waiting for the Red Army to drain the lifeblood from the Wehrmacht before they set a hesitant foot on the Continent. Their simulated preparations were part of a vast deception plan to keep the enemy in a constant state of alert.

But more convincing than any line of reasoning was the beautiful weather that flooded the coast with sunshine and made the channel as smooth as a lake. Staff officers and soldiers alike had the feeling that the Allies had missed their chance. May was the time when they ought to invade. This was an absurd idea: if Eisenhower had decided to attack in June or July, he was not going to change his plans because the sky was blue. The invasion of a continent cannot be set forward like a picnic. But the Germans were so tense that they could no longer think clearly. Wearied by all their waiting in vain, they imagined the same weariness in the enemy. They thought, consciously or not, that each of their false alarms was matched by a false start on the part of the Allies. Having arrived too early at the rendezvous, they finally convinced themselves that the enemy would never turn up.

And so, on both sides of the Channel, the mounting drama had been abruptly interrupted by a lull. In England, there had been the final exercises; in Normandy, the bringing up of reinforcements. As the Germans had groped their way toward the truth, the Allies had become increasingly anxious. Then suddenly there was a dead calm. For the Allies, the time of preparation was over. They had nothing to do but wait for D-Day and the green light from Eisenhower. For the Germans, the shifting around of divisions had ceased. Rommel was waiting for a reply to his requests.

The intermission was to last two weeks.

Like clowns entering the circus ring between acts, the men of FORTITUDE came on the scene. . . .

## 23. The Big Bluff

THE German reconnaissance plane had been picked up by radar even before it was over the Channel. It was headed for southeastern England. When the R.A.F. and the coastal antiaircraft batteries had been notified, the approach of the solitary aircraft was followed on the screens with almost loving care. Goering's pilots, hunted down by Allied squadrons, were showing great reluctance to fly over England. At night, the risk was acceptable. By day, it was almost suicidal.

This pilot was a brave one. Alone in the blue of the enemy sky, he continued his course towards the Kent coast with no regard for danger. Unlike many of his colleagues, he did not turn back, preparing a story of massive enemy reaction to justify the failure of his mission. He flew over Dover, which is directly opposite Pas-de-Calais. He had surely turned on his automatic cameras. He was undoubtedly pleased by the absence of Allied fighters, and was probably surprised by the remarkably inaccurate fire of the antiaircraft guns: their shells were bursting several hundred feet too low. Finally he turned back, still followed affectionately on the radar screens.

The Allies would have liked to see many more German reconnaissance pilots as brave as that one. He was going back to the Continent with photographs of a concentration of landing craft in Dover harbor. When German naval experts examined those pictures they would realize that Normandy was too far away for such craft, so that they must be intended for landings on the coast of Pas-de-Calais. It was precisely to make the Germans draw this conclusion that the landing craft had been brought to Dover, and the R.A.F. had been ordered not to intercept the reconnaissance plane, and the antiaircraft gunners had been told to shoot too low.

Landing craft had only to be moored, but with armored divisions it was another story. There were dozens of men keeping up a shuttle service from one part of the southeast to another. They arrived at night in their trucks and unloaded their equipment: piles and piles of folded rubber. These were pumped up, and became tanks, guns and half-tracks. They were left camouflaged on the edge of a forest, but not too well camouflaged. The last job was to leave tank tracks leading to the forest, and the men had special machines for the purpose. So when dawn came, there was an armored division opposite Pas-de-Calais, all ready to be sighted by a German reconnaissance plane. When the pilot had taken his pictures, the equipment was packed up and taken somewhere else.

There was another team whose job was to strew fields with hundreds of dummy gliders, and another that built plywood piers along the coast. Some of the engineers had become experts at giving the impression that a forest was crammed with war materiel: all they needed was a few trucks to make tracks in the surrounding fields.

Thanks to the efforts of these men, German pilots who were bold enough to fly over southeastern England were rewarded by the sight of a real fairytale landscape.

On the other hand, the bombs that were dropped on Pas-de-Calais were quite real. For every bomb on Normandy, two were dropped on Pas-de-Calais. This rule was strictly adhered to, despite the Allies' understandable temptation to concentrate their whole bombing strength on the selected invasion zones. If the Germans were keeping count of the bombs falling on them, in order to deduce which was the most threatened sector, the column for Pas-de-Calais was twice as long as the one for Normandy. This was what the Allies wanted.

The planners of Operation FORTITUDE had not waited until mid-May to use these stratagems. The traveling exhibition of rubber armored divisions had been touring the southeast since April. Allied bombers had obeyed the two-to-one rule from the beginning of the air offensive. Hitler and Rommel had not been deterred from sending reinforcements to Normandy, but the program was continued nevertheless. And rightly so, for the seeds of doubt are sometimes slow in germinating. It was only when a group of English communications specialists had begun to despair of success that their efforts were rewarded. They had set up a fake headquarters in Kent, opposite Pas-de-Calais, from which Montgomery was supposed to be directing his army group. His real headquarters was in Portsmouth, opposite Normandy. His messages were *telephoned* to the fake headquarters, so that they could not be picked up by the enemy, then were relayed to their destinations by *radio*, for the benefit of the German interception stations. On May 21, two weeks before D-Day, Rommel noted in his Diary: "The locating of Montgomery's headquarters south of London confirms that the center of gravity of the Allied forces is in southern and southeastern England." This was the first breach opened in Rommel's Norman convictions. It was a sizable one. Montgomery was the best English general, the man who had defeated the Afrika Korps; "my personal enemy," Rommel called him. If he was preparing to direct the invasion from southeastern England, it was improbable that Normandy was his objective. Rommel's interest in Pas-de-Calais increased sharply.

Bernard Montgomery wore thick-soled shoes in order to appear taller. He insisted on sporting a beret, although he had twice been ordered not to wear it because it did not befit his rank. He neither smoked nor drank. He read the Bible regularly. At the beginning of his staff conferences he gave his officers two minutes in which they could cough; after that, no coughing was allowed, except during very occasional one-minute breaks. Every week his troops, generals included, had to do a seven-mile cross-country run. He went to bed early; once when Churchill called him and asked him to come to Downing Street at midnight he had replied: "I can't, sir. I shall be in bed then." Montgomery was not exactly an accommodating man. But he agreed to something that the German generals, wrapped in their dignity, would have scornfully refused to do: he cooperated with FORTITUDE's team of clowns.

One day near the end of May a large official car passed through London on its way to Northolt airport. Each time it was stopped by a traffic light a small crowd gathered and shouted "Good old Monty!" In the car, Clifton James responded with the "Monty smile" and the "Monty salute." He was almost numb with stage-fright. Before the war he had been an actor with touring companies; he was now playing the part of a lifetime. His audience, indirectly, was the German Supreme Command. And he had been chosen because of his striking resemblance to Montgomery, except for a missing finger. But the fact that James had lost the middle finger of his right hand in the First World War presented no problem to the planners of FORTITUDE: a finger is easier to counterfeit than an armored division.

James had been recruited only three weeks earlier. He was strictly forbidden to say anything about his assignment to anyone, even his wife, to go to bars any oftener than necessary, or to write to his friends; he was even urged not to talk in his sleep. By accompanying Montgomery's staff on exercises he was able to study his model at close quarters. He noted Montgomery's stiff bearing, his habit of clasping his hands behind his back, the imperious way he held his head, the gesture he often made with his right hand—as though he were weighing an invisible object—during a discussion, and his tendency to pinch his left cheek between his thumb and forefinger. James then had many long conversations with Montgomery, carefully familiarizing himself with the nasal tone of his voice and his way of selecting his words with the greatest care, as though the fate of the world depended on his choice of an adjective. Finally came the dress rehearsal, when James addressed a small gathering of senior intelligence officers in Monty's crisp, man-to-man style.

Now he had made his entrance and the performance had begun; he was on his way to Northolt. In his pocket was a Bible (Montgomery always carried one) and he had a dozen handkerchiefs with the initials "B. M." which he would scatter in the course of his travels. Even the financial side was not overlooked: Clifton James was to receive a general's pay as long as he was wearing a general's uniform. He was about to fly to Gibraltar, where he would be received with the honors due to his rank. He would be driven to Government House—in an open car, so that the German agents who were swarming at Gibraltar, mingled with the Spanish workmen, could have a good look at him. The Governor, Sir Ralph Eastwood, had been at Sandhurst with Montgomery and was in on the secret. He would be on the steps to welcome James; the dialogue had been arranged beforehand: "Hullo, Monty, it's good to see you again!" "How are you, Rusty? You're looking very fit!" There was a manservant at Government House who had been Montgomery's batman for some years; he was sent away on some pretext or other—much to his annoyance. On the other hand, an "unexpected and unfortunate" encounter had been prearranged in the gardens between Montgomery's impersonator and two Spanish notables who were known to be in contact with the German secret service. They would hear James speak of a mysterious "Plan 303" and the French Mediterranean coast. The Germans might or might not believe in "Plan 303"; they might or might not come to the conclusion that Montgomery was taking command of the army believed to be preparing to land in the south of France. But they would have to accept eyewitness reports that General Montgomery was at Gibraltar in late May, and that he had left there by plane for Algiers.

If Montgomery was making a tour of Africa, the assault across the Channel could not be scheduled for the immediate future.

There were several aspects to the bluff. First, the date. Thanks to Clifton James, among others, the war of nerves continued. Then the place. The transformation of southeastern England into a false base for an attack on Pas-de-

Calais had a less obvious effect. But even if the Germans were not convinced *before D-Day* that the invasion would be in Pas-de-Calais, they might believe *after D-Day* that the Normandy landings were only a diversion and that the main attack was still to come where von Rundstedt expected it. If that part of the great bluff succeeded, the fifteen German divisions in Pas-de-Calais would go on waiting for an attack that would never come, instead of heading for the Normandy beaches. To achieve this important result, the men of FORTI-TUDE used what was, next to rubber, their favorite material: a general.

If anyone had told General Patton that he was as fiery as Murat, as brave as Ney and as wily as Davout, he would have been furious: he thought of himself as another Napoleon. Tall, athletic and admirably dressed, Patton was the star of the American army. He caused a sensation at the English court when he arrived with two pearl-handled pistols slapping his hips. His men had for him the kind of hate-tinged devotion that they could be expected to have for a commander who led them to victory but made them wear ties even in combat zones. The anger of American mothers had fallen on him when he slapped a young G.I. in a hospital in Sicily. The boy was suffering from shellshock but Patton felt that this was insufficient reason for giving up the joys of combat. The shrieks of protest from the home front rose so high that they almost reached Patton's stars. Eisenhower barely managed to save him. He made him apologize publicly to the slapped soldier, the hospital staff and the men of his division, then he took him to England with him, no doubt remembering, as a staff officer once commented, that "Patton pays off in ground gains as well as in occasional headaches." Patton promised to hold his tongue; he had felt the chill breath of dismissal on his cheek. But his urge to talk was as irrepressible as his urge to fight. He began by saying, with haughty disdain for politics: "Well, I'll tell you. This Nazi thing. It's like a Democratic-Republican election fight." There was an uproar in the press. His next public announcement was that after the war the world must be ruled, for its own good, by the United States and Britain. This greatly annoyed Stalin, and probably Charles de Gaulle. There was another storm. Eisenhower saved him from hell again, but this time he put him in purgatory. He was given command not of the American First Army, which was to attack in Normandy, but of the Third, which would not see action until the end of July. Eisenhower made this decision not so much to chastise Patton as to make best use of his talents. Patton's specialty was the swift advance. He would not be let loose on the Germans until the Allies had built up enough strength on the beachhead to crack the enemy's lines. Once the breakthrough had been made, the Third Army would plunge into the breach and gallop all the way to the Rhine.

It was a bitter blow for Patton, but fortunate for the FORTITUDE planners. The Third Army had not yet been formed, but it was given an artificial existence through the radio signals from a fake headquarters opposite Pas-de-Calais. The Germans picked them up, and learned that Patton was in command of the Third Army. To them, he was the American equivalent of Montgomery. He had driven them out of Sicily. They feared him like the plague. They would probably assume that Eisenhower had given the most important task to the Third Army rather than to Bradley's First Army. Tall and thin, with a sad face and steel-rimmed glasses, Omar Bradley looked like a morose preacher. When he spoke to journalists in his flat voice he seemed to imply that they should take his opinion only for what it was worth. The one eccentric thing about him was his first name (his mother, with surprising foresight, had chosen it to be original). He was a steadfast, upright man, who reread his favorite book, *Ivanhoe,* every year. He was also a great general, but he had not yet proved it. In May, 1944, he could not be compared with the flamboyant Patton. Furthermore, he was younger than Patton and had served under him in Sicily only a few months earlier. When the invasion began, therefore, the Germans should logically conclude that Bradley's First Army was only making a diversionary attack in Normandy while Patton was waiting to strike the main blow in Pas-de-Calais.

At least, that was the fervent wish of the FORTITUDE planners. If it was granted, the tribulations of the "cowboy general," as Hitler called Patton, would have paid high dividends. Meanwhile, for the man who always wanted to "take on the champion" it was an almost unbearable torment to play the dummy part that had been assigned to him. General Patton was FORTITUDE's most illustrious martyr.

## 24. Deceit and Sacrifice

THERE were martyrs more to be pitied. In his memoirs, published six years after the end of the war, Churchill wrote: "It would not be proper even now to describe all the methods employed to mislead the enemy." He set the tone in this matter, and was followed by most of the Allied commanders in their writings. Questioned twenty years later, they are quite willing to help in matters like finding the number of the first tank that landed on Omaha Beach and the ages of its crew, but they close up like clams when they are asked about Operation FORTITUDE. The men who directed the secret warfare on the Allied side are equally willing to enlarge on subjects like the rubber divisions or Montgomery's double, but although they admit there were other things, they refuse to be diverted from their inoffensive themes.

Twenty years after the event, "it would not be proper even now to describe all the methods employed to mislead the enemy." The mystery of FORTITUDE remains. But there is nothing to prevent one from trying to probe it . . .

Can it be that the Allies had an agent within Hitler's staff and that those who knew about it still want to protect him or his memory? Extremely unlikely. Hitler listened to no one. The most important members of his military entourage, Keitel and Jodl, were reduced to the positions of lackeys. None of the Nazi leaders had the power to influence him.

Technical stratagems analogous to the dummy divisions? Clever tricks that are being kept secret in case they should be needed later? Nuclear war would give no chance to use them.

"It would not be proper even now . . ." It is not to safeguard the future that FORTITUDE still remains veiled in secrecy—it is to give time for the past to be covered over with a crust of forgetfulness and become a dead thing that historians can harmlessly dissect.

If we want to discover the ultimate secret of FORTITUDE, perhaps we should begin by cutting into the scars left by operations NORTH POLE and STARKEY.

NORTH POLE first, with the Dutch parachutists whom the clever Giskes caught as soon as they landed, the transmitters he used for sending false information to London, the thousands of weapons that piled up in his storerooms. It was a remarkable success. But for whom, the Germans or the Allies? At the end of the war, three of the captured agents were still alive. All the others had been executed in Germany. One of the survivors was Hubert Lauwers, the radio operator whose capture enabled Giskes to establish radio communication with London for the first time and set up his operation. When he was accused of treason by the Dutch after the war, Lauwers talked.

He admitted giving Giskes his code; but at that time every radio operator dropped into occupied Europe was authorized to divulge his code if necessary: London recognized that otherwise it would be dragged out of him by torture. But radio operators were under orders to preserve the secret of their "security check" at all cost. This was a prearranged, deliberate mistake (an unnecessary letter, for instance) or a key sentence which had to appear in every message; its absence was an indication that the operator had been captured and was transmitting under duress. Lauwers had given Giskes a false security check. He assumed this would prevent London from falling into the German trap. But to his dismay London accepted his messages as genuine and replied by announcing the dispatch of more agents. Had there been a lack of attention? It was hardly likely, since each message was taken down by two operators working independently. Still, it was possible, for the men were overworked and not all were experienced. Lauwers thought of another way to warn London: by a clever combination of letters he succeeded in inserting the word "prisoner" into a message. London continued sending agents and weapons. Lauwers then got the word "prisoner" into a message three times. London asked him to repeat the text, and replied "Understood." Lauwers was exultant. But more agents were dropped into the waiting arms of the Germans. In prison he met another radio operator whose story was even more astounding: Giskes had used his code without giving the security check, and London had pointed out the omission, telling the agent to include it in the future!

Lauwers was by now convinced that it was all a put-up job by the Allies. For some reason unknown to him, it had been decided to deliver into enemy hands the men sent to carry out Operation HOLLAND. However, just in case, he managed to get through another warning, slipping into a message—under the eyes of the German experts at his side— a whole sentence: "Fooled by Jerries since 6 March." London took no notice.

Lauwers's revelations after the war caused an understandable outcry in Holland. A parliamentary committee made a two-year investigation. It asked the British government for an explanation, and the Foreign Office issued a statement: the absence of the security checks had not been noticed at first, then it had been decided not to take account of their omission. Why? Because agents quite frequently forgot to insert their security check, so it did not constitute a real test. A strange explanation! The system of security checks was the only means of knowing whether or not an agent had been "doubled" by the enemy, and the British kept trying to improve it all through the war. Nevertheless, the Foreign Office statement concluded solemnly: "The suggestion that the lives of Dutch patriots were deliberately sacrificed in the interests of other objectives, in the Netherlands or elsewhere, is both repugnant to His Majesty's Government and the British people." To the British government and the people? No doubt. But to the secret services? It is in the nature of the secret services of all countries to employ repugnant methods.

There is no real evidence to invalidate the statement of the Foreign Office. The fact that documents relating to Operation HOLLAND captured by the Germans indicated that the invasion was to take place on the Dutch coast may have been a pure accident. That Giskes and his organization were led to believe for eighteen months that the Allied invasion fleet would appear off the Dutch coast may have been a mere coincidence. The unexpected escape of the three Dutch prisoners, which caused the operation to come to an end, may have prevented Giskes's belief from turning into a certainty through the capture of more documents sent by London —and that would have been another fortunate accident.

So too much attention should not be paid to the stories still heard in Dutch Resistance circles twenty years afterwards. Stories like the one about the cyanide tablets that were given to the agents parachuted into Holland, in case they were captured. In many cases, it is said, the tablets were harmless pills, as though the Allies were making sure that the captured agents would tell the enemy what they wanted him to hear.

The doubts about Operation HOLLAND still in the minds of Dutch ex-Resistance men spring from a series of fortuitous circumstances. There was the matter of the security checks, to begin with; and the fact that the British deliberately ignored warnings sent by the Resistance members who had heard of the capture of several parachuted agents (one message even gave the names, and London ordered Resistance groups to break off all contact with the man who had sent it); the fact that the British, after being warned by the omission of security checks and by the Resistance, did not send over agents with the mission of clearing the matter up; the fact that they did not take this elementary precaution even when two of Giskes's prisoners escaped several months before the other three (the two managed to reach London to give the alarm, but they were imprisoned as soon as they arrived: Giskes had sent a message saying that the story of their escape was false and that they were working for the Abwehr); the fact that the British paid no heed to the pleas of Dutch intelligence officers, who were understandably worried; the fact that they never asked for the return to London of a single one of the fifty-three agents dropped into Holland—a circumstance that is probably unique in the annals of war; and finally the fact that they had set up a parallel Resistance group in Holland at the same time they were parachuting the fifty-three agents.

Such are the circumstances that explain the attitude of the Dutch. The Van der Waals affair may also explain it to some extent. Van der Waals was a traitor who had been of great use to the Germans in their fight against the Dutch Resistance. The Dutch police began searching for him at the end of the war, and eventually discovered that he was spying for the British in the Russian zone of occupied Germany. It took the intervention of the Dutch government to obtain his extradition. When the British finally handed him over he confirmed that the object of Operation NORTH POLE had been to deceive the Germans.

It had been planned and carried out by the Special Operations Executive. "The old firm," as it was called, was not an intelligence service. Its job was to organize sabotage and guerilla warfare in the occupied countries. Its headquarters was in London, in two buildings on Baker Street. But one last fortuitous circumstance has made it forever impossible to look for the truth about NORTH POLE in the files of the S.O.E.: all its records were burned at the end of the war, by order of high authority.

They might also have revealed the truth about the Resistance group *Robin.* Its leader, "Robin," was—and is— Swiss, Jewish and very rich.* In 1940, the second of these characteristics made him give up the security afforded by the first. He placed his courage, intelligence, contacts and wealth at the service of the Allies. He set up an active and reliable Resistance group in France, and financed it with his own money. In October, 1942, the British asked him to work for the S.O.E. and organize sabotage and guerilla groups. He hesitated. It was explained to him that the time was approaching when the fight against the Germans would have to be brought out into the open. He finally agreed, and the S.O.E. placed him in a network which covered a quarter of France, *Prosper,* led by the British major with that code name who had parachuted into France on October 1, 1942.

Early in 1943 Robin was told to step up his preparations: the invasion was going to take place that summer. He obeyed. In the following months, many warnings were received from London: D-Day was drawing near. But Robin's group was struck down at the height of its activity: nearly all its leaders fell into the hands of the Germans. Soon afterward, the whole *Prosper* network collapsed. The men were arrested by the hundreds, and their weapons were seized. Robin, however, escaped. He tried to build up his group again. But the Germans always seemed to know what he was doing; they thwarted all his attempts and continued to strike with unerring accuracy. Strangely unerring. One of the radio operators, an Englishman with the code name "Archambaud,"

---

* He has asked the author not to reveal his real name.

had been arrested. Maybe the Germans had "doubled" him. Robin warned London several times, through his own radio operator, that messages sent by Archambaud should be considered suspect. But disasters continued. Finally, Robin was ordered to abandon what was left of his group and flee to Switzerland, which he did.

He knew he had been betrayed. It was not unusual in underground warfare. But this time the Germans had known so much that he was convinced they could have learned it only from London. This might have been only the reaction of an embittered, hunted man. But Prosper, a major in the British army, who later died at the same time as Admiral Canaris, hanged from the same gallows in the Flössenburg camp, had expressed the same belief. And now that the dangers are gone and resentment has died down, nearly all the survivors of his organization still believe it today.

Archambaud had revealed his code to the Germans, as he was permitted to do. When questioned about his security check, he gave only half of the sentence, believing that London would thus be warned. But when he sent his first message under duress, London pointed out that he had omitted part of his security check . . . Although twice warned by Robin that Archambaud had been captured, London continued communicating with him and sending him information . . . Then an S.O.E. officer who had been dropped into France many months previously also informed London that some radio operators had been captured. He was told to mind his own business.

The captured members of the *Robin* group undoubtedly refused to talk when interrogated, and some may have continued to hold out under torture. They did not know that their courage was unnecessary, that it was quite permissible for them to reveal to the Germans that the invasion was going to take place within a few weeks. Those who did eventually tell what they knew were probably in despair at the thought that by weakening they were indirectly contributing to an Allied defeat. How could they have known that, instead, they were contributing to a victory on the part of Allied intelligence? The Allies had never planned to invade France in the summer of 1943. They only wanted to convince the enemy they were going to, and they succeeded. A vast campaign of deception, of which the sacrifice of the *Robin* group was only part, made the Germans leave divisions in France which could have been sent to reinforce their armies in the Mediterranean battle zones. This campaign was spread over a period of six months, and ended on September 8, 1943—the day before the Salerno landings in Italy—with Exercise STARKEY, which put all the German headquarters in the west on the alert. On that day, Luftwaffe reconnaissance planes reported that the roads of southern England were jammed with enormous army convoys, and that tens of thousands of troops were boarding landing craft in the ports; then, after nightfall, German radar picked up great air activity over the Channel. While von Rundstedt was expecting an assault on the beaches of Pas-de-Calais, Eisenhower was landing on the Italian coast.

Frédéric Léon Donet had begun the First World War as a sergeant and ended it a major. In those four years he had picked up four wounds and ten repetitiously worded citations: "outstanding courage," "a model of courage," "magnificent contempt for danger," "splendid courage." With his heavy mustache, bright eyes and deep, rugged voice, he might have stepped straight from an album of war heroes. He was the perfect example of the tough French sergeant who leaves the trenches with a handful of men and comes back with a machine gun and sixty prisoners. In the Second World War, as a lieutenant colonel, he acquired a bullet in the head and two more citations. The fall of France did not put an end to his war against the Germans: he joined the Resistance and became second-in-command of the *Mithridate* group. Thanks to their double agents, the Germans were aware of his importance and knew his pseudonym— Laflèche—but had not yet been able to capture him.

In April, 1944, the chief of *Mithridate*, Lieutenant Colonel Bressac, returned to France from London with an important mission for Donet. British technicians had perfected a new transmitter and were giving one to *Mithridate*. It was called "Ayesha," and would make it possible to communicate with London by voice, rather than in Morse code. From a security viewpoint it was a revolutionary development: the technicians guaranteed that it could not be picked up by enemy monitors. Thanks to this treasure, there would be an end to hastily tapping out messages reduced to the bare minimum so that the operator could finish before a German radio-detection unit arrived. Resistance groups had lost many of their members because their radio operators had been captured in this way. The use of Ayesha would eliminate this danger.

Donet was told to try out the transmitter. However, its inventors had said its range was limited; it had to be used within a hundred and fifty miles of London, and on level ground near the coast. This amounted to saying that it had to be used in Pas-de-Calais. *Mithridate* had no agent there who was able to keep Ayesha hidden away, so Donet got in touch with an old friend from the First World War, Michel Stoven, who lived at Renescure, near Saint-Omer. Stoven agreed to help, and on April 20 perfect communication was established with London. A month later, on May 19—two weeks before D-Day—Donet returned to Renescure to send his first batch of messages. There was a grand total of two hundred and fifty, including Donet's military record (he had been promoted to full colonel by the Free French, who wanted all his particulars) and an affectionate word for his son, who was serving with de Gaulle. After all, why restrict oneself when a wonderful instrument like Ayesha is available?

As Donet was trying to make contact with London, a group of German soldiers with submachine guns burst into the room.

During the next few days Donet was questioned by senior officers of German counterespionage. They discovered that the man they held was Laflèche, second-in-command of the *Mithridate* group and an important member of the French Resistance. He had been captured while trying to get in touch with London, using a new, perfected transmitter, and *in Pas-de-Calais*. After making a long telephone call to Paris, one of the German officers said to him with a broad smile: "Colonel, we now know where the Allies are going to land. We'll give them a reception that will enable us to carry the fight to England. That will be the happiest day of our lives."

Donet, who had been frantically wondering how the Germans had detected the transmitter, was given an explanation by his questioners themselves: Ayesha worked on the same wavelength as the radios of German tanks in Pas-de-Calais.

The British knew what that wavelength was, because they had been monitoring it, just as the Germans easily picked up radio messages exchanged by British tanks.

Donet remained stoically silent.

That the Allies made use of the Resistance in their plans to deceive the Germans appears likely in the cases of Operation HOLLAND, and the *Robin* group, and is obvious in the Ayesha episode. It served three purposes. One was to cover operations like the assault on Sicily or the Salerno landing. Another was to undermine the confidence of German counter-espionage in information obtained from the Resistance. But the chief purpose was to make the Germans believe that the invasion would not come in Normandy.

This is undoubtedly the ultimate secret of FORTITUDE.

Revolting callousness? Base treachery? The work of a secret service does not lend itself to categorical judgments. It is carried out in a sort of twilight world, with agents groping their way around and not knowing whether the next person is friend or enemy. Helped and guided by Giskes's "Resistance fighters," dozens of Allied airmen were able to reach Spain and, from there, England. The Germans regarded them as pawns not worth taking, because the end game might thereby have been lost. But for the Allies, the arrival of those airmen back in England was more than adequate compensation for the omission of a security check.

In any case, it is difficult to see clearly in this secret warfare. It was not unknown in London that the *Prosper* network had been penetrated by German agents. But how deeply? London may well have decided to maintain contact with the network, but also ply it with false information that the invasion was scheduled for the summer of 1943, for example. Yet a time came when London must have known that radio operators had been "doubled." Even so, it was necessary to maintain contact, to make the enemy think his trap was working; and the channel of communication that he himself had established provided another means of duping him. At a price, though: weapons and equipment. And men? The business of the false cyanide pills would be atrocious if it were true. But such extremes were not needed in order to dupe the enemy. It frequently happened, in 1944, that a Resistance leader succeeded in reaching London after his organization had been shattered by the Germans. After a few weeks he would want to return to his men. Permission was often refused, for death lay in wait for him at the end of the journey. Occasionally a leader was allowed to go back because only he could gather up the scattered remnants of the group. He was facing almost certain capture, and he knew it. Was there anything wrong in giving him false information ("Pas-de-Calais in July") which, revealed under torture, would help to deceive the enemy?

There was the case of Paul, one of the leaders of the *Carte* network, which had been penetrated by the double agent Michel, among others. Towards the end of 1943, the Germans arrested many members of *Carte,* but Paul managed to escape and reach London. He was one of those who wanted to return and was allowed to do so. The Germans captured him just before D-Day. He had been ordered, before leaving London, to give Michel (whose connection with the Germans was unknown to Paul) command of the Normandy group of the *Carte* network. This was not so astounding if London knew that Michel was a double agent. For then London could be sure that the false information given to Paul would reach the ears of the Germans.

The fact remains that men were deliberately sacrificed. Now, twenty years later, is it not time to acknowledge that they were, while admitting that the sacrifice was not in vain? Now that tears have dried and wounds have healed, is it not possible to accept the harsh truth? Colonel Donet, who was saved from the firing squad by a heroic act of the Belgian Resistance, had received his death sentence calmly: "When I led my company into action at the Battle of the Marne the sacrifice was the same." When Colonel Simpson of British intelligence said to him on September 8, 1944, "You know that you would not have died for nothing," Donet had already accepted his role. So had Robin, to whom another British officer said after the war: "You're a good businessman. You can understand these things. And you know it's sometimes necessary in business to write off five thousand francs to save half a million."

It was human lives, not money, involved, but the British and American leaders were well aware of that. They made their own compatriots, as well as members of the European resistance, pay heavily to keep the secret of D-Day. When they sent two commandos, Scott-Bowden and Ogden Smith, to explore the Pas-de-Calais beaches for nothing, they were exposing them to death in order to protect that secret. When they decided that the Allied fleet would open fire on the Wall only forty-five minutes before the assault, they were deliberately sacrificing the lives of hundreds of their soldiers. They knew from reports of amphibious operations in the Pacific and elsewhere that many hours of naval bombardment were needed to destroy pillboxes and bunkers and silence coastal batteries. But Normandy was not an island; the enemy could rush up reinforcements when warned of an attack, so Eisenhower limited the softening-up to three-quarters of an hour in order not to lose the advantage of surprise. This meant, however, that the leading assault waves would have to attack fortifications which were still strongly defended. The men who were cut down by their fire died less dramatically than the Dutchmen of Operation NORTH POLE or the Frenchmen of the *Robin* and *Mithridate* groups. They simply sprawled on the sand and no controversy ever arose over them. But their lives were sacrificed on the Normandy beaches, just as other lives were sacrificed months or years earlier in the tortuous maneuvers involved in duping the enemy.

The Resistance was an anvil on which both the Allies and the Germans hammered, but to some extent the success of OVERLORD was forged on it.

A strong chorus of double agents provided a background for the tragedies and comedies of FORTITUDE. The two soloists were Lily Sergueiev and Hans Schmidt, since the Germans regarded them as their most reliable sources of information, and they were supported by all the German agents captured and "doubled" since 1940. Their siren songs had been driving the Germans wild since April. For weeks they had kept the enemy thinking that the invasion would come the following night, and this had finally led to his lassitude in mid-May, and his growing conviction that there never would be an invasion.

It was then that the double agents really got going. Berlin was flooded with messages. Lily Sergueiev, instead of transmitting three times a week, was now sending messages three times a day, and they were getting longer and longer. Like Hans Schmidt, who was sending at the same rate, she played on two themes: July and Pas-de-Calais. She sent Kliemann a mass of information she said she had gleaned in trains, in clubs and canteens; she described the insignia of the divisions she had supposedly seen in the southeast; she reported concentration of armored units opposite Pas-de-Calais. As for her strategic information, she claimed to receive it from her friend Nelly, a young lady in whom General Koenig confided. Kliemann regularly congratulated her on her work.

At the same time, most of Schellenberg's agents in neutral capitals had been spotted by Allied agents. They were put on false scents (for example, by buying up all the Michelin maps of Pas-de-Calais available in Swiss bookshops). They were fed false information. Because of this, and because of the double agents busily tapping the keys of their transmitters in England, Schellenberg's services received a hundred and seventy-three messages in less than two weeks.

Some typical messages read:

"Technical difficulties have made the invasion impossible for the time being."

"The invasion will take place as soon as weather conditions permit."

"No invasion is to be expected in the near future."

"The assault will come in July between Dunkirk and Dieppe."

"The Allies will land in Denmark before June 18."

"Belgium will be invaded between May 15 and May 22."

"The assault troops have all embarked. The fleet is about to get under way."

"There will be an attack in Pas-de-Calais at the end of May. This will be only a diversion. The British and Americans are not yet agreed on the location of the main attack."

"Many parachutists will be dropped on northern France beginning May 20."

"Because of the ever-increasing strength of the Wall, the Allies have decided to call off the invasion."

"The invasion is scheduled for the night of May 20."

"The invasion will come in July, in Pas-de-Calais."

And so on.

Perhaps there really did exist after all some German agent who had succeeded in getting into Britain and escaping Allied counterespionage. The odds were greatly against it, considering the crude blunders that led to the capture of the spies sent by Canaris and Schellenberg. One thing is certain: if such a hero had existed, his voice would have been drowned by the cacophony from the double agents. Each valid item of information he sent would have been contradicted by a score of other messages. Even if he had transmitted the secret of OVERLORD to Berlin, why should the Germans have believed him rather than Lily Sergueiev or Hans Schmidt?

In May, 1945, Allied intelligence officers discovered in captured German files the texts of two hundred and fifty messages received from agents before D-Day. Most of them indicated July and Pas-de-Calais. Only one message gave the exact date and place of the invasion. It had come from a French colonel in Algiers. For a time he had actually worked for the Abwehr, but the Allies had unmasked him and put him to work for them. He too was used to mislead Berlin—used and abused. The Germans were so often deceived by him that they ended by treating all his information as worthless. But they kept in contact, for it is always useful to know what the enemy wants you to believe. With rare audacity and truly admirable perversity, the Allies had the colonel announce that the invasion would take place on the coast of Normandy on the fifth, sixth or seventh of June. For the Germans, his message was absolute proof that the invasion would come on any day *except* the fifth, sixth or seventh of June, and anywhere *except* Normandy.*

This is one of the few cases in which intelligence work can be regarded as one of the fine arts.

It is impossible to tell which of FORTITUDE'S many facets was the most effective. Was it the rubber divisions or Patton's prestige? The false information gathered from the Resistance or Montgomery's false headquarters? In all probability it was the sudden flow of messages from double agents, for they gave support to arguments which had not previously been considered decisive. In any case, the fact remains that in two weeks Hitler and Rommel covered half the distance that separated them from von Rundstedt. On May 15 they believed the invasion would be in Normandy. On May 31 they still thought Normandy would be attacked, but they believed that it would be only a diversion and the main assault would be in Pas-de-Calais.

---

* The Colonel's stock with the Germans shot up after D-Day, so that the Allies were able to use him to good account for the rest of the war.

# JUNE

## 25. The Last One Hundred and Fifteen Hours

*June 1. 115 hours before D-Day.** *

THE British assault divisions begin to embark. The Americans, who have a longer crossing to make, began going aboard their landing craft two days ago.

The troops began leaving their camps on May 26. They were taken to assembly areas near ports, called "sausages" because of their oblong shape. When they entered them they still did not know their destination. The maps issued to them gave no clue; Caen was called Warsaw, and the rivers of Normandy had been given Russian names. The amount of marshland shown on the maps given to the American paratroopers made them think Denmark was their most likely objective.

When the assault divisions were in the "sausages," two thousand Field Security and Military Police took up positions to prevent all contact with the outside world. French money was issued to the men. The British received a leaflet which began: "A new B.E.F., which includes you, is going to France. You are to assist personally in pushing the Germans out of France and back to where they belong."

The officers received real maps. Then the men were given photos of the beaches where they would land. These photos had been taken from sea level and showed the coast exactly

---

* British time, one hour earlier than German time.

as the men would see it from the landing craft. Then they were shown photos of the strongpoint they were to attack. They recognized it: for months they had practiced attacking an exact replica of it. The photos were so clear that they could even make out the faces of the German soldiers they had to kill. They were given a detailed inventory of the enemy's weapons and shown on models where they were hidden. They also learned the locations of ammunition dumps, minefields and barbed-wire networks. Then they were told what means would be used to overcome those defenses, and the part each man would play.

When the assault troops left the "sausages" for their landing craft, morale was higher than when they had arrived. They now felt that they had all possible information about the enemy. Fear of the unknown had been banished. They had been given a tough assignment, but they knew how to carry it out. They had been told the whole truth. They were much more reassured than the German troops who, during preparations for Operation SEA LION in 1940, were issued "psychological maps" showing England so close to the Continent that the Channel could apparently be crossed in one step.

Now the troops are packing into the landing craft, and must remain in them. At night, a smoke screen covers the ports to prevent the Luftwaffe from discovering the invasion fleet with its flares. British and American pilots have been warned that any aircraft flying over the ports will be shot down, even if it bears Allied markings.

The invasion is still scheduled for June 5.

*114 hours before D-Day.*

Luftwaffe intelligence reports: "Considerable increase in parachuting of weapons since the full moon of May 28. Officers in uniform have been dropped in small groups. Since they can hardly stay underground for long, there is reason to regard the period beginning June 12 (moon's last quarter) as dangerous."

German headquarters in the west expect better things of the Luftwaffe. Its job is not so much to report on parachute drops into France as to observe invasion preparations in England. Night reconnaissance flights have reported a great deal of road traffic on the southwest, apparent because the drivers are careless about lights. Von Rundstedt believes

that this "carelessness" is deliberate, that the enemy is trying to make him think the landing will be in Normandy rather than Pas-de-Calais. Daytime reconnaissance flights are very rare. Rommel complained of this in his weekly report dated May 21: Air reconnaissance has provided *no* information."
Strong forces of Allied fighters prevent Luftwaffe from approaching the ports in the southwest.

Yet a few Junkers have been flying over southeastern England with very little opposition. They report that the number of landing craft at Dover and Folkestone is about the same, if not slightly smaller. This reassures von Rundstedt. As long as the ports opposite Pas-de-Calais are not full of assault craft he feels there is nothing to fear. On May 30 he reported to Hitler: "It is true that the day of the invasion is drawing near, but the extent of enemy air attacks gives no indication that it is imminent."

Staff officers at headquarters in Saint-Germain-en-Laye carefully mark enemy units on a map of England, using in formation provided by Schellenberg's spies. Divisions are accumulating in the southeast of England. There are hardly any in the southwest.

*112 hours before D-Day.*

At SHAEF headquarters near Portsmouth, Eisenhower has just received a furious letter from Churchill. The Prime Minister has heard that an American reporter for the Chicago *Tribune* was allowed to return to the United States. He is indignant about this special favor at a time when members of Allied governments, foreign diplomats and British civilians are forbidden to leave the island. Eisenhower orders an immediate investigation and is able to assure Churchill that he has been misinformed: the reporter is still in England. The incident cheers Eisenhower up. "The old boy's in good form," he says.

Group Captain Stagg is studying the weather reports. Eisenhower has been testing his forecasts for several weeks, with highly satisfactory results. There are five weather requirements for OVERLORD: a wind of under fifteen miles an hour on the beaches, under twenty miles an hour out at sea; visibility of at least three miles; cloud ceiling no lower than three thousand feet; and not too bright a moon. These conditions are needed for at least three days. They prevailed throughout most of May. Even last night, there was a glorious sunset; but today there is no sun, the sky is gray. Stagg notes: "Fairly optimistic, but obviously a very marginal and difficult situation."

Records over the last hundred years show that there is only one chance in thirteen of all five weather requirements prevailing in the Channel during the month of June.

### 99 hours before D-Day.

After the B.B.C. news in French, twenty-eight personal messages are broadcast to the Resistance. They are picked up by German stations in Holland, Belgium, France and Germany and sent on to Schellenberg. Through his double agents in the Resistance, he is well acquainted with the warning system arranged by the Allies. The twenty-eight messages on his desk were to be broadcast on the first, second, fifteenth or sixteenth of the month. They were broadcast on the first, and were intended to put the Resistance on the alert. The second group of messages—the "B" messages—should soon follow, meaning that the invasion is imminent. In the following forty-eight hours the B.B.C. will broadcast the code sentences that will be the signal for guerilla and sabotage operations in selected areas.

But it has not yet come to that. Perhaps this is only another attempt to deceive the Germans. In 1943, when Exercise STARKEY was about to take place, the B.B.C. broadcast the "A" messages. Schellenberg will have no certainty until he hears the "B" messages.

At Fifteenth Army headquarters in Pas-de-Calais, Colonel Meyer, head of the monitoring station, has just picked up one of the messages: "The long sobs of the violins of autumn." This, the first line of the poem *Chanson d'Automne* by Paul Verlaine, is a two-part signal to be completed later by the second line of the poem. Meyer reports it to higher authority, and also to the Fifteenth Army's chief of staff, who orders the troops into a state of alert. They have been in that state almost continuously since the first of April.

In France, the Resistance receives the messages with surprise and enthusiasm. After such a long wait, it had seemed that they would never come. Final preparations are immediately begun. Each group will have its part to play in the four plans that have been worked out. The "Green Plan" is the disorganization of the French railway system by sabotage. The "Tortoise Plan," as its name indicates, is the slowing down by guerilla action of enemy reinforcements moving by road. The "Violet Plan" is the cutting of long-distance telephone lines, and the "Blue Plan" is the disruption of power lines.

Each leader has received his instructions in a sealed envelope. He must not open it, on pain of death, until he has heard the message telling him to go into action. Obviously these messages will not all be sent at the same time to all the groups in France. During the spring, agents from London explained to the Resistance leaders that the folly of a general uprising must be avoided. On D-Day only the groups near the landing zone will be sent into action. The others will be called upon only as the Allies advance inland. If they were to come out into the open too soon, they would be massacred.

Some groups are already commanded by Jedburgh teams consisting of three officers (usually one American, one British and one French). These are the "officers in uniform" parachuted into France and reported by Luftwaffe intelligence. They have been sent to lead the sabotage and guerilla operations.

The Sussex teams have been sent to obtain tactical information before the landing and during the French campaign. They are forbidden to enter into contact with the Resistance, which is considered to contain too many German double agents.*

Gathered around their radios, Resistance members are now waiting for the messages that will tell them whether or not they are among the elect.

*88 hours before D-Day.*

Heavy bombers are pounding the French coast. Two bombs on Pas-de-Calais for each one on Normandy. The ninety-two German radar stations between Dunkirk and Le Havre are

---

* The number of Sussex teams proved insufficient, so Justin O'Brien of the American O.S.S., Professor of French at Columbia University and a great admirer of Proust, started Operation À LA RECHERCHE DES HOMMES PERDUS. This consisted in tracking down candidates previously rejected for the Sussex teams. The code name of each mission was the name of one of Proust's characters.

being attacked by medium bombers. They are well protected by antiaircraft guns and losses are heavy.

### 78 hours and 45 minutes before D-Day.

German monitoring stations again pick up the twenty-eight warning messages for the Resistance. This repetition surprises Schellenberg. The messages were supposed to be broadcast once. Probably the Allies want to be sure they have been heard.

### 78 hours and 30 minutes before D-Day.

Eisenhower sees Stagg and the other meteorologists. Their news is not good: "The situation is not what we hoped for . . . Still mainly favorable from wind point of view but very uncertain about cloud."

### June 3. 70 hours before D-Day.

Warships leave ports in Scotland and Northern Ireland at three o'clock in the morning and make for the zone off the Isle of Wight where the invasion fleet will assemble. The zone has already been nicknamed "Piccadilly Circus."

### 65 hours before D-Day.

Schellenberg informs the various commanders-in-chief that he has again intercepted the twenty-eight messages, and warns that the invasion might well take place within the next two weeks. Admiral Doenitz and his staff consider it to be just another episode in the long war of nerves.

### 63 hours before D-Day.

A young British officer on liaison duty between Portsmouth and London makes a short detour to call on his parents. He tells them that the landings will take place in Normandy on June 5. His parents denounce him to the police, and Security officers place him under arrest.

Coastal batteries and radar stations along the French coast are heavily bombed.

The embarkation of the assault divisions is complete.

### 54 hours before D-Day.

The crews of the Mulberries have taken their places on their huge concrete caissons, but will not be towed away until dawn on D-Day. The construction of these two artificial

ports, each the size of Dover harbor, has been one of the big
headaches for the planners of OVERLORD, mainly because of
the difficulty of keeping such an enormous enterprise secret.
When those in charge made requests for men or materials
they often met with the remark: "Mulberry? What ship is
that?" They hated the code name they had been given; it
was unwarlike and unimpressive. They would have preferred something like "Tiger's Teeth."

The crews of the caissons are listening to the English
traitor "Lord Haw-Haw" broadcasting from Germany. His
words are directed to them. "We know exactly what you intend to do with those concrete units," he is saying in his
smooth, silky voice. "You intend to sink them off our coast
in the assault. Well, we're going to help you, boys. We'll
save you some trouble. When you get under way, we're going
to sink them for you."

The men listening know what wonderful targets they offer
on these caissons which are as big as houses. For once, Lord
Haw-Haw has shaken them.

*53 hours before D-Day.*

Rommel meets General Kramer, who has been released
by the British in an exchange of prisoners. Kramer assures
Rommel that the Allies will attack in Pas-de-Calais.

*51 hours and 45 minutes before D-Day.*

German monitoring stations pick up the twenty-eight messages for the third time.

*51 hours and 30 minutes before D-Day.*

The Allied weather officers make their report. It is 9:30
at night, June 3. The first American convoys are already at
sea. Stagg's forecast is pessimistic: high winds, low cloud and
even a little mist along the Normandy coast. There is, however, a measure of uncertainty in the reports that have come
in from weather stations. Eisenhower decides to hold another conference in six hours and make his decision then.
The convoys continue on their way.

*49 hours before D-Day.*

In London, an Associated Press teletype operator is prac-
ticing her speed. She types the "flash" that every journalist
would like to be able to send: "URGENT ASSOCIATED PRESS NYK

FLASH EISENHOWER HQ ANNOUNCED ALLIED LANDINGS IN
FRANCE." Her "flash" is accidentally sent out. Twenty-three
minutes later the Associated Press issues a retraction, but
the "news" has already been repeated by Radio Berlin and
Radio Moscow.

### June 4. 45 hours before D-Day.

It is four o'clock in the morning when Eisenhower holds
his conference. It is a clear, windless night. But Stagg re-
peats his gloomy forecast. Eisenhower decides to postpone
D-Day from June 5 to June 6. Orders are given to re-
call the convoys already at sea.

### 43 hours before D-Day.

At his headquarters in La Roche-Guyon, Erwin Rommel,
up before dawn as usual, signs the weekly report that will
be sent to von Rundstedt today. It stresses: ". . . the sys-
tematic and distinct increase in air attacks, and of mine-
laying in the approaches to our ports . . . indicates that
the enemy has reached a high degree of readiness. Concentrated air attacks on the coastal defenses between Dunkirk and Dieppe strengthen the supposition that a large-scale
landing will be made in that area . . . Since June 1 an increasing number of warning messages has been broadcast to
the French Resistance (but judging from previous experience,
this does not necessarily mean that an invasion is imminent). Air reconnaissance has not observed a great increase in the number of invasion craft in the Dover sector.
*No* flights have been made over the other ports along the
south coast of England. It is essential to send reconnaissance
planes over all the harbors of the south coast."

Despite the order to return, for some unknown reason an
American convoy is still proceeding towards Utah Beach.
A seaplane is sent after it, and succeeds in alerting it.

Rommel's aide-de-camp, Captain Lang, brings him the
Luftwaffe intelligence report: "The enemy is becoming increasingly successful in protecting the approaches to the
south coast of England against air and sea reconnaissance.
This probably means he is concentrating transport in readiness for the invasion."

"Probably . . ." Rommel wants certainties, not probabilities.

He finds them in the second document that Lang hands him: the daily weather forecast. It is the work of Professor Walther Ströbe, now a colonel and head of the Luftwaffe meteorological section in Paris. It predicts rain, high winds and low cloud. At this moment another meteorologist, Major Lettau, is writing that no landings will be possible for the next two weeks. His report says: "The enemy has not taken advantage of the three recent periods of good weather, and it is far from certain that there will be any in the coming weeks."

Rommel has not yet seen Lettau's report, but he is satisfied with Ströbe's. There is nothing to fear in the near future. The weather situation gives unexpected and powerful support to what Friedrich Hayn, intelligence officer of the 89th Corps, called the "official doctrine": "Since they haven't taken advantage of May, they won't move before August."

The navy has assured Rommel that the Allies need five consecutive days of good weather in order to consolidate their landings. They will not have them during the coming week.

*42 hours before D-Day.*

Seven o'clock in the morning. Daniel stops the black Horch in front of the building. Rommel shakes hands with his staff officers. "It eases my mind," he says to Admiral Ruge, "to know that while I'm away the tides will be very unfavorable for a landing. Besides, air reconnaissance gives no reason to think it's imminent."

Having said this, Rommel gets into his car and leaves for Germany. He intends to go first to his home at Herrlingen to celebrate his wife's birthday on June 6, then to Berchtesgaden, to see Hitler. He has decided to use the privilege of a field marshal to have direct access to the Führer. He has already telephoned to his friend Major General Rudolf Schmundt, Hitler's adjutant, to ask for an interview. Schmundt has replied that it might be possible between the sixth and ninth.

Rommel hopes to get the two armored divisions and the antiaircraft batteries which he considers necessary for the defense of Normandy. At this moment, he probably thinks that the main attack will be in Pas-de-Calais, but the base of the Cotentin peninsula is thinly defended, even against a diversionary assault. All his previous requests have been turned down. He is up against the opposition of staff officers who prefer to stick to the rules of strategy and keep the armored divisions some distance from the coast in order to be able to throw their whole weight against the enemy at that point.

There is only one way in which Rommel can overcome this opposition: by obtaining Hitler's support. But Hitler has changed his mind since the beginning of May. He, too, now believes that the main attack will come in Pas-de-Calais, and therefore prefers to keep his armor in reserve, so that he can use it against the most important beachhead. General Guderian, chief exponent of the use of armor, has warned him against putting his Panzers "in the shop window." "If you do, it will be impossible to withdraw and engage them elsewhere quickly enough." It is obvious that if they are to be thrown into battle in Pas-de-Calais it is better to leave the 12th S.S. at Lisieux and the Panzer Lehr at Le Mans rather than sending them to Normandy.

Rommel admits that this is sound theory, but in practice Allied air supremacy makes it meaningless. He knows what such supremacy meant in Africa. He foresees that the armor will be under continuous air attack while it is moving from one position to another. He would rather have it on the coast, where it can do some good, than inland, where it can only be a target for enemy fighter-bombers.

The Führer's change of mind has reduced Rommel's chance of success, but he intends to press his point: that the armor should be on the coast and not inland, whether Normandy or Pas-de-Calais is believed to be the most threatened area.

As he speeds toward uncertain discussions, he has at least one certainty: the landing won't come while he's gone. Rain is spattering the hood of the Horch. The trees along the road are bending before the strong wind.

Yes on May 17, nineteen days earlier, Rommel addressed the men of the 6th Parachute Regiment. "Don't think they'll come on a clear day and notify you in advance," he told them. "They'll suddenly drop from the sky in a flurry of wind and rain."

*39 hours before D-Day.*

Two British counterespionage agents call at Leonard Dawe's house in Leatherhead, Surrey. He and his friend

Melville Jones are the compilers of the *Daily Telegraph* crossword puzzles. On May 27 one of the clues was: "But some bigwig like this has stolen some of it at times." The answer, published on June 2, was "Overlord." On May 30 the puzzle contained the following clue: "This bush is a centre of nursery revolutions." The answer was "Mulberry." A clue on June 1 was "Britannia and he hold to the same thing," and the answer was "Neptune"—the code word for the naval operations in the invasion.

Since "Utah" and "Omaha" also occurred among the answers, a total of five important code words involved in the invasion have appeared in the *Daily Telegraph* in less than a month. A strange coincidence, say the two spy-hunters. An extraordinary coincidence, agrees Leonard Dawe. But he easily proves his innocence: he composes and sends off the puzzles months in advance. It was only by a fantastic trick of chance that all the suspect clues appeared in such a brief space of time.

When informed of the Associated Press "flash" incident, Eisenhower merely shrugs his shoulders.

*36 hours before D-Day.*

Rommel's weekly report has just reached von Rundstedt. In the eyes of the elderly field marshal it shows the progress made by the "Boy Marshal." "Concentrated air attacks on the coastal defenses between Dunkirk and Dieppe strengthen a large-scale landing in that area." That is, in Pas-de-Calais. Rommel has seen the light at last! But before he could arrive at the truth that von Rundstedt had discovered by strategic reasoning alone, the enemy had to open his eyes by bombing Pas-de-Calais twice as much as Normandy.

As for Rommel's remark about the messages to the Resistance, von Rundstedt is in complete agreement. He received the news of the interception of the twenty-eight code sentences with the same blasé indifference as Admiral Doenitz. At the time of Exercise STARKEY in 1943, he learned how much credence could be placed in orders to the Resistance from London. As Rommel has written, "Judging from previous experience, this does not necessarily mean that an invasion is imminent."

In any case, on the evening of June 1, the commander of the German armies in the west did not deem it necessary to put them on the alert.

*29 hours before D-Day.*

The Allied air commanders decide that both Pas-de-Calais and Normandy will be bombed tomorrow. The plan was that on D minus 1 the objectives in Pas-de-Calais would be abandoned if it was obvious that the enemy was expecting a landing in Normandy. But there is nothing to indicate that he has such foresight.

This rather unexpected success of FORTITUDE has prompted Eisenhower to ask for an extension of the security measures in Britain, particularly as applied to foreign diplomats. He wants to keep from the Germans as long as possible the fact that the Normandy landings are not just a diversionary attack. It is for this reason, too, that he has forbidden any public reference to the Mulberries even after D-Day, because they would indicate the extent of the effort concentrated on Normandy.

*27 hours and 30 minutes before D-Day.*

The Allied commanders meet to hear the verdict of the meteorologists. It is a wet, gusty night, with gales in the Channel. But Stagg forecasts a period of relative calm that will last from the night of June 5 through the morning of June 6.

Eisenhower decides to go ahead. One of his reasons, and probably the main one, is the necessity of keeping the secret of OVERLORD. A negative decision would mean that the attack would have to be put off for two more weeks. The assault troops now know their objectives. There would be little hope of maintaining secrecy if they were to stay in England two weeks longer. An attack undertaken in such poor weather conditions will involve risk and sacrifices. Eisenhower chooses to take the risk and accept the sacrifices rather than lose the advantage of surprise.

*June 5. 21 hours before D-Day.*

The rain has stopped. After Stagg has confirmed his forecast, Eisenhower says "O.K. We go."

*19 hours before D-Day.*

From many different ports, the five thousand ships and landing craft of the invasion force are converging on "Piccadilly Circus."

In Paris, Walther Ströbe, the meteorologist, has given his

officers the day off. Since he forecasts that bad weather will prevent any enemy raids, the antiaircraft gunners are also given leave. When the weather forecast is telephoned to von Rundstedt's headquarters, the staff officers consider it very satisfactory.

Neither Ströbe nor his colleague Lettau has the means of knowing that weather conditions in the Atlantic have changed, that a new front giving improved conditions is on its way. Unlike the Allies, they have no network of weather stations and well-equipped weather ships. The revelation of this deficiency came as a complete surprise to Lily Sergueiev. At her meeting with Kliemann in March he asked her to give the London temperature, wind direction and cloud formation in all her messages. "The temperature is the most important," he added. "But a thermometer placed on the ground, or even on a window ledge, won't do. The best plan would be to tie a long string to it and then go into a park and swing it around above your head, so that you can get the temperature at a certain height."

"Don't you think that would look a bit odd?" Lily exclaimed. "I might attract some attention if I started swinging a thermometer in Hyde Park. It's not a very common sight."

"You'll obviously have to do it when there's nobody around," was Kliemann's curt answer. "It's very important for us."

### 18 hours before D-Day.

Luftwaffe intelligence report: "The enemy is still trying, by every trick in the war of nerves, to prevent us from discovering his plans."

He is not only trying: he is succeeding. Today, June 5, while five thousand ships are sailing toward Normandy, a German pilot takes off on a reconnaissance mission. In accordance with his orders, he carefully scrutinizes the sea off the coast of Holland.

### 16 hours before D-Day.

In Wales, Mrs. Ogden Smith, wife of the commando sergeant, wearing her best clothes, is about to take a train to London. She has received an invitation to go to Buckingham Palace, where the king is going to decorate her husband with the Military Medal. She is just leaving for the station when she receives a telephone call telling her that the ceremony has been postponed because her husband has been detained by other obligations.

### 15 hours before D-Day.

At Cherbourg, Rear Admiral Hennecke is informed that the powerful radar station at La Pernelle has detected abnormal activity on its screens. He asks his weather officer about the possibility of an invasion. The reply is that "high seas, bad visibility and strong winds make it unlikely that even enemy bombers will be over. No improvement, even temporary, can be expected for the next two days."

A convoy due to leave for Brest is ordered to remain at Cherbourg because of the storm.

### 12 hours before D-Day.

Von Rundstedt signs the weekly report to be sent to the Führer. Then he goes to the Coq Hardi to have lunch with his son, a young lieutenant. He plans to make a tour of inspection in Normandy tomorrow, June 6, and is looking forward to showing the Atlantic Wall to his son.

His report to Hitler states: "The continued air attacks on Dunkirk and the coast as far as Dieppe lead us to suppose that the enemy will attack in that sector. . . . However, it is unlikely that the invasion is imminent."

### 9 hours before D-Day.

The 124 fighter planes of the German 26th Wing take off from airfields in the west of France to reach new bases in the east. They are moving out of range of the Normandy coast—and there are only 160 fighter planes, including these 124, in the whole of France.

### 8 hours before D-Day.

The invasion fleet is assembling at "Piccadilly Circus."

### 7 hours before D-Day.

The ground staff at British airfields now see why tons of white paint have been delivered during the last few days: they have been ordered to paint three white stripes on the wings of all aircraft. This is to enable friendly planes to be more easily distinguished from enemy ones in the D-Day mixup. The order has been given at the last possible moment so that the Germans will not be able to copy these new markings.

There are some ten thousand planes to paint before night-fall.

*6 hours and 30 minutes before D-Day.*

The B.B.C. begins to broadcast a number of personal messages. French Resistance members are told to stand by for further messages.

*6 hours before D-Day.*

Lieutenant Colonel von der Heydte is informed that a score of conscripted Alsatians serving as drivers with his 6th Parachute Regiment have all deserted during the afternoon. He orders a group of his noncoms, out on an exercise, to return to headquarters at once.

In London, the French Resistance hero Colonel Rémy is having a discussion with Colonel Miller and his chief assistant, Neave, of the American O.S.S., about the advisability of parachuting arms into Normandy. Miller is reluctant. Glancing at a map of France, Rémy happens to put his finger on Omaha Beach and says, "Suppose the landings took place tomorrow, right here . . . You'll have to admit that my proposal would be interesting then!"

For the first time, his two friends treat him coldly. He soon leaves, offended. He is not a Bigot. Miller, who is, immediately calls Security. They suggest arresting Rémy to keep him out of the way for a time. But Miller guarantees the Frenchman's discretion.

*5 hours before D-Day.*

In Caen, the weekly staff conference at the headquarters of the 716th Division is just ending. General Richter finishes on a humorous note, telling his colonels that a "high authority" has told him the landing will take place between the sixth and tenth of June. He adds that he has received the same warning at every new and full moon since April 1.

*4 hours and 30 minutes before D-Day.*

The headquarters in Normandy have lost a few generals and colonels. They have set off for Rennes, where there is to be a *Kriegsspiel*—a map exercise. Its theme is: "Enemy landings in Normandy, preceded by paratroop drops." The practice alert scheduled for the night of June 5 has therefore been canceled.

The Seventh Army's chief of staff, worried by this exodus, telegraphs an order at the last minute: "Divisional Commanders and senior officers participating in the *Kriegsspiel* are requested not to leave for Rennes before dawn on June 6."

But most of them, reassured by the storm, are already on the way to Rennes. Among them are General Heize Hellmich of the 243rd Division, General Karl von Schlieben of the 709th Division, and General Wilhelm Falley of the 91st Division. All these divisions are in the Cotentin peninsula.

Admiral Krancke, chief of naval forces in the west, sets out for Bordeaux. He has informed von Rundstedt that no German vessel has been able to leave port that day because of the storm. There will be no patrols at sea during the night.

At the headquarters of the 84th Corps in Saint-Lô, the staff officers are planning to celebrate General Marcks's birthday with Chablis at midnight, German time.

Rommel's chief of staff, Hans Speidel, is giving a small dinner party at La Roche-Guyon. Among his guests is the author Ernst Jünger.

*2 hours and 45 minutes before D-Day.*

After its 9:15 news report, the B.B.C. French service broadcasts *all* the "B" messages and *all* the personal messages ordering *all* the Resistance groups into action.

In London, the Free French officers are stunned. Since they are not in on the secret of OVERLORD, they have prepared four different plans so that wherever the landing is made the Resistance groups and the Maquis in different areas will gradually be brought into the struggle. The Allied leaders have given their approval. Everyone has agreed that a widespread uprising would only bring about a bloodbath, and that must be avoided at all costs.

And now the bloodbath is to take place tomorrow, set off by such innocent sentences as "I am looking for four-leaved clovers," "The tomatoes should be picked," "The dice are on the table," "It is hot in Suez," "Children are bored on Sundays," "Soothe my heart with monotonous languor," and the others. All of them. Tomorrow thousands of men of the Maquis will throw themselves almost barehanded against the

German armored columns. Tomorrow men will fall by the hundreds in Ain, Vercors, Ardèche, Savoie, Dauphiné, Haute-Province. History will forget them. When it adds up its totals after the landing, it will count only the corpses in uniform lying on the beaches of Normandy. But the underground fighters who are about to die in French fields, forests and towns will also have paid their tribute of blood to OVERLORD.

The German monitoring stations have picked up the B.B.C.'s messages too. They are immediately relayed to Berlin. Schellenberg is probably just as surprised as de Gaulle's officers. The special messages for each group have been broadcast at the same time as the "B" messages, instead of forty-eight hours later. They will unleash guerilla warfare and sabotage all over France. That was not foreseen. It all seems so insane that Schellenberg may now have doubts about the worth of reports from his double agents in the Resistance.

In any case, the setting off of a general uprising has prevented him from drawing any conclusion about where the landing will take place. By sacrificing the French Resistance, the Allied leaders have destroyed Schellenberg's hopes. He cannot inform the headquarters in the west that the landing will be made at such-and-such a place. He can only tell them that the invasion will begin at any moment. He does this. But he has already done it so often before . . .

At Fifteenth Army headquarters in Pas-de-Calais Colonel Meyer has picked up the second line of Verlaine's poem: "Soothe my heart with monotonous languor." He immediately notifies von Rundstedt's headquarters, then bursts into the room where the Fifteenth Army's commander, General Hans von Salmuth, is playing bridge with three officers. Meyer tells him the news. Von Salmuth gives his usual reply: "State of alert." As Meyer hurries away, the general picks up his cards again. "I'm too old to get excited about that," he grumbles.

When news of the interception of all the "B" messages is received at von Rundstedt's headquarters a staff officer exclaims: "Does anyone really think the Allies are crazy enough to announce their arrival over the radio?"

Naval headquarters at Cherbourg also receives the news. It is entered in the log with this comment: "Of course, nothing will happen."

Speidel's dinner party at La Roche-Guyon is going well. Conversation ranges over Italy, Russia, French politics, the situation in the United States, the French navy and Adolf Hitler's lack of education, but no mention is made of the "B" messages.

The Seventh Army, on which the defense of Normandy depends, has not been informed of the interception of the messages. No one in Saint-Germain or La Roche-Guyon has seen fit to alert it. Ten times in the last two months the intelligence services have announced the invasion for the following day—and the weather was good. There is certainly no reason to believe them now that the bad weather makes a landing out of the question.

As the Allied invasion fleet heads for the coast of Normandy the Germans still have a chance of detecting it. If they take that chance, they will still have time to get their troops ready for combat, bring up the guns and ammunition moved from their emplacements at Le Hoc, Riva-Bella, La Madeleine and Morsalines because of the bombing attacks, and bring all available fighter planes to Normandy.

Their last hope lies in their radar stations. They have suffered 1668 air attacks since May 10, but, thanks to the efficiency of the repair units, there are still enough screens in service to pick up a fleet of five thousand ships. Surrounded by uncertainties, the German generals have always been sure of one thing: that their radar will give them at least a few hours' warning of the invasion.

*2 hours and 10 minutes before D-Day.*

Six Albermarle transport planes take off from the airfield at Harwell. They are carrying the sixty "pathfinders" who will parachute into the Orne valley to mark the drop zones of the British airborne troops. C-47's carrying the American pathfinders are taking off from Newbury.

*1 hour before D-Day.*

Eight planes of Cheshire's 617th Squadron take off for France. Each aircraft has two pilots and two navigators. Inside the fuselage is a pile of paper-and-tinfoil strips, black on ⟨on⟩e ⟨si⟩de and shiny on the other, and three men to throw ⟨them⟩ ⟨⟩ut.

The chance for action has come just in time for the men of the 617th. A short time earlier, to liven the monotony of their exercises, Cheshire conceived the idea of having pistols, submachine guns and grenades issued to them, on the pretext that there might be an attack by enemy paratroopers. For lack of enemy paratroopers, the airmen waged an entertaining but dangerous little war among themselves. Grenades went off outside the mess hall, and anyone venturing out at night ran the risk of encountering submachine-gun fire. The flight order came as a great relief to their superiors.

The flight approaches Le Havre, then turns east and follows the coast. In single file, the planes fly back and forth thirty-five seconds in one direction, and thirty-two seconds in the other. Each time they turn to take the thirty-five-second direction, the three men in the fuselage throw out a bundle of tinfoil strips.

This will go on for two hours, then another group of eight planes is to take over. This relay is the most delicate part of the operation, because the new group will have only three seconds to take the old one's place. Altogether, the 617th will have planes in the air for eight hours.

If the maneuver is carried out with absolute precision, German radar screens will pick up what will seem to be the image of an enormous convoy, fourteen miles long, proceeding up the Channel towards Pas-de-Calais at a speed of seven knots. But a four-second gap will be enough to enable the radar operators to spot the subterfuge.

Below Cheshire's eight planes are eighteen small British vessels plowing through the waves, each towing a balloon. On German radar screens, these balloons will appear as the big warships escorting the convoy.

*45 minutes before D-Day.*

All over France the sabotage groups are at work. In Normandy, they are damaging the railroad lines between Paris and Cherbourg, Paris and Granville, and Saint-Lô and Coutances. They are cutting the telephones that connect German army headquarters with one another, and the Paris-Cherbourg cable has been sabotaged.

*40 minutes before D-Day.*

Radar stations near the Normandy coast report intensive

"snowing" of the screens. Those in Pas-de-Calais, which have purposely been spared by Allied bombers, report great activity in the Channel.

All available German night fighters are ordered to patrol the Straits of Dover.

*30 minutes before D-Day.*

General Falley is driving towards Rennes. General Hellmich and General von Schlieben are already there.

At La Roche-Guyon, Speidel's guests are just getting up from the table to take a stroll in the garden.

At Cherbourg, Rear Admiral Hennecke and his staff officers have been to a concert and are now having supper with the performers.

At Saint-Lô the officers who have prepared the little birthday party are wondering how the rather stern General Marcks will take it.

At Herrlingen, Rommel is savoring the joys of family life.

At Berchtesgaden, Hitler is receiving a few Nazi leaders and their wives. They are going to listen to Wagner.

*D-Day. Midnight*

There are 1087 airplanes on their way to Normandy. Inside them are 18,000 paratroopers who will jump in an hour and a quarter. Below them, 5000 vessels, carrying 185,000 men and 20,000 vehicles, are only two hours away from the anchoring berths that have been assigned to them off the Normandy coast.

In France, which is on German time, D-Day is still an hour away.

# 26. "By Sheer Weight of Numbers"

THE secret war ended more or less at the same time the fighting began. On the morning of June 6, any machine-gunner above Omaha Beach had more influence on the fate of Germany than Walther Schellenberg did. The success of OVERLORD now depended on the American paratroopers jumping from their C–47's, and no longer on the men who had labored for so many months to prepare and protect the operation.

When the first shots were fired, the secret service men all became more or less like Clifton James. While the invasion fleet was moving toward Normandy, he was asleep in a room at Shepheard's Hotel in Cairo. He had finished being Montgomery, he was now Clifton James again. And all the spies and agents likewise withdrew from the stage as the curtain rose on the drama they had helped to prepare.

Among the few exceptions were the two commandos Scott-Bowden and Ogden Smith. At General Bradley's request they were guiding the American assault waves towards Omaha Beach. This was their third visit to it, and it was to be far grimmer than the other two.

Some agents had disappeared forever. Douin the sculptor and Thomine the fisherman heard the rumble of the airplanes from their cells in Caen prison, but at six-thirty on the morning of D-Day they met their death as the guns of the liberating fleet boomed out. Others had disappeared only temporarily, such as Duchez, who was with the Maquis, and his wife, who was in the Mauthausen concentration camp. A few felt a strange nostalgia at the thought that their clandestine activities were now over. Dominique Ponchardier was sleeping in one of his Paris hideouts; when he awoke and heard the news he said to himself, after his first outburst of joy, "From now on, life will be stupidly calm and safe." As for the sweeper-up spy, he had never been near enough to the footlights to be dazzled, so the shadows backstage did not seem dark when he returned to them. Now that the *Feldwebel* was about to move out of his house and the battery was going to leave his meadow, he could take up his life again where he had left it. He would remember the period he had just lived through mainly as a long fear.

Because he had the courage to be afraid, the soldiers preparing to land in France had more chances of killing than of being killed. He had told them as much about their adversary as it was humanly possible to find out. He also made —humanly—a few mistakes. At Merville, for instance, sixty-six of Colonel Ottway's paratroopers gave their lives to capture an objective that was hardly worth taking. The battery there turned out to be composed not of 150-millimeter guns, but of short-range 75's. Was the local spy mistaken? Not necessarily. The Allies may have been misled by their tendency to judge the size of a gun by the thickness of the concrete protecting it.

Greater bitterness was felt by Colonel Rudder and his Rangers, who lost one hundred and thirty-five men in scaling and capturing La Pointe du Hoc, only to find that there was no battery at the top. Yet the *Centurie* group had sent a message to London reporting that the guns had been withdrawn a mile or so inland. The message may not have gotten through. Or it may have arrived too late, as in the case of the movements of the German 352nd Division. In May the Resistance had announced that the 352nd had been stationed on the hills overlooking Omaha Beach. The homing pigeon carrying the message had been shot down. So had the second pigeon, carrying a confirmation. The Resistance eventually got the information through to London, but by then the troops had already embarked and it was too late to make any changes.

Nevertheless, the Resistance in Normandy did accumulate a vast amount of precise information about the coastal defenses. The sweeper-up spy was later able to read this tribute paid to him by Eisenhower: "We sailed for France possessed of all the tactical information which an efficient intelligence service could provide." But his real reward was to know that the Allied soldiers went into battle with a confidence born of his anguish.

It was because of the Allied secret services that Montgomery was able to write in *From Normandy to the Baltic*: "We realized that the Germans would be alerted during the night of D—1, as our forces were approaching the coast of Normandy . . . We know now that we attained a degree of surprise far beyond what we had imagined."

Past masters in the art of deception, conjurors, implacable hunters, masterful humorists: the heads of Allied intelligence —especially the British—were all those things. They were the cold-blooded mathematicians, prepared to subtract a few lives, or a few hundred, or a few thousand, on the truly irrefutable principle that it is sometimes necessary to sacrifice a little in order to gain a lot. Lily Sergueiev, who had a romantic soul, could not get used to such pragmatism. She broke with the British soon after D-Day, tired of being treated like a machine; she eventually went to America, and died there seven years after the time that had been set by her doctors. As for Hans Schmidt, he was allowed to go on living in England, for he would have run grave risks by returning to his own country. Although they did not go so far as to reproach him for having betrayed his original masters, the British made it quite clear that they were not at all grateful to him. It is a common fate for a double agent; he usually becomes contemptible as soon as he ceases to be useful.

These are trivial details compared to the results obtained by the Allied intelligence services. First they cleaned house, sweeping up all the spies in Britain. Then they succeeded in imposing on that liberal country more stringent security measures than any dictatorship had ever known. They erected an impenetrable wall around the great secret. Despite a few close calls, they won the defensive battle that they fought on the threshold of OVERLORD. It required only stubborn determination. But it had taken talent to succeed in duping the enemy with regard to the landings in North Africa, Sicily and Anzio, at the same time destroying his confidence in his intelligence services. And it took much more than talent to bring off Operation FORTITUDE. Juggling rubber armored divisions, General Patton, Montgomery's double and a handful of double agents, the heads of Allied intelligence, brilliant sleight-of-hand artists, made Normandy vanish and pulled Pas-de-Calais out of their hat before an audience of bewildered Germans.

It was almost midnight in France. There was not a single German officer or soldier who really believed that in a few moments D-Day would begin for him. The troops had been placed on the alert far too often; their intelligence services had stretched their nerves too much, sent too many false warnings. The troops in Normandy would believe in enemy airborne landings only when the paratroopers tumbled on top of them, and would believe in the invasion fleet only when they saw the hordes of ships and landing craft. They believed in the bad weather because they saw the rain pelting down and heard the trees rustling in the wind. For the first time in two months they had a certainty: the storm ruled out the possibility of a landing for the time being. Compared to that almost palpable reality, what was the story of those "B" messages? Only more rantings from Berlin, of which there had already been too many. After hearing so many false alarms the army had decided to stuff its ears and stop straining its eyes for the sight of imaginary convoys. It wanted to touch before believing. And by an extraordinary quirk of fate, that army so intent on having tangible evidence was going to be vanquished by an army of phantoms.

It all began with the Allied raid on Dieppe. Colonel Roenne, head of an intelligence section with the special task of assessing Allied intentions, sent in a report saying that the attack was not an attempt to invade the Continent. For Goebbels to proclaim the contrary was only natural; it was part of his job. But General Zeitzler, then von Rundstedt's chief of staff, was going beyond his when he congratulated the Führer on having repulsed an enemy invasion. He soon got his reward: he was appointed head of the German General Staff. Colonel Roenne, who was little interested in promotion, protested strongly against a deformation of the facts which seemed to him dangerous. After submitting several reports in this vein he received a curt note from on high telling him that his section spent too much time turning out reports and would do better to engage in more constructive work.

Roenne and his section were from then on regarded as pessimists and defeatists of the worst kind; they became known as always looking on the dark side of things and little notice was taken of their estimates of the Western Allies' strength. Reassured, Hitler began moving divisions from the west to bolster up the eastern front. What could Colonel Roenne do to prevent this folly which was draining the best forces from the west? His second-in-command, Lieutenant Colonel Michael, supplied the answer: commit the sin of falsifying intelligence reports. Roenne did so, toward the end of 1943, and the exodus of German troops from the west was brought to a halt.

But then came D-Day; and with Hitler, Rommel and von Rundstedt all agreed that it was only a diversion, that the main assault would come in Pas-de-Calais, Roenne and Michael were probably exceedingly worried men by the time Cherbourg fell to the Allies, who then had fourteen divisions in Normandy and were opposed by German forces with the strength of only six or seven divisions. There were fifteen German divisions in Pas-de-Calais, but they remained there, as though the disasters in Normandy did not concern them. Hitler was holding them to meet the Allied assault still to come. They were going to throw back the fresh divisions that Eisenhower was keeping in reserve. Only Roenne and Michael knew that those divisions did not exist, because they had invented them at the end of 1943—thirty divisions with one stroke of the pen!—to convince Hitler not to empty the west of its last troops.

It is easier to invent thirty divisions than to make them disappear. Neither Roenne nor Michael could think of a way to do it. They left their thirty paper divisions where they were, and Hitler left his real ones in Pas-de-Calais while the Allies pushed theirs into Brittany.

"The German Fifteenth Army," Eisenhower wrote later, "if committed to battle in June or July, might possibly have defeated us by sheer weight of numbers."

Hitler did not let go of it until the end of July. By then the German front had been cracked and the battle for France had been practically decided. German intelligence, driven mad by four years of self-delusion, had given the final touch to the masterpiece of deception that had been elaborated in London.

French clocks were about to strike midnight. In the sky, the British and American paratroopers were standing up in their planes, ready to jump. The fleet was only an hour away from its anchoring berths.

The German soldiers were sleeping in their concrete fortifications or in their tents. In a few more minutes they would begin opposing Operation OVERLORD with their usual courage and determination. It would take them a long time, and cost them much blood and suffering, to discover that another operation, called FORTITUDE, had already sealed their fate before the twelve strokes of midnight began.

# Appendix

"I cannot overemphasize the decisive value of this most successful threat [FORTITUDE] which paid enormous dividends, both at the time of the assault and during the operations of the two succeeding months."

—DWIGHT D. EISENHOWER,
*Report by the Supreme Commander*

"Our intelligence service failed in this completely [predicting the invasion], even though a few reports subject to caution had indicated that Allied preparations had been completed. An invasion of northern France had been expected since the spring of 1944, as soon as the weather was favorable. The Normandy landing was reported in time, but only the usual alert was given, as it had been given so often before —an alert which, in varying degrees, had become almost a habit with the German troops, because of the frequent raids by Allied commandos.

"German military intelligence knew nothing of the real state of Allied preparations. Even when craft carrying Allied troops were approaching the coast of Normandy, the highest state of alert was not ordered."

—WILHELM KEITEL,
Hitler's chief of staff, replying to reporters the day after he was sentenced to death as a war criminal at Nuremberg

"While the enemy's Seventh Army, overworked and understrength, struggled to pin us down in the beachhead during July and August, the German High Command declined to reinforce it with troops from the Pas-de-Calais. There for seven decisive weeks, the Fifteenth Army waited for an invasion that never came, convinced beyond all reasonable doubt that Patton would lead the *main* Allied assault across that narrow neck of the Channel. Thus while von Kluge was

being defeated in the Battle for France, fewer than 100 miles away the enemy immobilized 19 divisions and played directly into our hands on the biggest single hoax of the war."
—OMAR N. BRADLEY, in *A Soldier's Story*

"Secrecy and the factor of surprise were strictly safeguarded by the enemy during the preparatory work and the landing itself."
—GENERAL STAFF OF THE GERMAN NAVY

"We sailed for France possessed of all the tactical information which an efficient intelligence service could provide . . . We learned how inadequate was the enemy's intelligence concerning the Allied intentions."
—DWIGHT D. EISENHOWER, *op. cit.*

# Bibliography

Historical research is never simple, but the study of secret history, that is, of intelligence work, is particularly difficult. The participants, bound to secrecy by vocation and obligation, usually do not relate their memories. Yet they constitute the only accessible source, for while official archives are sometimes published, those of secret services practically never are.

There is one notable exception to this rule: Nazi Germany. Victorious Allied troops took a considerable amount of historical booty which is now available to the public. Among the mass of captured documents were the files of the S.D., the main German intelligence service. I have made use of these documents for everything concerning the German side of the secret war that preceded the Normandy invasion. I also questioned many former members of the Abwehr and the S.D. They were willing and able to answer my questions, inasmuch as the defeat of Germany had put an end to their intelligence activities and released them from the requirements of professional secrecy.

The contribution made to D-Day by the Resistance was, of course, quite easy to study. Even in the thick of their underground struggle, members of the Resistance never regarded themselves as professionals. These talented amateurs had no reason not to speak. They were extremely cooperative and I would like to express my gratitude to them.

Officials of the American and British intelligence services were not able to display the same helpfulness. Unlike their German counterparts, many of them are still engaged in intelligence work. Unlike members of the Resistance, they rightly regard themselves as professionals. Even those who have ceased all activity are still constrained to secrecy by rigorous laws. This presented a delicate problem. I would not have been able to solve it without the help of Constantin Melnik, formerly assistant to the French Prime Minister and in charge of French intelligence operations. He was kind enough to place at my disposal the many friendships and acquaintances he formed with his American and British colleagues in the course of his work. Thanks to him, these men were willing to grant that revealing details of an invasion that took place twenty years ago would not endanger the security of the free world. I am especially grateful to M. Melnik; without him it would not have been possible to write this book.

No previous work has dealt with the totality of intelligence operations that preceded and prepared D-Day. There have, however, been many works dealing with D-Day itself. They were extremely valuable to me. They study the visible part of the iceberg; the precise image they give of it enabled me to orient my research by suggesting the contours of the submerged portion.

The bibliography employed naturally includes a certain number of general works devoted to military operations, historical figures in the war, the various intelligence services, and so on. I have limited myself to listing books that fall within the private domain. In general, official publications and works by the historical services of various governments do not appear on the list below.

ABSHAGEN, KARL HEINZ. *Canaris* (Hutchinson, 1956).

ARON, ROBERT, and GEORGETTE ELGEY. *Vichy Régime, 1940–44* (Macmillan, 1958).

BLOND, GEORGES. *Great Migrations* (Macmillan, 1956).

BRADLEY, OMAR NELSON. *A Soldier's Story* (Holt, 1951).

BRICKHILL, PAUL. *Dam Busters* (Ballantine).

BUTCHER, HARRY CECIL. *My Three Years with Eisenhower* (Simon and Schuster, 1946).

CARELL, PAUL. *Invasion—They're Coming!* (Harrap, 1962).

CHURCHILL, WINSTON S. *Memoirs of the Second World War* (Houghton Mifflin, 1959).

COLVIN, IAN GOODHOPE. *Chief of Intelligence* (Gollancz, 1954).

COOKRIDGE, EDWARD H. *Secrets of the British Secret Service* (Sampson Low, 1947).

COURTABESSIS, BERNARD. *Percée du mur d'Atlantique* (Paris, 1947).

CRANKSHAW, EDWARD. *Gestapo: Instrument of Tyranny* (Viking, 1956).

EISENHOWER, DWIGHT D. *Crusade in Europe* (Doubleday, 1948).

FULLER, J. F. C. *The Second World War* (Meredith, 1963).

GILBERT, F., ed. *Hitler Directs His War* (Oxford, 1951).

GROUSSARD, GEORGES ANDRÉ. *Service Secret, 1940–1945* (Paris, 1964).

HERVAL, RENÉ, ed. *La bataille de Normandie: récits de témoins* (Paris, 1947).

HOWARTH, DAVID ARMINE. *Dawn of D-Day* (Collins, 1959).

INGERSOLL, RALPH MCALLISTER. *Top Secret* (Harcourt, 1946).

JAMES, M. E. C. *I Was Monty's Double* (McGraw–Hill, 1954).

LEMONNIER, ANDRÉ GEORGES. *Les cent jours de Normandie* (Paris, 1961).

LEMONNIER–GRUHIER, FRANÇOIS. *Battles of the 6th June, 1944* (Saint-Pierre-Église, 1962).

LEVERKUEHN, PAUL. *German Military Intelligence* (Praeger. 1954).

LIDDELL HART, BASIL HENRY. *Defence of the West* (Morrow, 1950).

MAUPERTUIS (pseud.). *La vie en Normandie, 1940–1945* (Caen, 1947).

MILLER, MAX. *The Far Shore* (McGraw–Hill, 1945).

MONTAGU, EWEN. *The Man Who Never Was* (Lippincott, 1954).

MONTGOMERY, BERNARD. *Memoirs of Field-Marshal Montgomery* (New American Library, 1958).

——————. *Normandy to the Baltic* (Hutchinson, 1947).

MOOREHEAD, ALAN. *Montgomery: A Biography* (Hamish Hamilton, 1946).

MORGAN, FREDERICK. *Overture to Overlord* (Doubleday, 1950).

MORISON, SAMUEL ELIOT. *History of United States Naval Operations in World War II*, vol. I: *The Battle of the Atlantic, 1939–1943* (Little, Brown, 1947); vol. XI: *The Invasion of France and Germany* (Little, Brown, 1960).

MOYZISCH, L. C. *Operation Cicero* (Coward–McCann, 1950).

NORD, PIERRE. *Mes camarades sont morts* (Paris, 1947).

NORTHWOOD, ARTHUR, JR. and LEONARD RAPPORT. *Rendezvous with Destiny* (Infantry Journal Press, 1948).

PINTO, ORESTE. *Spy-catcher: World War II* (Harper, 1952).

REITLINGER, GERALD ROBERTS. *The S.S.: Alibi of a Nation, 1922–1945* (Heinemann, 1956).

RENAUD, ALEXANDRE. *Sainte-Mère-Église* (Monaco, 1945).

RENAULT–ROULIER, GILBERT. *Memoirs of a Secret Agent of Free France* (McGraw–Hill, 1948).

ROMMEL, ERWIN. *Krieg ohne Hass* (Heidenheim, 1950).

RYAN, CORNELIUS. *The Longest Day: June 6, 1944* (Simon and Schuster, 1959).

SCHELLENBERG, WALTHER. *Labyrinth: Memoirs of Hitler's Secret Service Chief* (Harper, 1957).

SHIRER, WILLIAM L. *The Rise and Fall of the Third Reich* (Simon and Schuster, 1960).

SHULMAN, MILTON. *Defeat in the West* (Dutton, 1948).

SPEIDEL, HANS. *Invasion—1944* (Regnery, 1950).

STANFORD, ALFRED. *Force Mulberry* (Morrow, 1951).

STJERNFELT, BERTIL. *Alarm: Atlantvallen* (Stockholm, 1953).

THOMPSON, REGINALD WILLIAM. *The Price of Victory* (Constable, 1960).

TURNER, JOHN F. *Invasion '44* (Putnam, 1959).

U.S. WAR DEPARTMENT—HISTORICAL DIVISION. *Omaha Beachhead (6 June–13 June 1944)* (Washington, 1945).

WICHTON, CHARLES. *Heydrich: Hitler's Most Evil Henchman* (Chilton, 1962).

——————, and GÜNTER PEIS. *They Spied on England* (Odhams, 1958).

WILMOT, CHESTER. *Struggle for Europe* (Harper, 1952).

YOUNG, DESMOND. *Rommel: The Desert Fox* (Harper, 1951).

# Index